The Definition of Literature

The Definition of
Literature

and other essays

W. W. Robson

Cambridge University Press

Cambridge

London   New York   New Rochelle

Melbourne   Sydney

Published by the Press Syndicate of the University of Cambridge
The Pitt Building, Trumpington Street, Cambridge CB2 1RP
32 East 57th Street, New York, NY 10022, USA
296 Beaconsfield Parade, Middle Park, Melbourne 3206, Australia

First published 1982

Printed in Great Britain by
Western Printing Services Ltd, Bristol

Library of Congress Catalogue card number: 82–4196

British Library Cataloguing in Publication Data
Robson, W. W.
The definition of literature and others essays.
1. Criticism
I. Title
801'.95 PN81

ISBN 0 521 24495 1

W P

To Anne and Hugh

Contents

Preface

Recent attempts to make literary criticism more 'rigorous' have sometimes only succeeded in alienating it from many authors and readers. The discussions that follow are written in what I hope is plain and straightforward language. But I concede to the rigorists that plain and straightforward language can beg questions and gloss over problems, and I have tried to avoid this by being as fully explicit as possible about the standards, criteria, and methods which I favour. I believe that this is the only permissible way of arguing about literary questions at a time when there is so much disagreement about matters of principle.

The first four essays deal with general questions. In 'The Definition of Literature' I have attempted, not to fix on a specific formulation, but to decide what *kind* of definition is preferable. 'On Liberty of Interpreting' examines the much-canvassed question of the relevance or otherwise of authorial intentions to criticism. Its purpose is to bring out what seems true in both 'intentionalism' and 'anti-intentionalism', and to discard what in both seems false. 'Evaluative Criticism, and Criticism without Evaluation' argues that one widely favoured account of literary appraisal is in fact empty. 'The Novel: a Critical Impasse?' raises a general problem about prose fiction. It may serve as an introduction to the three following essays, which discuss some famous novels in detail. A contrasting kind of approach is used in the essays on Tennyson and Frost, which survey a writer's work as a whole. The last four discussions adopt one more method of considering literary questions, through the study of what some distinguished poets have thought about them.

My general aim has been to take conversation about prose and poetry out of the limited and specialised 'literary' or 'academic' world in which it so often takes place, and to turn it towards the broader world of thought which is shared by all reflective people, whoever and wherever they are.

I am grateful to Mr Michael Black for his invaluable help in the selection and preparation of these essays.

W.W.R.

Bibliographical note

'The Definition of Literature', 'On Liberty of Interpreting', 'Evaluative Criticism, and Criticism without Evaluation', and 'The Novel: a Critical Impasse?' have not been published before.

'The Sea Cook: a Study in the Art of Robert Louis Stevenson' is revised from an essay that appeared in *On the Novel*, ed. B. S. Benedikz, Dent, 1971.

'On *Kidnapped*' appeared in *Stevenson and Victorian Scotland*, ed. Jenni Calder, Edinburgh University Press, 1981.

'On *The Wind in the Willows*' appeared in *The Hebrew University Studies in Literature*, vol. 9, no. 1, Spring 1981.

'The Present Value of Tennyson' was the Sir Charles Tennyson centenary lecture, delivered 31 October 1978. It appeared in *Studies in Tennyson*, ed. Hallam Tennyson, Macmillan, 1981.

'Robert Frost' appeared in *The Southern Review*, Autumn 1966.

'Hopkins and Literary Criticism' was the Hopkins Annual Lecture for 1974, published by the Hopkins Society, 1974.

'T. S. Eliot: a Poet's Notebook' appeared in *The Literary Criticism of T. S. Eliot*, ed. D. Newton de Molina, Athlone Press, 1977.

'I. A. Richards' appeared in *The Times Literary Supplement*, 26 February 1970.

'Yvor Winters: Counter-romantic' is based on material that appeared in *Essays in Criticism*, vol. XXV, no. 1, January 1975.

I
The Definition of Literature

Someone who asked for a definition of literature might want various things. He might want a concise formulation of what he already knew, such as might be found in a dictionary. Or he might want a witty *aperçu*, which looks at a familiar feature of our experience in an unexpected way. Or he might be a philosopher, asking for the necessary and sufficient conditions for the employment of this word; or a historian of ideas, interested in tracing the modulations of its meaning since Greco-Roman times. My object in raising the question is to isolate, as far as possible, the field of inquiry of literary criticism, to determine its subject-matter and doctrine of relevance. I am interested, not so much in trying to find a particular formula which satisfies these requirements, but in asking what *kind* of definition is most likely to be useful.

For this purpose definitions of literature may be divided, without remainder, into the descriptive and the honorific; the honorific being those which refer to value or quality, and the descriptive those which do not. In an age when the natural sciences are in such high repute it is usual to look first for a descriptive definition since this, it is hoped, will reduce the constituent of subjectivity and confine itself as far as possible to properties which can be recognised, without rhetorical persuasion, by anyone.

Two possible candidates for descriptive definition may be ruled out at once. The first is the special use of 'literature' in the expression 'the literature of a subject', that is what has been published about a subject. That this *is* a special use is indicated by the presence of the definite article: 'the' literature. The other rejected candidate may, in fact, be only a hypothetical one. I myself have never come across the usage, but it is sometimes claimed that 'literature' can mean the entire written documents of a community. If this definition were adopted, the only demarcation-disputes would arise over things such as films or TV performances, or folk ballads, or the floating verbal concoctions of everyday life: limericks, jokes, witticisms, and so on; would they count as literature only when they were written down? But I propose to ignore this usage because, if it exists, it must be very unusual. I have never met anyone who would include bus-tickets or ballot-papers among literary works. It might be said that there are literary collages, comparable to pictorial ones. Pound's *Cantos* offer some examples, and Eliot includes the items of a military parade in his *Coriolan* and a list of London Underground stations in his *Burnt Norton*. Such things can be *parts* of literary works. But they are not usually regarded as literary works by themselves. By themselves they belong to the history of a civilisation as a whole, rather than to its literature.

At the other extreme from this, and I think equally impractical, is the equation of literature with a determinate list of texts, on the analogy of a sacred scripture. Some might remark that this reflects actual school and university practice. And certainly the traditional notion of 'classics' – in China or, in European cultures, the Greco-Roman deposit, or parts of it – has been something like this. But however things may have been in the past, today even the most obstinately conservative among us would hardly be happy with a definition which confines literature to a list that cannot be added to or changed. Some communities may have segregated their literature in this way, but all of them certainly do not, and we belong to the dynamic Western culture which, for good and ill, is aware of perpetual change. We live in the age of *le musée imaginaire*. New things are added to the museum from time to time, and other things are removed to the basement. In our culture the proposal to close the literary canon is not a live option.

Various other proposals for a descriptive definition have been made by literary theorists. But only two of them seem at all plausible. The first is the kind of definition which refers to a special use of language. The uses of a language might be divided up, as Wellek and Warren suggest in *Theory of Literature* (1949), into the ordinary, the literary, and the scientific. Much work has been done by linguists on the possibility of defining the literary use of language. (I need refer only to Roman Jakobson.) If this could be done our problem would be solved: a literary work would be defined as a text written in literary language. On the face of it, this possibility looks promising. There are obviously all sorts of ways in which the language of literary works can have a distinctive character. In many communities, for example, there has been a special diction for poetry, which at once marks off the poetic from the everyday. And even where, as in many modern literary communities, the use of 'poetic diction' is frowned on, there are usually all kinds of devices to distinguish poems from casual speech. Even William Carlos Williams, who came nearer than most poets to the assimilation of them to everyday utterances, set them out in lines, like traditional verse. And this is clearly not just a typographical preference. The effect of setting them out in this way is to require a slower, more reflective response than that which is given to casual utterances, a different pace and emphasis, a more careful attention to the actual words chosen, especially in their sensuous character. And of course many other poets, ancient and modern, have gone much further to indicate to the reader that they make such demands. As for the demarcation between poetic and scientific language, this seems even easier to draw. Poetic and everyday language are both composed of words. But scientific language sometimes abandons the use of words altogether for a special symbolic notation. And even when words are used, every effort is made to divest them of their overtones of pluri-signification, variable emotional suggestiveness, allusiveness, and all the other potentialities which the ordinary speaker struggles with and the poet exploits.

Much useful work has been done, and is still being done, by linguists to separate the poetic use of language from other uses. (And it should not be forgotten that grammar and syntax have to be considered as well as vocabulary.) But I doubt whether this approach is the right one for our purpose. To start with, the attention of linguists interested in this subject has until recently been mainly concentrated on poetry, and, at that, on the most idiosyncratic linguistic features of poems. But there is a great deal of poetry which does not differ in diction and syntax from everyday uses, or from prose uses, as Wordsworth long ago pointed out. Moreover there is a great deal of writing which is not poetry, but which has a *prima facie* claim to be considered as equally literary, yet does not use poetic licence. Modern readers will at once think of the novel. Now it may be that prose fiction has its own specific linguistic devices. Indeed the fact that an experienced reader can usually tell at a glance that some page of writing comes from a prose fiction strongly suggests that this is so. But the special devices of the novelist do not appear to be of great importance. Literary critics, like ordinary readers, usually take them for granted. They are more interested in what a particular novelist does with them. In any case it is not difficult to show that, just as literature often incorporates ordinary speech, everyday speech has picked up many literary phrases, metaphors, and other figures of speech. It would be strange in a time of widespread literacy if this were not so. The written and the spoken are too much mixed up in our language for the distinction between them to be the basis of differentiation, or the main feature of a literary work. It is surely easier to regard the poetic, the everyday, and the scientific, not as sharply differentiated, but as belonging to a series of gradations. At one end of the series are the symbols of the scientist; at the other, the utterances of the mystical poet, which are without literal meaning, or the labyrinths of sound created by the word-musician, in which meaning of any kind has almost disappeared. In between is the great middle ground inhabited by most poetry, ornate prose, plays, prose fiction, essays, histories, political speeches, ordinary conversation. . .and all the rest, one shading into the next. At any point on the scale, between the two extremes at which words disappear, there can be literary language.

The other plausible descriptive definition is much more popular; I imagine it is the one that most of us, for practical purposes, unreflectively accept. This is the simple assumption that literature is fiction. Wellek and Warren support that view. Having maintained that the centre of the art of literature lies in the traditional genres of lyric, epic, and drama, they remark that in all of these 'the reference is to a world of fiction, of imagination'. I will leave for a moment the (to me) rather worrying apposition, 'of fiction, of imagination', which seems to imply that there is not much difference between these two terms, and speak only of the 'fiction' part of it. Does defining literature as fiction help to get it under the glass bell? The *prima facie* objection that springs to mind is that 'fiction' includes a lot of writing which no one, neither author nor reader, would dream of calling literature. But it must be remembered that the proposed definition is descriptive, that is, neutral with regard to value, quality, general esteem, and so on. It allows us to speak, without insufferable paradox, of bad literature.

In an article reprinted in *Aesthetics and Language* (ed. William Elton, 1954) the philosopher John Passmore, arguing for the definition of literature as fiction, has worked out some of the consequences of that view. *Middlemarch,* and all the fictional works that are in generally high esteem, are literature. But so is *The Way of an Eagle.* It may not be good, but it is literature. On the other hand, history by Gibbon and philosophy by Hume, works that are of comparable standing in their own fields with works like *Middlemarch* in its field, are not literature. Passmore reserves a special category for some literary works which are fictional, and are widely admired and loved, but which do not seem remotely comparable with *Middlemarch.* He means, for example, *Alice's Adventures in Wonderland.* Some people may even prefer such books to some at least of the supposedly more central works. Edmund Wilson declared that the *Alice* books were better than most Victorian novels. But on Passmore's view, though they may be good, these anomalous works are not literature. Evaluatively speaking, then, the standards are set by *Middlemarch* and its peers. Lesser works, like *The Way of an Eagle,* may not come up to those standards, but they are judgeable by those standards; descriptively speaking, they belong to the same category as *Middlemarch,* whereas Gibbon and Hume do not.

Should we adopt this way of speaking and thinking about literature? It involves us in some difficulties. Many people – including some very great names – have valued literature because they think it tells the truth. A character in a novel by Bernard Malamud recommends Dostoevsky's *The Idiot* to a friend, who says, 'I haven't read it. Is it fiction?' The character replies, 'It's the truth.' Now it is sometimes held that the 'truth' such people are thinking of is compatible with fiction. It is held that there is a distinction between truth about matters of fact – the sense of the word 'truth' in its everyday employments – and some higher kind of truth, in which the poet or novelist excels. (Wilde's *Decay of Lying* derives much of its persuasive force, as well as its humour, from ignoring this distinction.) It has been suggested that we might formulate the distinction as that between 'truth-about', truth in the matter-of-fact sense, and 'truth-to', which has a wider and deeper sense. We might think here of Aristotle's way of contrasting the poet with the historian. This is too large a question to go into here. I will merely observe that, leaving the difficult question of 'truth' out of it, many literary works mingle fiction with *fact*. Truman Capote and Norman Mailer are by no means the first to do this. Tolstoy did it. Napoleon's invasion of Russia is described in *War and Peace*, and there really was a Napoleon and he really did invade Russia. It has been suggested to me that in this context we should put 'Napoleon' in inverted commas, to indicate that what we are talking about is not the Napoleon of history, but an imaginary figure invented by Tolstoy. But should we then put 'Russia' in inverted commas? The novel, of course, has always been thought the literary form which was closest to the raw material of life, the one most bound up with temporal society and the grain of reality. Indeed, Henry James was worried about *Middlemarch* because it seemed to him too like a historical work. 'If we write novels so, how shall we write history?' Once we have put fiction at the centre of literature, it is difficult not to find ourselves putting realistic prose fiction at the centre of that. But then the edge of the distinction we wanted to draw has been taken off.

The mingling of fact and fiction could, perhaps, be dealt with by deciding to regard the factual element in literature as subordinate, not central. But greater difficulties arise from the exclusion of memorable non-fictional works, such as Gibbon's *Decline and Fall*. Does it not seem plausible to say that the things it has in common with a great novel are more important than the things a great novel has in common with a novelette? Gibbon, of course, was a historian, and we can read the *Decline and Fall* to find out some facts of Roman history. But many people do not; they are not interested in Gibbon's accuracy, but in his point of view. In any case, what is a historian? Was Sir Walter Scott a historian? Certainly much in Scottish history that survived only in oral tradition would have been lost without his work. And whether Scott himself should be called a historian or not, he certainly influenced historians. Macaulay and Carlyle are very different from eighteenth-century historians, and it seems clear that one important reason for the difference is that they had learned from the Waverley Novels. It is true that a modern historian like G. R. Elton would consign Macaulay and Carlyle merely to 'literature'. Considered as historians, they seem to him picturesque anachronisms in an age whose standards are set by historians like Maitland or Namier. But without going into these professional and terminological problems, we must surely agree that there was a profound revolution in historical thinking after the eighteenth century – the recognition, which Macaulay had and Gibbon had not, of the deep differences, in vital respects, between other periods or cultures and our own. Modern historians may take this for granted; but that they do so is an unconscious tribute to the pre-scientific literati.

Once again it might be possible to reconcile this with the view that literature is primarily fictional. We might see literature as a class of utterances in part defined by the fact that we do not raise the question whether the entities they refer to exist or not. That is to say, whatever may be the existential status of the people or environments mentioned in literature, in practice we treat them all as if they were fictional. Gibbon's Rome, Tolstoy's Russia, even Joyce's Dublin – the most accurately portrayed city in all literature – are all equally countries of the mind (to use Middleton Murry's fine expression). Their relation to external realities does not matter. I find this view hard to hold. A map of the Dublin of *Ulysses* would be the map of Dublin in 1904. But it seems possible to hold such a view about less reportorial authors.

Given a certain stretching, then, it would seem that the concept of fictionality might do as the basis for a descriptive definition of literature. But there are other difficulties. Is the

Bible literature? And if so, is it fiction? Some of the Bible seems to me to be clearly fiction, and meant as such, the book of Jonah for example. But equally clearly, even to the non-fundamentalist, a great deal of it is not fiction – not, at any rate, meant to be read as fiction. (The early chapters of Genesis may have been meant to be read as myth, but that is a different matter.) Yet it seems hard to deny literary status to, at any rate, a great deal of the Bible.

However, this may not be a live issue. It may be that the Bible is read today, if at all, as Scripture. Let us then put it aside as a special case. But what about secular poetry – poetry in general? Is poetry fiction? This is a more serious question, for if a definition of literature cannot accommodate poetry there must be something wrong with it. Well, it is obvious that poetry often contains a good deal of fiction. We need only mention the *Odyssey*. Even *Paradise Lost*, which as we all know was written to 'justify the ways of God to Man', contains much that to Milton himself was fictitious, as well as to his readers. But we would hesitate to say that the whole of *Paradise Lost* was fiction to Milton. Then there are those short, or fairly short, poems in which the poet seems to speak in his own person, the kind of poems usually, though not happily, described as 'lyrical'. Are they fiction? It is common nowadays to argue that the mere choice of verse as a mode of expression, together with other literary devices, is enough to signalise to the informed reader that the speaker is not 'really' the poet, but a *persona*, not to be identified with an actual human being.

Now certainly poetry, even lyrical poetry, is not autobiography. And there are many poems in which the presence of a *persona* is obvious – Browning's dramatic monologues, for instance. But what about 'One Word More', or other poems in which the poet actually says that he is speaking in his own person? What about all those poems of Wordsworth, Coleridge, Shelley...and many others, in which, without conformity to a critical dogma, we should normally take it for granted that the speaker *is* Wordsworth, or Coleridge, or Shelley? This is not to say that poetry, even this kind of poetry, is simply autobiography. Autobiography itself is not a simple concept. Literary scholars and biographers have shown us how much fiction is really autobiography, and Proust has shown us that much auto-biography is fiction. The traditional distinction between memory and imagination is not a simple one, when applied to a man telling the story of his life. But the point I want to make is that the mere presence of verse form cannot be taken as an infallible indicator that what is being said is fiction. When a poet makes some general statement in verse, is he to be taken as signalling, by his use of the verse form, that he 'doesn't really mean it'? On the contrary: by using verse form on these occasions he may be doing his very best to ensure that his readers take his utterance with the utmost seriousness, take it as *his* utterance, his *auctoritas*, remember it, make it a personal possession. In any case, there is something odd about a definition which obliges us to say that *The Prelude* is fiction and Mill's *Autobiography* non-fiction, solely because one is in verse and the other in prose. Suppose *The Prelude* had been written in prose (and it must be confessed that, as it is, a good deal of *The Prelude* is rather prosy). Would that make it non-fiction? Why?

It might be objected that the lack of fit between 'poetry' and 'fiction' is merely due to an unfortunate accident of the English language. Other languages, it is said, have a common word for both poetry and fiction, and so these problems do not arise. And we can avoid them in English if, instead of speaking of poetry or fiction, we employ the rather clumsy term 'imaginative litera-ture'. But I do not think the problem can be solved by this substitution. In spite of the advantage of having the word *Dichtung* as a single word for 'imaginative literature', German critics have had to wrestle with it quite as much as English-speaking ones. And it might be argued that, so far from its being a nuisance that our language has different words for poetry and fiction, this is really an advantage, because it draws attention to a distinction that ought, in the nature of things, to be made. And it seems to me that this is in fact the case.

But can we then find our definition of literature by confining it to 'imaginative literature', and then trying to be as precise as possible about the meaning of 'imaginative'? It is at this point that I would like to make a demur against Wellek's and Warren's assimilation of fiction to imagination. I do not want to make too much of their incidental coupling of these terms. It is plain that Wellek and Warren were here using 'imagination' in an ordinary popular sense, as when we say, 'There's nothing there, it's just your imagination'. But, perhaps without intending to, by using this wonder-word they have quietly reinforced the plausibility of their argument for taking fiction as the type of literature. 'Imagination' is a word both vague and powerful in suggestion – too much so, it seems to me, to figure in what is intended to be a descriptive definition. Let me make the case for excluding it by elaborating on the suggestion that imagination, whether or not it has anything particular to do with literature, has nothing particular to do with fiction.

There is an episode in *The House with the Green Shutters* in which the hero's son, John Gourlay, a student at Edinburgh University, goes in for a literary prize. He is over-sensitive, morbidly fanciful as the author sees it, but un-intellectual. The subject set for him is 'An Arctic Night'.

He saw a lonely little town far off upon the verge of Lapland night, leagues and leagues across a darkling plain, dark itself and little and lonely in the gloomy splendour of a Northern sky. A ship put to sea, and Gourlay heard in his ears the skirl of the man who went overboard – struck dead by the icy water on his brow, which smote the brain like a tomahawk.

He put his hand to his own brow when he wrote that, and 'Yes,' he cried eagerly, 'it would be the *cold* that would kill the brain! Ooh-oh, how it would go in!'

A world of ice ground round him in the night; bergs ground on each other and were rent in pain; he heard the splash of great fragments tumbled in the deep, and felt the waves of their distant falling lift the vessel beneath him in the darkness. To the long desolate night came a desolate dawn, and eyes were dazed by the encircling whiteness; yet there flashed green slanting chasms in the ice, and towering pinnacles of sudden rose, lonely and far away. An unknown sea beat upon an unknown shore, and the ship drifted on the pathless waters, a white dead man at the helm.

'Yes, by Heaven,' cried Gourlay, 'I can see it all, I can see it all – that fellow standing at the helm, white and stiff's an icicle!'

Yet, do what he might, he was unable to fill more than half a dozen small pages. He hesitated whether he should send them in, and held them in his inky fingers, thinking he would burn them. He was full of pity for his own inability. 'I wish I was a clever chap,' he said mournfully.

But his professor, nicknamed 'Thomas Aquinas', prefers quality to quantity and awards him the prize. In his preliminary disquisition, before announcing the winner, 'Thomas Aquinas' makes some interesting observations about imagination. Of course, he says, there are various kinds.

'In its lowest form it merely recalls something which the eyes have already seen, and brings it vividly before the mind. A higher form pictures something which you never saw, but only conceived as a possible existence. Then there's the imagination which not only sees but hears – actually hears what a man would say on a given occasion, and entering into his blood, tells you exactly why he says it. The highest form is both creative and consecrative, if I may use the word, merging in diviner thought. It irradiates the world. Of that high power there is no evidence in the essay before me. To be sure there was little occasion for its use.'

'Thomas Aquinas' here distinguishes four kinds of imagination, which we may call A, B, C, and D. 'A', the ordinary popular sense of 'imagination', does not concern us, and we may leave 'D', the 'creative and consecrative imagination', to Coleridge and his followers. It is 'B' and 'C' that are most easily identifiable and most relevant, 'B' which 'pictures something you never saw, but only conceived as a possible existence', and 'C', 'the imagination which not only sees but hears'. Now of these only 'B' clearly involves the notion of fiction (though it could also be the quality which distinguishes the ingenious inventor in any field). And Gourlay's effort belongs to fiction, since he had never seen an Arctic night. But suppose he had. Would his effort be then less imaginative? Surely not. I suppose we would feel that in some way he deserved more credit for having made the whole thing up. But his essay itself might be no different. In 'C' the notion of fiction is absent. A good historian or reporter could show imagination in that sense – indeed, could he be a good historian or reporter without it? A historian must not make up his facts; but without the use of his imagination some of the most important facts are inaccessible to him. To use Collingwood's language, he finds himself trying to think the thoughts of people in the past. How can he do that without imagination? And surely some writers of fiction have lacked imaginative power, while some writers of non-fiction have had it abundantly. Besides, imaginative power can show itself in all sorts of human activity. There seems no good reason for identifying imagination with fiction. In fact there seems no good reason for supposing that there is any special relationship between them.

But nothing I have said so far rules out the possibility that fiction, while not the whole of literature, is in some way exceptionally distinctive of it. And it may be that some critics, especially those of a strongly moralistic bent, need to be reminded from time to time that invention and fiction play an important part in literature. Poets do indeed feign. And one of Shakespeare's characters even says that 'the truest poetry is the most feigning'. But I would plead for a distinction to be drawn here. 'Poets feign' is not – to use old-fashioned terminology – an analytic proposition, like 'poets make poetry'. We can seriously discuss whether a poet on a particular occasion is feigning or not, as the great critics have done. It is better to say that poets *sometimes* feign. It is one of their privileges, not one of their defining characteristics.

One incidental advantage of abandoning this emphasis on fiction might be to correct the tendency, very notable since the time of George Eliot, to over-value the dominant form of modern literature, the novel. I do not deny that some novels are great books, but I do not believe that all great books are novels. To believe that seems to me historical parochialism.

But if literature cannot be defined as fiction, the last plausible candidate for a descriptive definition of literature disappears. We are left with honorific definitions. And these, I am sure, are more in keeping with normal usage. Yet they have not resulted in the emergence of any satisfactory agreed term. '*Belles-lettres*' is unattractive, and H. L. Mencken's translation of it as 'beautiful letters' is worse. Erasmus's *bonae litterae* is more appealing, but H. W. Garrod's translation of it as 'good letters' has not caught on. That is not important. What most people have in mind, when they talk about literature, is the great and good works, of whatever genre. But these do not constitute a fixed list. Everyone's list is different. This is what distinguishes the honorific definition from the 'great books' kind of descriptive definition. But then the notion of 'literature' becomes very elusive.

Perhaps it is easiest to pin it down by contrast. One contrast, especially pertinent at the present day, is with journalism. Journalism, however brilliant, does not survive its immediate occasion. If some journalism has become literature, this is because we read it although we are no longer interested in the immediate occasion. This transcendence of occasions seems to me a distinctive 'note' of literature (in the honorific sense). We come nearer still to the mode of its existence when we contrast works that are alive and kicking with the discarded works that have been forgotten, that are never read except by scholars. On a descriptive definition they would be literature, on an honorific definition they are not. It seems to me that literary theorists have not paid enough attention to these discarded works. Why have they been discarded? Many of them never fell into the category of ephemeral journalism. They were meant to be permanent literature; they aspired to the great tradition, but they never 'made it'. In some literatures they have disappeared altogether, so that we have to hope that what scholars and critics in those cultures preserved for us are the works we should have liked best. But in our culture many of them remain, and their existence presents us with a problem.

Some literary historians have urged that we should pay more attention to these discarded works. They point out that in many cases these works were very popular, filled a need, were even thought to be great literature. And they have also demonstrated that some of them, if only in virtue of belonging to the same period or cultural phase as some acknowledged great work, have a lot in common with it. So they have pleaded for the fuller study of these rejects, not for their own sake, but in order to throw fresh light on the classic works. But in practice, if not in theory, this is bound to lead to an upgrading of these works, since no one wants to spend time on what is agreed to be rubbish.

Whether he wants to or not he will, if he persists, come to feel some kind of affection, if only an exasperated one, for these un-rescued Cinderellas. The result is, either that the honorific definition of literature is eroded, and we are back with descriptive definition; or the canon is enlarged, and the honorific sense of the word becomes so extended as to be meaningless.

Now I have been assuming that we have a clear idea of what these discarded works are, the works that are merely documents of their time. But when we ask which works *are* discarded, we come to some rather embarrassing considerations. From the point of view of the great world it often looks as if most of literature, including works that we have been taught to venerate as classics, has been discarded. I wonder how many voluntary readers some famous books really have – whether they are actively current influences on imagination and taste, whether anyone reads them (to use a phrase of F. R. Leavis) 'as we read the living'. On the other hand, if we look at our literary heritage through the eyes of academe, we have an opposite picture. From this point of view it sometimes seems as if the category of 'discarded works' has almost disappeared. Expert after expert urges on us the historical, if not the intrinsic, importance of some neglected author, some piece forgotten by the world. Once it was possible to feel, optimistically, that natural selection operated in the field of literature; that the mere action of time eliminated much that was not worth reading; that most authors are dead, not only in the sense that they have undergone the divorce of body from soul which is the lot of all men, but in the sense that their *world* has died with them. It is correct, in their case, to give a literal significance to the word 'past'. But in the age of the Ph.D. industry is it possible to speak of a 'dead' author? It is true that often there is no sign of life in these exhumed figures. But how do we know that sometimes a spark does not pass from the subject to the student – or from the student to the subject?

Certainly it is important not to canonise contemporary taste, to make it an absolute. Unfashionable authors may have something to give us which fashionable authors do not – something which we need, all the more because it is not fashionable. It is also important to recognise that *kinds* of literature which happen

14

to be unfashionable just now may have great virtues. They are still available, if anyone wants them. Even those whose chief concern is to be in the fashion should pause to reflect that there are many occasions in literary history when the stone that the builders rejected has become the foundation. Authors out of favour have come back and have become the fashion in their turn. To confine oneself to works favoured by fashion is to run the risk of becoming, one of these days, old-fashioned oneself.

So what is known as 'the test of time' is far from infallible. There are too many counter-examples. 'Time', if by that is meant fashionable opinion, or academic convention, has frequently failed to spot what a later age comes to think of as the best work of its day. Many discarded authors have simply had bad luck. Their theme or subject perhaps no longer has a topical significance; they have failed to touch a contemporary pre-occupation. They are not 'relevant'. But is 'relevance' relevant, I wonder?

All the same, it is impossible not to believe that some works have been *justly* discarded. We may reasonably predict that they will never be current again. And it does seem possible to distinguish an accidental lack of topicality, which time may remedy, from some deep failure of vitality in the structure or content of those works. The most plausible reason for their failure to survive is that they only give us something which is better done by better men. They are not 'originals', they lack the spiritual signature of a truly distinguished writer. This unique quality is one of the most important 'notes' of literature; it is sometimes called textuality, and its unmistakable mark is the resistance of the texts that possess it to all kinds of paraphrase, synopsis, or translation. In Kipling's story 'Regulus' (in *A Diversity of Creatures*) the Latin master King is asked by his pupil Winton about a passage in Horace. 'If it's a free translation mightn't *obstantes* and *morantes* come to about the same thing, sir?' King replies: 'Nothing comes to "about the same thing" with Horace, Winton.'

Some people want to use the word 'style' here. Yeats liked to quote Sainte-Beuve's remark that 'there is nothing immortal in literature except style'. 'Literature', says Evelyn Waugh, 'is the right use of language irrespective of the subject or reason of the utterance. A political speech may be, and sometimes is, literature; a sonnet to the moon may be trash. Style is what distinguishes literature from trash.' Unfortunately the word 'style' has often come to have the meaning of a decorative extra, something added to an otherwise satisfying functional structure. This is not the meaning intended. But when it is ruled out, 'style' ceases to have any clear meaning. That 'literature is the right use of language' seems to be true, but I do not see how we can tell when it *is* right irrespective of subject. Right for what? But however we may cavil at details, this seems to be the best *sort* of definition, at least negatively speaking. It is not the subject, or the motive for writing, that makes a work literature.

But what, positively, *does* make it literature? To say that it is style is to say no more than that there is an X-factor which has kept the work alive. And at this point a perplexity arises. Suppose we contrast standard literature not, this time, with the discarded works which were once thought good, Addison's *Cato* and the like, but with works that plain men enjoy, that we all enjoy, but which do not seem to be candidates for the great books, or paradigms of 'style'. These are works that have an obstinate habit of survival, though disparaged or ignored by academic and highbrow opinion. I mean things like *Ben Hur*, or *Little Women*, or *King Solomon's Mines*. We could all make our own list. And we should all, I think, feel discomfort at pronouncing them to be literature, in the honorific sense. Yet such works have 'stood the test of time' in a robuster sense than, say, *The Faerie Queene*, or *Paradise Lost*, or, perhaps, Joyce's *Ulysses*. Would *those* works really survive if they were not in the intensive care unit? Far more books and articles are written about them than about the sub-literature, but have they really given more genuine enjoyment to more people than the sub-literature? I do not pretend to know the answers to these questions; I do not know how we could possibly find out. I think it probable that many older works would not survive without academic attention. But this is an argument for the existence of academics, not an admission that these works are no good. To judge them no good would be barbarous. Some old books, or books like

Ulysses that are technically very unusual, require a great deal of preparation on the part of the reader, but they amply repay it. And it may be that they give a more inclusive and lasting pleasure, to those who are able to read them, than more popular works; though it would be hard to prove this.

All the same, genuine survival, without academic or fashionable attention, is strong evidence in favour of a work from the past. The 'good bad poems', the Longfellows and Mrs Hemanses that everyone laughs at, have their place in our affections. But it may be that they have a place in literature as well. One thing they all seem to have in common is the conviction with which they are written. There is no fumbling. In this respect they have qualities in common with some greater works and not with some fashionable modern productions that are too self-conscious and turned away from the reader. I am not suggesting that these robust survivors are the best works, or even that they are especially good. But if we are going to adopt an honorific definition of literature, while we may be as fastidious as we like in making distinctions of kind and judgments of scale within that definition, we must not be too exclusive about what we admit to be literature at all. Most of the literature that has survived was 'what the public wanted' – Shakespeare's plays, or the novels of Dickens.

This must not be construed as a sell-out to the commercial interest. Public taste at any one time may be bad, just as any individual's taste may be bad. But a popular work which entertains several different publics, in different generations, must have some genuinely literary quality. And at least it can be said in favour of the authors who are enjoyed by the great public, but not by the critics, that the element of pretence, on either the writers' or the readers' side, is minimal. The great public does not bother to pretend that it has been entertained if it has not, whereas some highbrow success may be *totally* without merit (remember the Emperor's new clothes).

We should, then, be prepared to admit to literary status work that is not itself of high pretensions, but is not harmed (as middlebrow literature is) by being read in the light, or shadow, of greater work. But one tendency which might seem at first sight to be in the same direction must be resisted. This is the recommendation of work because it is in agreement with opinions of the proper brand, or invites our sympathy for the oppressed people who produced it or read it. There may be genuinely moral and practical reasons for paying attention to such work, but let us clear our minds of cant. If we do not ourselves think that it is literature, we must not smuggle it into literary studies on some other ground. The insistence on not confusing literary value with other values has sometimes provoked the charge that this conception of literature is reactionary and elitist. The idea has got about (I have encountered it in both French- and English-speaking critics) that 'literature' in this honorific sense is a comparatively recent notion, the invention of the late nineteenth-century bourgeoisie. But this is quite wrong, as René Wellek has shown (in *What is Literature?* ed. Paul Hernadi, 1979). Cicero speaks of *litterae* and even of *litteratura* in the required sense.

To sum up what this essay has tried to do. I have suggested practical arguments against the descriptive kind of definition of literature, as not useful for critical purposes, and argued in favour of the honorific kind, which commits its user to decisions about value and quality; and, within that kind, for the type of definition which picks out transcendence of originating contexts as a central characteristic of literature; and within that type, for definitions which turn on ideas of 'textuality' – linguistic adequacy, propriety, and excellence. This recommendation may be criticised on the ground that it is too formalistic, too neglectful of subject-matter. But it does have the advantage that it is equally compatible with a 'high', a 'middling', and a 'low' view of the subject-matter of literature. It is compatible with the high view, which sees literature as the pre-eminent means for giving form and outline to what Sartre (1979) has called the most important questions: what is man? what does he want? what does he expect? It is compatible with the middling view, which sees literature as an open forum for the free exchange of thoughts, the 'current of ideas' so much longed for, in closed societies, by the authors and consumers of samizdat. And it is compatible with the low view, which finds the value of literature in its contribution to happiness, in its capacities as entertainment or pastime or anodyne, and judges it according to how far it promotes or prevents human cheerfulness and contentment. And it seems to me that all these compatibilities are essential, because literature – or even, at different times, one single work of literature – can be all these things.

2
On Liberty of Interpreting

To understand the meaning of an utterance, is it necessary to know the intention of the utterer? (I use 'utterer' to cover both writers and speakers.) In order to get a preliminary grip on this question I shall distinguish three ingredients of meaning. First, there is who or what the utterance refers to. If someone says, 'He made a great mistake in invading Russia', we cannot fully understand this statement unless we know who 'he' is, unless we know the reference of the statement. We may guess that it probably refers to Hitler, or Napoleon, or Charles XII, but without the context the total meaning is uncertain. Next, there is what is said about the person or thing referred to; in this example, the mistake the subject made in invading Russia. This may be called the sense of the statement. And to understand this we have to be acquainted with a great many things. For instance, we have to know what sort of thing making a mistake is, or invasion. And of course in order to know that these notions are involved we have to know the relevant vocabulary and grammar in which the statement is made – in this case the English language. The necessary conditions for understanding the sense and reference of a statement are quite numerous and quite complex.

One of them, sometimes overlooked by students of the written word, is inflexion. Thus, in the example I have given, the meaning varies according to which words receive more or less stress. For instance, 'He made a great mistake in invading *Russia*' (as it might be, not in invading Norway) is different from 'He made a great mistake in *invading* Russia' (as it might be, in not undermining Russia, or penetrating Russia in some way). It is clear that the inflexion is part of the sense and that these statements, though they are closely linked, differ in meaning.

Supposing we have got the sense and reference right, do we then understand the meaning of the utterance? Not necessarily. A third ingredient of meaning has to be taken into account: the way the utterer says what he says. Here we must bear in mind one difference between the spoken and the written word. The written word has no tone. This is one of the problems for the novelist: how to convey to the reader the way people actually say things, communicate their meaning, over and above mere sense and reference. In our time, Kingsley Amis is a master of this art.

What is meant by tone is the speaker's attitude to what he is saying, and his attitude to his audience. 'He made a great mistake in invading Russia' can be said in different tones. It might be offered as a mere statement of reported historical opinion, revealing nothing of the speaker's own feelings about the matter, if he has any. Or it might be said regretfully, or in a satisfied, complacent voice. And there are many other possibilities. Quite often it is possible to understand an utterance without knowing the tone in which it is supposed to be spoken. Indeed many utterances have no individual speaker, like 'Keep Off The Grass'. It is, of course, possible to imagine this being said in a gruff official voice. But we do not have to imagine a voice at all to understand this injunction fully. On other occasions, however, the tone must be picked up if we are to know what is being said. 'Can I help you?' sometimes means just what it says, an offer of assistance. But more often than not it means 'What are you doing here? What are your credentials?' So much in speech and writing is not literal, not to be taken at its face value, that it seems impossible to limit the meaning of an utterance to its sense.

But if the tone is part of the meaning of an utterance, then the intention of the utterer is part of it. For it is the tone that distinguishes the *user*'s meaning, over and above the public meaning, the meaning determined by vocabulary and grammar. It is true that many utterances are toneless, and many more are tonally ambiguous. But this only shows that the linguistic environment of a human being is not always intimate or intelligible. Fortunately it often is. People do talk to each other, do understand each other.

And indeed it seems to me that the relevance of the user's meaning to the understanding of what is said goes beyond tone, into sense and reference. Imagine that there is a Grim-Barbary language, in which the phonetic sequence corresponding to the

English words 'Good-morning' happens to be identical with the sequence that to a Grim-Barbary hearer conveys the meaning 'Your dictator is a nasty piece of work.' An unfortunate Anglophone might be in dire need to convince the authorities that the sounds he uttered were meant to represent English words, not Grim-Barbary words. Here the question of intention is absolutely crucial. ('What language were you speaking?') But I think it is often quite central on countless other, much more everyday, occasions.

It seems common sense to conclude that the intention of the utterer is an indispensable ingredient of the meaning of an utterance. We are not usually concerned with what such-and-such a sequence might convey in some other language, or even with what far-fetched interpretation could be placed on it in English, but only with what so-and-so meant to convey by it.

But there is an influential school of thought which holds that, whatever may be the case with utterances in general, where this class of utterances is concerned the intentions of the utterer are irrelevant to the meaning (they may even be unknowable). The class of utterances in question is that of literary works. Some theorists hold that the peculiarity of literature – possibly one of its defining features – is the independence of its meaning from the intentions of its authors. This is the question I now wish to discuss.

The late W. K. Wimsatt said in 1968 that 'the design or intention of the author is neither available nor desirable as a standard for judging either the meaning or the value of a work of art'. The part of this pronouncement to be considered here is the assertion that 'the design or intention of the author' is not 'available'. Wimsatt was known as one of the leading antiintentionalists among literary theorists, and this is what we should expect him to say. But surprisingly his view seems to be partly endorsed by E. D. Hirsch, who is known as one of the leading intentionalists. Referring to the argument 'which states that the author's intended meaning cannot be certainly known', Hirsch says: 'This argument cannot be successfully met, because it is self-evidently true. I can never know another person's intended meaning with certainty because I cannot get into his head to compare the meaning he intended with the meaning I understand, and only by such direct comparison could I be certain that his meaning and my own are identical' (*Validity in Interpretation*, 1971). Now if we take Hirsch as saying that we can never know what anyone else means, then this applies to his own statement: as I cannot get into Hirsch's head I cannot know what he means, and so further discussion is pointless. But it seems necessary to lay stress on the words 'with certainty' in Hirsch's formulation of his position, and to assume that he would grant that on innumerable occasions of everyday life we can know what another person means, without reasonable doubt, without being able to get into his head. Indeed it is hard to imagine how any kind of social life could be carried on if that were not the case. Similarly we should perhaps interpret Wimsatt as saying that we can never know beyond reasonable doubt what is the intention of the author of a work of literary art. And this seems a discussible view.

But it is also most implausible. Even to call something a novel or a play or a poem is already to allot it to the category of things done with a conscious purpose which we recognise. And we can go further than that. It seems to me that I know beyond reasonable doubt a great many of the intentions of the author of (say) *Great Expectations*. For example, I know beyond reasonable doubt that he intended to compose a work entitled *Great Expectations*; that he intended it to take the form of the personal narrative of an imaginary character called Philip Pirrip; that he intended to introduce various other imaginary characters (list follows); that he intended some of them to amuse his readers (Joe Gargery, Mr Pumblechook), and others to puzzle or mystify them (Miss Havisham, Jaggers). . .and so on. And we might even judge it beyond doubt that he wished his work to convey certain morals or lessons to his readers and to have certain 'atmospheric' effects, etc. Of course I am not saying that we know this sort of thing in all cases. The further back we go in time the more do such considerations become problematic. It is by no means beyond reasonable doubt that the author of *Piers Plowman* intended to compose a single poem of that name, or that there really is such a thing, or that there was only one author. I am saying only that there *are* cases where we do know many of the author's intentions, even though no sensible critic would bother to write them all down; he simply takes them for granted, and quite rightly. It is what is *not* beyond reasonable doubt that is, precisely, the sort of thing a sensible critic *does* bother to write down; what, if he is an intentionalist, he believes to be the un-obvious intentions of the author; or what, if he is an anti-intentionalist, he believes to be part of what the work says, although he has no way of knowing whether or not the author meant to put it there. And it is at this point that we reach something that is, for practical purposes, worth discussing; whether there is, in any intelligible sense, a distinction to be drawn, as Wimsatt draws it, between the intention of the author and the meaning of a work of literary art.

But this last expression needs elucidation. What *is* 'the meaning of a work of literary art'? As is well known, inquiries into meaning occupy modern philosophers a great deal. Wittgenstein's *Brown Book* begins with the question 'What is the meaning of a word?' And this inquiry leads him into deep waters. But in practical life the question 'What is the meaning of this word, X?' is not as a rule difficult to understand. It can often be answered simply and univocally. If, as an English-speaker, I ask a German-speaker, 'What does *Sperling* mean?' I am perfectly content with the answer, '*Sperling* means sparrow.' But a question like 'What does *Henry Esmond* mean?' is different. In an ordinary conversational context it might be taken as an inquiry about the meaning of the *name* 'Henry Esmond'. But after it is made clear that the reference is not to the name of a character in the work, but to the work itself, it becomes difficult to see what sort of answer is required. This is no longer an ordinary question, but a strange question, a literary critic's question. How is it to be understood?

There are many ways in which it can be understood. I shall consider three. The first way is to take it as referring to what I shall call the textual meaning of the work, that is, the meaning of the words of which it is composed. But does the term 'meaning' have the same force in the two expressions ('the meaning of the work' and 'the meaning of the words in which it is composed')? There is a difficulty here. It is well known that the meanings of words change. ('Indifferently' when the Prayer Book was written meant 'impartially', but it doesn't now.) Does it then follow that the meanings of texts change? In *Paradise Lost*, v. 434, the Archangel Raphael, sitting down to dinner with Adam and Eve, says 'Think not I shall be nice.' Presumably the sense intended by the author does not include the modern sense of 'nice'. But is it none the less permissible to construe it in the modern sense? Gray in 'The Progress of Poesy' speaks of 'Dryden's less presumptuous car'. There were no cars, in the modern sense, in the time of Dryden or Gray, but is it permissible to take this word in the modern sense? P. D. Juhl, in an article entitled 'Can the Meaning of a Literary Work Change?' (in *The Uses of Criticism*, ed. Foulkes, Frankfurt, 1976) cites a striking example in which the old and the modern meanings are exactly opposite: Hamlet's 'I'll make a ghost of him that lets me.' This sense of 'let' has only survived in tennis and in 'without let or hindrance'. But may we none the less construe Hamlet as meaning that he will kill anyone who allows him to follow the Ghost?

Surely the answer to these questions is no. Liberty of interpreting cannot apply to *words*. Words can only be validly interpreted according to what they meant at the time of their use, within the language system used by the writer. There are, of course, special cases, *Finnegans Wake* for example, where Joyce does many strange things to English words. Or there are those poems of Dylan Thomas in which he puts together words that cannot normally be put together in standard English ('Once below a time', and so on). Or there is the more frequent case when an author uses a more or less normal language system, but gives his own meaning to particular words. In Yeats, for example, 'wisdom' often means something pejorative, grey, bloodless, 'bleareyed', 'a something incompatible with life'. And there are puns to consider, and the Empsonian ambiguities and Mallarméan polyvalences that modern critics love to discover. But this sort of thing does not affect the general principle that words can only be validly interpreted according to what the writer meant when he used them. The only difference it makes is that we may have to define a particular author's language system very carefully.

In this sense, then, the meaning of a literary work cannot change. Surely there is no serious disagreement about this. Schoolboy howlers may amuse us, and we may even admire some of Ezra Pound's 'creative translations'. But they cannot be defended as valid interpretations of a work's textual meaning. No translation can convey the meaning of its original unchanged; but this does not mean that all translations are equally inaccurate. Some meanings, especially of ancient texts, may be irretrievable, as Heidegger and others have argued. But in that case that is what they are, irretrievable, and we have to accept that the given words have no meaning for us. We are not allowed simply to make it up.

But sometimes a modern critic who accepts the stated principle will none the less defend an anachronistic interpretation. Wellek and Warren in *Theory of Literature* (1949) are prepared to grant that in the lines

> My vegetable love would grow
> Vaster than empires, and more slow

Marvell probably did not have in mind something like a huge cabbage, and they quote another commentator as suggesting that in the seventeenth century 'vegetable' meant 'vegetative', in the sense of pertaining to the life-giving principle. But they urge the allowability of retaining the modern association in this line as 'an enrichment of its meanings'. Now if the 'cabbage' meaning was merely improbable, it might be retained on the ground that Marvell, writing in the metaphysical tradition, might have permitted himself outlandish fancies. But suppose it was shown beyond reasonable doubt that the 'cabbage' meaning was not known in Marvell's time. Surely in that case a responsible critic would have to rule it out as part of the meaning of 'To his Coy Mistress'. Some mistranslations of Biblical or classical passages seem to me more beautiful than what the originals meant. But they remain mistranslations.

Examples of this kind are the only ones P. D. Juhl gives in his article and the result, it seems to me, is to give him an easy victory over those who hold that the meaning of a literary work can change; the pluralists, as we may call them. But a defender of their cause might reply that this kind of thing is not what a pluralist has in mind when he says that the meaning of a literary work can change. Questions about the meaning of 'To his Coy Mistress', or any other literary work, are not to be taken as questions about the meaning of this or that word or sentence or passage. But how then are they to be taken? This brings us to the second way of interpreting the question about meaning.

What the questioner may have in mind is a possible non-literal meaning. The textual meaning remains primary: you cannot understand the other meaning without understanding it. If you do not know what 'rose' means you cannot understand *The Romance of the Rose*. And it should be remembered that understanding the meaning of 'rose', in this context, includes understanding the aesthetic, emotional, and other implications of 'rose' in the culture in which the poem was written; the 'matrix of equivalences', to use a phrase of E. H. Gombrich. And, incidentally, you must have some feeling for the nature of roses themselves; as C. S. Lewis puts it, *The Romance of the Rose* could not without loss be rewritten as *The Romance of the Onion*. But to know these things is not enough to understand the poem. It is not merely a rigmarole about a youth who tried to pluck a rose. It has a second or latent meaning, and Lewis in *The Allegory of Love* explains what that is. Similarly *The Pilgrim's Progress* tells the story of a man's search for salvation; the Musical Banks in Butler's *Erewhon* refer to the churches; *Animal Farm* alludes to the Russian Revolution and the subsequent history of Russia ...and so on. This discovery of allegory has been thought, especially in some periods, our own included, to be peculiarly the province of the critic or interpreter, or 'hermeneutist', to use a fashionable word. This is understandable. The textual meaning of a work is an area well trodden by historical linguists; the manifest story can be left to vulgar readers who read on to find out what happened to the hero. So it is widely held that the proper field of interest for the critic is the latent meaning. Frank Kermode has put forward as an interpreter's charter 'the right to affirm, and the obligation to accept, the superiority of latent over manifest sense' (*The Genesis of Secrecy*, 1979). And whether we agree with this or not, there can be no doubt that many works do have a non-literal meaning.

But do they all have one? Certainly a determined critic can read an allegorical sense into any story whatever. But to say that a story can be given an allegorical sense is clearly not the same as saying that it is an allegory. Some rabbis maintained that the Song of Solomon is an allegory of God's love for Israel; some Christian Fathers saw it as an allegory of Christ's love for his Church. And it is fortunate that they had such ideas, since otherwise these beautiful poems might not have been preserved. But the rabbis and the Fathers were probably mistaken. In any case, it is possible to give an allegorical sense to what is without doubt a plain narrative of fact. A report in a newspaper could be used as a text – or a pretext – for a sermon, though in itself no more than a record of literal events. The allegorical or symbolical element in literature must not be belittled. I believe it is something that comes near to being a characteristic aspect of literature: the transcendence of particular occasions. And, at a lower level, no one can deny that the impulse to construct such things as cryptograms, rebuses, and puzzles is as widespread as the wish to uncover and decode them.

But equally there can be no doubt that quite often interpreters who see this or that latent sense in a work are merely imagining things. Of course they have every right to do that: it is one of the pleasures of literature that it stimulates our fantasies in this way. But many other things can do that – an ink-blot, or flames in the fire – especially when aided by a suitable drug. We have to distinguish legitimate interpretation from mere day-dreaming, or free association. But how can we do that? How can we decide whether a particular work really is an allegory? Is *The Odyssey* an allegory? Some works are obviously allegorical, like some of Hawthorne's tales, but are all Hawthorne's tales allegorical? And in an obviously allegorical tale by Hawthorne, is everything allegorical, or only some things? How can we tell? Is Jane Austen an allegorical writer? There is a scene in *Mansfield Park* (chapter X) which several critics have judged to contain important symbolic elements, but does that make *Mansfield Park* an allegory?

Similar considerations apply to, and similar problems are raised by, the equally old notion of a lesson or moral inculcated by a work. Writers have sometimes denied that they were drawing one. 'This story has no moral', says the author of 'Frankie and Johnnie'. But she belies her own words.

> This story has no moral,
> This story has no en';
> This story only goes to show
> That there ain't no good in men;
> He was her man
> And he did her wrong.

Contrary to what she says, she does draw a moral; she elicits a general inference from a particular instance. And the same process is evident in many other works: Defoe's term 'moral fable' can be applied very widely. But, as with allegory, it is not always certain whether these lessons or morals are really part of the story. And they may differ, according to what point of view you take. The moral of 'Red Riding Hood' is one thing from Red Riding Hood's point of view, but quite another from the wolf's; and since he is the character who gets the worst deal in the story, I have heard it suggested that he is the main character and cautionary instance, and the moral is 'Keep away from innocent-looking young girls.' But is this what the story means? When the author does not explicitly draw a moral there is usually a doubt about it. *Charley's Aunt* has a lesson to teach us. It teaches us that the power of greed over a man's mental faculties may be so great that it blinds him to the grotesque unlikeness of Lord Fancourt Babberley to Charley's aunt. (For me this reading received negative confirmation when Danny La Rue played the part: a brilliant impersonation takes away the point of the play.) But did Brandon Thomas know about this? Wasn't he just writing a farce? It is the same question as with allegory. We may use a story homiletically; but are we justified exegetically? And does it matter?

Perhaps these examples will be thought too trivial. Modern critics are too sophisticated to talk about the lessons or morals of a work they consider important. They agree with Charles Lamb that 'a Moral should be wrought into the body and soul, the matter and tendency of a Poem'. They prefer to talk about themes and significances. This may not only be because they dislike open didacticism, and prefer 'immanence'. It may also be because they do not want to beg the question whether the author has actually put the meaning that interests them into the work. But suppose we do want to know this. How can we know, beyond reasonable doubt?

In some cases we can know because the work gives us obvious verbal signals. In the case of allegory there is the occurrence of names like Mr Great-heart, or the Delectable Mountains. And a moral or lesson is sometimes tagged on at the end – to quote Lamb again, 'like "God send the good ship into harbour" at the conclusion of our bills of lading'. There may not always be these verbal signals, but there can be; and they may be sufficient to make further inquiry into the author's intentions unnecessary; they are part of the panoply of his work. But there is one kind of non-literal meaning where there seems to be no panoply. I am thinking of irony. In speech the presence of irony may be unmistakable, because of the speaker's intonation, or the expression on his face. But what are the equivalents for these in a passage of literature?

How shall we excuse the supine inattention of the Pagan and philosophic world to those evidences which were presented by the hand of Omnipotence, not to their reason, but to their senses? During the age of Christ, of his apostles, and of their first disciples, the doctrine which they preached was confirmed by innumerable prodigies. The lame walked, the blind saw, the sick were healed, the dead were raised, demons were expelled, and the laws of Nature were frequently suspended for the benefit of the church. But the sages of Greece and Rome turned aside from the awful spectacle, and, pursuing the ordinary occupations of life and study, appeared unconscious of any alterations in the moral or physical government of the world. Under the reign of Tiberius the whole earth, or at least a celebrated province of the Roman Empire, was involved in a preternatural darkness of three hours. Even this miraculous event, which ought to have excited the wonder, the curiosity, and the devotion of mankind, passed without notice in an age of science and history. It happened during the lifetime of Seneca and the elder Pliny, who must have experienced the immediate effects, or received the earliest intelligence, of the prodigy.

Each of these philosophers, in a laborious work, has recorded all the great phenomena of Nature, earthquakes, meteors, comets, and eclipses, which his indefatigable curiosity could collect. Both the one and other have omitted to mention the greatest phenomenon to which the mortal eye has been witness since the creation of the globe.

> Edward Gibbon, *The Decline and Fall of the Roman Empire*,
> chapter xv.

Few readers would doubt that this passage is ironical. But how do we know? Not, it seems, on purely linguistic grounds. The panoply of Gibbon, his flowing Ciceronian periods, remain the same in passages where no one would suspect irony. The element of unction could be found in many eighteenth-century sermons; indeed, Gibbon seems to be slyly borrowing their language. Yet most people would agree that the reader of this passage is being invited to draw the conclusion that the darkness during the Crucifixion never happened, all the more persuasively because the author refrains from drawing this conclusion himself. We are convinced that this thought could not have *not* occurred to someone as intelligent as we judge the author to be. We have a secret understanding with the author. But how can linguistic analysis show this? The ironic element does not seem to be textual.

In this respect irony appears to differ from allegory, or moral fable. They can be marked by characteristic linguistic devices, but irony cannot. And the reason for this is not hard to find. Irony consists in the author's adoption of a *persona* who speaks quite un-ironically. What makes what he says ironical is our sense that the author dissociates himself from, and in some way ridicules or criticises, what the *persona* is saying. It is therefore in the nature of the case that irony tends to be elusive, and is often missed altogether, as anyone who attempts it in a 'Letter to the Editor' will soon discover. Thus critics constantly disagree about Defoe. There are many passages in *Robinson Crusoe* which sound ironical to present-day readers, such as the pious Crusoe's account of his treatment of the Moorish boy Xury. But it is hard to decide how the real author saw them. It all turns on the difficult question whether Defoe was a very subtle or a very naive author.

Other cases, which seem more straightforward, can present us with problems if the interpretation is questioned. Take, for example, the work usually known as the *Modest Proposal*. Surely this is obviously ironical? But suppose this view were challenged. We could only reply by pointing to the monstrous conduct recommended, on commercial grounds, in the *Proposal*, the outrage to our moral assumptions. But humanity has always shown a recurrent liking for infanticide. Without common moral assumptions, can the correct interpretation of the *Proposal* be settled, unless we reveal that the masked author is Swift, and use as evidence what can be known of *his* moral assumptions in what we know of him in his other writings? Similarly the question whether Gibbon was writing ironically in some passages of the *Decline and Fall* could only be settled, if at all, by reference to a wider historical and biographical context. The local linguistic indicators are insufficient.

But at this point we come up against a widespread opposition to this kind of procedure; in fact, to the argument for liberty of interpreting. It goes like this. With texts in general, the utterances of speakers or writers, it is perfectly in order to refer, when disagreements about intention arise, to their context of origin. To take a simple case from everyday life: when we do not understand something a speaker has said, we may ask him to explain it. But the case is different with a literary work. Here the utterance is determinate: 'what I have written I have written'. It is not only that the authors are often personally inaccessible, being dead. Even when they are accessible they might be reluctant, or unable, to offer explanations. They might feel that their explanations would tend to limit the meaning of the work too much. And even if they do offer explanations, are their explanations necessarily privileged? Many writers would agree with Paul Valéry that 'once published, a text is like a machine which each person may use as he will and as he can; there is no certainty of the maker's operating it better than another'. In a similar vein Roland Barthes asks us to see the author as like the dummy hand at bridge. 'He played his part in the establishment of the contract, his hand is there on the table for all to see, but he does not play it; his partner, the reader, does that.'

Now there are certainly well-known difficulties about the search for an author's un-obvious intentions. As every reviewer knows, a work can fall short of an author's intentions; all too often. What is sometimes forgotten is that it can also exceed them. Lewis Carroll in the *Alice* books gave us a profound study of English life and character, but did he mean to do that? And where are we to look for the author's intention? What was Spenser's intention in book II of *The Faerie Queene*? The sketch of it he gives in the Letter to Raleigh appears not to fit what actually happens in book II. Assuming that these cannot be reconciled, in which are we to look for Spenser's intention?

Some historically minded critics are aware of such problems, and accept that recovery of all the author's intentions may often be difficult or even impossible. So they have suggested that the validation of interpretations should instead be sought in what his first readers made of his work. But in practice this is often just as hard to discover. Few readers have left their impressions on record, and such opinions are less available the further back in history we go. And in attempting to infer them from the author's text the historical critic finds himself arguing in a circle. In any case, the first readers or audiences were all individuals, as much as any readers or audiences are; they presumably varied from each other in intelligence, insight, relevant information, moral assumptions, interest in what the author was saying, just as much as their modern equivalents. Why should it be assumed that their reaction was homogeneous? (The late A. J. A. Waldock, in *Sophocles the Dramatist*, 1951, has some interesting observations on the tendency of classical scholars to make that assumption.) And why is it supposed that the views of the first audience, even if we could know them, must be of more value than the views of later audiences, or our own views? This is the strength of the case for liberty of interpreting. What is it, after all, that makes us call a literary work great? Surely it is its continuing appeal to other ages than its own. We may imagine a great work of art, a picture for example, hanging in a gallery, while an endless stream of admirers and students file past it through the ages. Are the reports of the first ones to see it necessarily the best? Surely it might well be held that later viewers see more.

For one thing, they could have the benefit of whatever illuminations the earlier viewers may have had.

Even the historically minded may be ready to agree that there is some justice in this opinion when it is applied to the generally agreed classics of art and literature. It is a commonplace that their meaning is inexhaustible. But there is likely to be more resistance to liberty of interpreting when it is proposed to extend it generally. Yet why should we not do this? Why may we not hold that this transcendence of the historical situation, or context of origin, is not only an occasional feature of some literary works, but the defining property, the *differentia*, of literature in general? On this view, to reconstruct the hypothetical first context of a work – the author's putative design, or the readers for whom it was in the first place intended – is not only very difficult – we would all agree about that; it is misguided in principle. In making this sort of investigation we are undoing the author's work. He made something which only fulfils its reason for existence when it is recontextualised. The new context in which it should be interpreted is the whole field of literary works to which, by virtue of having survived to be appreciated in another time and place, it now belongs. Something like this point of view is anticipated in the famous essay 'Tradition and the Individual Talent', in which Eliot claims that the appearance of a new work of art modifies the previous works among which it takes its place; it can act retrospectively, as well as prospectively. Or we might think of Northrop Frye's 'order of words', the whole realm of literature seen synchronically, not period by period, ahistorically coexisting.

This argument for liberty of interpreting seems to me to point in the right direction. But its conclusion itself needs some interpretation. Are we to reject all historical considerations and probabilities? Can we make a work mean whatever we like? Some critics seem to hold that view. 'There are no interpretations', says Harold Bloom, 'only misinterpretations, and so all criticism is prose poetry.' Taken literally, this statement presents difficulties. The word 'misinterpretation' only has force in the language as a contrast to 'correct interpretation'; if there are no correct interpretations, there are no misinterpretations either.

But I see what he is getting at. If rational decision between variant interpretations is impossible, it may well be that the critic has nothing to do but rhapsodise. But other advocates of liberty of interpreting would disagree. They admit that considerations of textual meaning are relevant. The dictionary can still be consulted. But they would strive to eliminate 'the author' as far as possible, to give priority to communal and co-cultural meanings over his (hypothetical) personal intentions. On this view it is impermissible to use other works of an author – say, works B, C, or D – to interpret work A, except in so far as they can be said to belong to the same cultural matrix. They have no *special* status in virtue of having come from the same personal source. The libertarian interpreter tries to maintain, as far as possible, the self-sufficiency of a work taken by itself, severed from the umbilical cord that once linked it to its author. The meaning of the work would, on this view, not be something (so to speak) embedded in it for us to dig out, but rather a locus for potentialities of meaning, some of which were perhaps actually realised by the author, but others of which remained for him and earlier readers merely incipient, to be actualised (or not, as the case may be) by later readers.

Thus Salvador de Madariaga, in his book on *Don Quixote* (Oxford, 1935), regards as futile the question whether Cervantes meant to give his characters the symbolic values which we now attach to them.

Had Cervantes meant to symbolize abstractions, he would have failed to create a work of art. He was, however, purely concerned with creating characters, and that is why he succeeded in giving the world eternal symbols. For even as a stone that strikes the water, though merely intent on obeying the law of gravity, will cause ever-widening circles to rise on the surface of the liquid, even so the creator who succeeds in touching the sea of the spirit will stir circles on it beyond the bounds of his limited sight. Not what Cervantes meant, but what he did, is our patrimony, and when speaking of *Don Quixote* we can choose any of the infinite number of circles which surge wider and wider round the spot where the book first fell.

All this is so metaphorical that it is not certain what limits, if any, Madariaga is prepared to draw round valid interpretations.

At any rate in his own discussion he goes beyond anything Cervantes could possibly have had in mind, interpreting the windmills Don Quixote mistook for giants' castles as modern factories, and so on.

It seems to me that when interpretation is as free as this, it becomes indistinguishable from *application*; and as a fundamental canon of exposition we surely must be able to draw this distinction. If there is any rationale for ignoring it, the only one I know is that which underlies the practice of what the rabbis called *midrash*. (In what follows I am indebted to the discussion of it by M. D. Goulder in his *Midrash and Lection in Matthew*, 1974.) The word *midrash* derives from *darash*, to probe or examine. Secure in the belief that Revelation is a bottomless mine of wealth, and that there are seventy faces to Scripture, the midrashist, the *darshan*, made things up to his heart's content. Not, of course, that he thought of himself as making things up. The derivation of the *midrash* was the guarantee that what he was digging for was there before. As he saw it, he was not inventing. One passage of Scripture would show him what was missing in another. His activity was nothing but examining one passage in the light of other passages. There is no need to ridicule the *darshan*, or cast doubt on his good faith. *Midrash* can result in things of great value and beauty. But where modern critical inquiry is concerned the activity of the *darshan* offers a cautionary tale, not a model to be followed. The subject-matter of modern criticism is not Scripture; and even if it were, Scripture itself does not have the plenary and total inspiration and unity which the *darshan* supposed it to have. Still less is the modern critic divinely inspired. His only guides are more prosaic ones, historical possibilities, respect for the facts, and, if he is lucky, a certain quality of imagination (so long as it is the same kind of imagination as the author's) which saves him from crass pedestrianism. So far from supposing that his interpretation will be accepted as finally authoritative, or even as a contribution to an ultimate final interpretation, the best he can hope for is that a few readers may think he has made a good or at least a plausible point now and then.

Liberty of interpreting goes astray if it tempts the critic or interpreter to put himself in the place of the author. There is an ethical objection to this, canonised in the Ninth Commandment (the one about false witness). But there is also an epistemological objection, which may be clarified as follows. Suppose that, instead of talking about texts, we talk about men and women. There are the men and women who create stories, poems, plays, who have the power to express and give coherent and enduring form to their imaginings. And there are the men and women who receive these things, who appreciate and enjoy them and for the time being live in them. Many of the former undoubtedly thought of themselves as having things to say to the latter. Some of them thought these things were true and important, even desperately important, and they did their best to convey them in a form their readers would understand. Today these men and women are dead and gone, and the people for whom they wrote in the first place are dead and gone too. And it may be that we no longer understand the forms in which they wrote. They can no longer address readers directly. Now I would agree with the libertarians that a preoccupation with old fashions and conventions, while entirely proper in the historian, is detrimental to the lover of literature. These obsolete forms are distracting, because they introduce a strangeness into the work of the dead poet which is irrelevant. We study these things in order to forget about them, so that we can grasp that which in the poet's work is or ought to be the common possession of humanity. But – and this is the epistemological objection I referred to – unless and until the forms through which he worked are understood there can be no true liberty of interpreting. Unless there is common ground between the old readers and the new, a 'semantic constant' as we might call it, the poet's work is no longer there to interpret. Expert opinions naturally differ about what, in the case of a particular work, constitutes its semantic constant. To my mind the most important consideration here is the sincerity of the reader's search for it. Generally speaking, if we have a sense of the whole tenor of a writer's work – established on the basis of passages about which there is no serious disagreement – we shall have a pretty good idea which interpretations are improbable. We should try to maintain our links with the dead poet, even though we know that as time goes on more and more of them will be broken, and even though we may be keenly aware that any reconstruction of the past must be at best partial and tentative. But it is worth persevering. The interpretation of Virgil and Ovid by the medievals – Virgil a sorcerer and Ovid a moralist – Lionel Trilling's description of Jane Austen as 'an agent of the Terror' – such things show a sad breach of cultural continuity. A new work has been put in place of the author's, and it may well be an inferior one.

Finally there is a third sense of 'meaning', when we talk of the meaning of a literary work, that I have not so far mentioned. And where meaning in this sense is concerned liberty of interpreting seems not only inescapable but proper. What I have in mind here is what may be called the direction of the reader's sympathies. After we have conscientiously, using all the knowledge we have at our disposal, endeavoured to read a work in accordance with the author's intention, 'with the same spirit as he writ', it may still be the case that the work we read is not, for us, the work he intended. Many of us find Macaulay's James II an oddly likeable person, which is certainly not how Macaulay saw him. Similarly, modern Milton scholars have succeeded admirably in describing the poem Milton probably intended to write in *Paradise Lost*. Yet we might accept their reconstructions, and still feel that Satan in books I and II, and Adam and Eve in book IX, attract more sympathy than the poet intended. What are we to do about this? It would be distasteful if we were to anaesthetise our emotional reactions, to try to make ourselves feel what we do not feel in the interest of some historical dogma, or theological assumption and, worse still, to denature beautiful poetry and adopt the least generous and most ignoble of interpretations in the effort to 'save the appearances'. Of course if you are quite happy about Milton's God, if for you Milton has justified his ways to Man, there is no more to be said. But we must not try to put out of court those sincere and well-informed readers who are *not* happy, by calling them 'Satanists', or convicting them of theological ignorance. There is nothing wrong with finding, on occasion, that we have to defend a work, or a character, against what appears to be the conscious will of the author. We need not talk about the Unconscious, or Kipling's Daemon, or the Muse, or 'inspiration', but we have to recognise that in all cultures, though they have used different terminology, poets themselves have testified to the fact that much in their art is not at their conscious beck and call. A writer probably intended his work to have a certain emotional effect, but there is no way in which he can ensure that it actually has that effect. In this sense, then, liberty of interpreting is our prerogative as readers. It means freedom of judgment, of personal decision whether or not the writer has actually performed what he seemed to promise.

3
Evaluative Criticism, and Criticism
without Evaluation

Literary criticism has traditionally been regarded as evaluative, or judicial. But over the centuries this notion of it has come to be questioned, and itself 'evaluated' adversely. With the recent deaths of leading figures – Edmund Wilson, Lionel Trilling, F. R. and Q. D. Leavis – who were critics of this kind, the Anglo-American literary scene has been left for the present without a great critical pundit. And I cannot help wondering whether there is likely to be another. Is the idea of evaluative criticism really compatible with rational discussion, as that is understood nowadays? Does it belong with other, now discredited ideas of authority in regions of discourse where no authority can respectably exist? This seems a suitable moment to have another look at the notion.

The first thing to note is that evaluative criticism is not itself a distinct literary genre. There are such things as 'critiques', but they do not by any means make up the entire field. Much valuable criticism occurs in letters, or in records of conversation. It can be found in novels, or poems: Shelley's *Peter Bell the Third* contains some illuminating criticism of Wordsworth. It can appear, as we would expect, in biographies of writers, such as Johnson's *Lives of the Poets*. Conversely, most critics have seen it as their business to inform their readers about other matters besides the value of authors' work. And of course the reviewer of new books cannot make his remarks intelligible unless he conveys to his readers something of what the work he is discussing is like; and if he is as fair-minded as he ought to be he will do his best to make his preliminary account of it as non-evaluative as possible. But obviously much criticism, whether of current works or old ones, consists very largely of value judgments.

As a rule these are offered without justification. It would seem that the critic's personality or manner, intimidating or cajoling, is regarded as a sufficient substitute. We may infer, then, that these judgments are persuasive, not rational. Critical writing is a form of rhetoric, not argument.

Still, evaluative critics have been known to offer reasons for their judgments. And anyway it is usually possible to deduce a rationale from the *œuvre* of a notable critic, even if he is unwilling or unable to formulate his principles for himself.

What principles have been proposed? On the face of it the literature of criticism swarms with precepts and doctrines, far too many to enumerate, let alone discuss. But the situation may not be so chaotic as it looks. There seem in fact to be only four kinds of justification for evaluative criticism, though these are usually concealed within the very large (and mainly figurative) vocabulary employed by critics. Some critics have been known to use all four, though this, as will be seen, involves them in inconsistency. And few leading critics can be pinned down to one kind. All the same, these four kinds seem to be distinct.

First there is the kind that appeals frankly to general criteria of value – moral or ideological, religious, political, etc., many of them extra-literary. This kind of criticism is apt to be prescriptive (authors are told what to do) and proscriptive (what not to do). It is a very old kind, and adorned with great names. Of these, Plato's is the greatest. He held that literature should serve the State, and judged and condemned it accordingly. Another great writer, Tolstoy in *What is Art?* (first English edition 1898), held that literature should serve the Brotherhood of Man. Work that was (to use a modern expression) elitist could not bring men together, because too few of them could understand it, so Tolstoy condemned it root and branch – including *War and Peace* and *Anna Karenina*. Other critics of our own days, though with less candour and consistency than Plato or Tolstoy, have taken a similar line. Irving Babbitt condemned many works because they offended against, or did not positively serve to strengthen, traditional morality. It is well known that many Socialist and Communist critics have condemned writers on political grounds. Writers have been applauded (or denounced) as Catholics, or as Protestants. Anti-pornographers campaign on hygienic grounds. And so on.

Two recurrent features of ideological criticism may be noted.

41

It is often censorious. And it takes no account of a writer's intentions. The Roman *Index Expurgatorius* ignores them. If a Russian writer's work is viewed by Soviet authority as 'objectively' aiding United States imperialism it is no use his protesting that he did not mean to do this. It may seem curious that, since most of these critics are moralists, they do not allow mitigation on grounds of good intentions. Good intentions have usually been regarded as a sufficient defence against condemnation in the moral sphere (if not in the aesthetic). No doubt these critics would draw a distinction between matters of private and public morality. At any rate, the essential claim is that the Church, or the State, or the Party, or some other community for which the critic is the mouthpiece, takes the decision about what the author's work is like, not the author himself, or his public.

The liberal-minded do not like this notion of evaluative criticism, and in some societies the brave ones among them have actively fought against it. But the historical fact must be faced that a great deal of criticism, perhaps most of it, has consisted of moral or ideological propaganda. Some modern critics have denied that this is true of their work. F. R. Leavis was at pains to insist that his appraisals did not entail ideological commitments. He liked to describe his criticism as taking part in 'the common pursuit of true judgment'. But his opponents have accused him, not merely of ideology, but of sectarianism. Similarly Marxist critics have claimed that what they are writing is science, not propaganda. If they are serving a progressive purpose by tearing away masks, stripping away bourgeois illusions, this from their point of view is merely a fortunate by-product of their impartial inquiries. Notwithstanding this, it is well known that they themselves have been often accused of flagrant bias. And they in turn have not been slow to accuse their liberal–democratic opponents of begging fundamental questions by tendentious talk of what is 'rational', or 'objective', or 'common sense'. And we all know that what seems obviously true and reasonable to one person may seem to another hopelessly class-blinkered, or mere camouflage for sexism, or racism, or some other objectionable tendency.

Can poetry be put out of reach of all this fighting? As vernacular literature became a subject for academic study the

Academy tried to find it a haven from these contending winds of doctrine. Traditional literary scholarship had great things to its credit. But it had failed to supply a generally agreed doctrine of relevance with which to exclude all this barbarism. The need for this brought about the rise of formalism in university and college teaching in the twentieth century – what came to be known in the Anglo-American world as the 'new criticism'. In Continental Europe this movement was associated with a non-evaluative conception of criticism, as in the Russian formalists, with their background in linguistics. But, inspired by some early pronouncements of the poet–critic T. S. Eliot, the Anglo-American movement retained the old notion of criticism as judgment, in an up-to-date version of aestheticism. 'When you judge poetry', said Eliot, 'it is as poetry you must judge it, and not as another thing.'

The three other kinds of justification have, then, been employed by critics who worked in the spirit of this saying. They all agree that poetry – imaginative literature in general – must be judged as poetry. But they interpret this injunction differently, and their different interpretations have generated different schools of criticism.

The least satisfactory way of interpreting it is that which involves a large general conception of literature. The critic, we are to suppose, forms a philosophic view of the whole universe and the scheme of values which includes literature. From literature's place in that scheme, its relation to other values, he deduces a literary standard, which he applies to particular instances. This conception of literary criticism was the life-long dream of Coleridge. The trouble is that neither Coleridge nor anyone else has achieved this total, generally accepted *Weltanschauung*. It sounds more like an ambition of Continental European thought, with its 'huge cloudy symbols', than of Anglo-American; and the Continental Europeans have not only not convinced the Anglo-Americans, they have not convinced each other.

The blunt truth is that 'poetry' is too vague a term for the injunction 'it is as poetry you must judge it' to have a clear meaning. We need to know what poetry is being contrasted with here, and we are not told. What tends to happen in practice, as Eliot in later years came to realise, is that the poet–critic

43

covertly identifies poetry with the kind of poetry he himself writes, or wants to write. Eliot had said in *The Sacred Wood* (1920) that 'the important critic is he who is absorbed in the present problems of art, and wishes to bring the forces of the past to bear on the solution of these problems'. The trouble with this is that there are no 'present problems of art'. There are only the problems that (say) T. S. Eliot, or Ezra Pound, may have had in *their* art, in 1920 or whenever. But these problems were very different from the problems that Sean O'Casey or Ivy Compton-Burnett may have in *their* art. Who is to say *which* present problems are the important ones?

There is an element of unconscious arrogance in the poet–critic. I must explain at once that I do not wish to say anything against the criticism of poetry by poets. On the contrary, I believe it to be the most valuable criticism we have. Poets can tell us things about poetry that only poets can know. But of necessity the personal equation bulks large in what they say. Good poets are often (not always) engaged in making a literary revolution. They are thus bound to be ruthless to their peers and predecessors. The perspective and balance of a Goethe or a Baudelaire are rare. Many poets have felt themselves to be engaged in a struggle against 'influences'. Yeats felt he had to 'get Milton off my back'. So apparently did Eliot. The discovery by poets of what they need, or don't need, in other poets' work can be illuminating for the rest of us. It has been urged that Eliot would not have discerned certain qualities in the metaphysical poets, and so helped us to discern them, without his practitioner's interest. And this may well be true. But the claim for the poet–critic cannot be generalised. Poetry does not belong to one poet, however gifted, or to one school of poets. It belongs to all its lovers and appreciators, whoever and wherever they are.

The relevant point here is that without some very particularised conception of 'poetry' the injunction to judge poetry as poetry has no meaning. But if the conception is particularised, the criticism that is controlled by it is too restrictive. Here the problem of all appraisive criticism is focussed. To mean anything, criteria have to be specific, narrow. But if they are specific and narrow they are too cramping.

Episodes from literary history suggest, then, that appeals to a large general conception of literature either result in vacuity, or its tendentious redefinition by a special interested group. But there has been another kind of attempt to judge literature by purely formal standards, which at first sight seems to promise more objectivity, because the controlling idea is more definite. This is the revival of the old idea of genre, which has some great names attached to it, the greatest being that of Aristotle in his *Poetics*. The details of Aristotle's treatment of the question, and its interpretation and misinterpretation from the Renaissance onwards, are of great historical and cultural interest, but they need not now concern us. Even those critics, like the Chicago School, who call themselves neo-Aristotelians are well aware that some of Aristotle's famous phrases are very obscure in meaning. And the historical situation, and the field of literature available to us compared with that available to Aristotle, are too different for direct adaptation of the *Poetics* to be helpful. What matters is the spirit of the thing.

Genre criticism can be tried in different ways. One way seems bad. The critic dreams of an imaginary 'tragedy' or 'novel', embodying the good-making features of all the ones he thinks good, and judges actual works according to a non-existent pattern-work laid up in some Platonic heaven. A more sensible sort of genre critic proceeds differently. He brings together literary works that seem obviously comparable, and chooses what he thinks the best as the standard for that class of work. If he is sufficiently sensitive to the immense variety among works and authors, he will probably confine himself to the *œuvre* of a single writer. Suppose the genre in question is 'Shakespearean tragedy'. The genre critic might decide that *Macbeth* was the best play of this kind. He could give reasons: *Macbeth*, he could say, is the most tense and gripping of these plays, because it has least in it that is irrelevant to the plot. So he would judge it superior to *Hamlet*, which is leisurely and long-winded, and has much in it that appears to be irrelevant to the plot (the grave-diggers, Osric). The advantage of this sort of criticism is that it is fairly definite. Whether or not we adopt the criteria proposed, there is some way of finding out whether they have been met or not.

But the drawbacks are obvious. Why should not Shakespeare, or any other writer, have produced works that were good in quite different ways? Why should only one of his works be used as the standard? And why should we adopt 'relevance to the plot' as the decisive criterion? That many people do, as a matter of fact, accept such a criterion is shown by the number of attempts that have been made to show that the 'irrelevances' of *Hamlet* are not really irrelevant. But there is no compulsion to accept this criterion. Why should not a work be loosely knit and rambling? Some people prefer that kind of work.

There is a further, more subtle argument against the notion of genre. It is convenient to define literary kinds, like many other things, *per differentiam*. Contrast is a well-tried method of criticism. But it would be a logical error to infer that the qualities of a work that are best suited to exhibit differentiation are necessarily those that make for its value. A dramatist might be classified with a certain group on account of his dramaturgy. But the valuable thing in his work might be its poetry; and this might be more aptly comparable to the work of some other, and perhaps non-dramatic poet.

Yet the notion of genre seems to have some basis in reality. Certain works do seem to be obviously comparable, whether for genetic reasons (all produced by the same school or author) or not. And 'genre' is a more definite idea than 'poetry' or 'literature'. It does offer some guidance about what is likely to be relevant, and, at least with minor genres, or sub-genres, it could be made quite precise. And that it is a commonsense notion is in its favour. At a purely descriptive level there is something to be said for it. The trouble begins when it becomes prescriptive. If Aristotle, or R. S. Crane, or Wayne Booth, lays down that this or that mode of characterisation, or mixture of characters, is unlikely to succeed, we can be sure that some clever writer will prove them wrong. Imagination is a 'licentious and vagrant' faculty, said Johnson, the most sensible of corrective critics; and he did not mean this as a reproach. It is simply a fact of life and art.

It seems to me that the practical value of the notion of genre lies not in making but in combating arbitrary stipulations. For example, the appeal to stylistic norms can be opposed in this way. The bad grammar in *Huckleberry Finn* for long kept it out of the canon of American literature. The recognition that what might be out of place in an Addisonian essay could well be in place in a different kind of work may seem obvious enough now. But it took a long time to sink into educated minds. In our time even a conservative critic like Evelyn Waugh, concerned with standards of 'good writing', could defend the bad grammar in a novel of Henry Green.

But it is surely plain that the most effective defence of such deviations is to be found, not so much in considerations about literary kinds, as in an account of the particular, individual, unique thing that a Mark Twain or a Henry Green is doing. And this brings me to the last of the purely 'literary' justifications that have been offered for evaluative judgments, and surely the only one that is a live option: the judgment in terms of an author's particular intention in a particular work. Whatever a critic's pretensions, however portentous and baffling his language may be if he is writing about established work, when it comes to current literature and he is faced with a new work that he has to try to judge fairly, I do not know of any literary criterion that he can apply other than 'What did the author intend here? How far did he fulfil his intention?'

Historically speaking, it took a long time for literary criticism to get here, and there are still many critics who, in practice if not in theory, refuse to accept this approach. Yet its advantage is obvious. It recognises that a writer, if he has enough freedom in the choice and treatment of his *donnée* to be called an artist, is a unique species. He is not concerned with Poetry, or The Novel, but with a particular thing, indescribable till he has done it. The right of an author to be viewed in this light may be called the privilege of singularity. The recognition of this peculiarity of literary art, or of art in general, is usually credited to Benedetto Croce. But it appeared much earlier: much of the credit for it is, I believe, due to the romantic movement, German, French, and English, although regrettably that movement left no one famous essay or manifesto in which it was definitively stated and enshrined – perhaps Victor Hugo's preface to his *Cromwell* comes nearest. And this is one legacy of the romantics to the moderns that has not been altogether repudiated. Critics committed to a censorious doctrine are, of course, bound to oppose it; and some of the neo-Marxist theorists, with their talk of 'literary production', spokesmen for our technological–collectivist age, have denounced its individualism. All the same, it is the only aesthetic theory (if it is to be called that) which is widely accepted by both artists and plain men.

But once the unique, the unrepeatable, the irreducible are recognised by literary criticism its own status becomes problematic. What becomes of the traditional critic, speaking as he does about 'standards'? Standards are no more than recipes, formulas, rubber-stamps – the last thing an original writer is interested in. He wants to do something quite particular. But since his aim is chosen by himself, what right has anyone but the artist himself to decide whether or not he has accomplished it?

And it is fashionable today to say that we can never know what an author's intention was. But this seems an over-statement. And it leads to logical difficulties. For example, such a view cannot be consistently held with regard to all forms of authorship – otherwise an anti-intentionalist would be unable to formulate his own doctrines. There would be nothing to prevent a reader, without the possibility of correction, from ascribing the most rigidly historicist doctrines to a Barthes or a Derrida. It may be answered that their view applies only to artistic writing, not to discourse. But to decide that this or that is artistic writing or discourse is itself a critical judgment. Total anti-intentionalism would reduce discussion, language, meaning to total nonsense. And indeed some of the latest French criticism seems to be well over the edge into nihilism. Words have become merely mounds of ink, or noises, generating more mounds of ink, or noises. Perhaps it should all be blamed on 'the age'.

But without surrendering to insanity we must admit that where works of art are concerned the notion of the artist's intention is sometimes not clear. In some cases we do not know, we have no way of knowing, whether the author intended this or that. He may be dead, or otherwise unavailable for comment. We cannot telephone Molière to find out what he thinks of his latest producer. And even when we are in a position to ask the author, he may be unwilling or unable to answer. He may be better at creating beautiful things than at explaining them; the two faculties rarely go together. He may have forgotten what he meant. He may change his mind about it, or lie. It is always open to him to answer: 'It means what it says.' An author does not 'own' the meaning of his work, he has no privileged access to it. Its meaning belongs to a public world.

I agree with all this. But I think it is still an over-statement to say that we never know what an author intended. We know it in innumerable cases. Nothing so contrary to common sense and reason as the extreme anti-intentionalist doctrine can possibly be acceptable. The concept of intention cannot be dispensed with in literary criticism if it is to be part of rational discourse. This would be too obvious to need saying, if it were not that there are at the moment spectacular literary pontiffs who deny it.

What is wrong with some traditional, 'intentionalist', criticism is that it is too presumptuous. The critic discovers, from his inspection of the work, and perhaps also from external, biographical evidence, what the work before him ought to have been. An ideal work floats before his eyes, with which he compares the very imperfect work before him. This is a fine procedure when the critic is the artist himself, engaged in revising. It is ludicrous when the critic is not the artist. It is worse than genre criticism. At least the genre critic can point to an actual achieved work as his standard, however unfair, in a particular case, it may be to do that. The critic who plays at being the artist is referring to a work which exists only in his imagination. Like Ulrich Brendel in Ibsen's play, he has spared himself the sordid task of writing a single word of it.

To particularise the author's intention is thus absurd. It puts the critic in the place of the author, or above him. To speak instead of the author's general intention is to avoid these absurdities; it is perfectly proper, and in some cases helpful (for example, here and there it may be necessary to point out that a writer was trying to be funny).

The trouble is that, gross misunderstandings apart, it is usually not very helpful to talk about general intentions. Art resides in minute particulars. Statements about intention need to stick closely to the author's own terms of reference, to the details of his text. But then I wonder whether they are necessary. Why repeat in a weaker way what the author has already said better?

If we grant the privilege of singularity, and if we restrict criteria to purely formal and literary ones, the enterprise of evaluative criticism is empty.

Is there any escape from a wholly negative conclusion of this kind? Many have decided that there is not. Criticism without evaluation is a better prospect. It appeals to modern scepticism about values. As far as matters of taste are concerned the climate of opinion favours complete relativism. But there is still respect for the expert, the specialist. And this is now the fashionable role for the critic. It is held that an ordinary reader of a work of serious literary pretensions needs information to appreciate it, other than what is supplied by the work itself, and his own feelings about it. Informative criticism, leaving judgment to the reader, is in some esteem.

The common objection to it is that a critic cannot but evaluate, since he has to select the things he wants to talk about, and decide what in them is important, or less important, or un-important. But this objection is not cogent. It would apply, *mutatis mutandis*, to any field of inquiry.

Another objection is that it is tedious. This objection has some force in the Anglo-American world. All the great British and American critics have been literary journalists, who had to write in a lively and interesting way. The attempt at criticism without the personal equation does lead too often to heavy, graceless writing, with many abstractions and would-be technical terms. But again this does not seem a fundamental objection. Some gifted writers have been able to deal clearly and succinctly with very abstruse subjects.

And we could put up with an ugly style if we could agree that we were being brought nearer to the truth by it. As Bacon says, 'Truth is a naked and open daylight that doth not shew the masks and mummeries and triumphs of the world half as stately and daintily as candlelight.' But is it truth that we are getting?

No short answer can be given. There are too many varieties of non-evaluative criticism for it to be possible. They range from the myth-criticism of Northrop Frye, or the incandescent utterances of Wilson Knight, to the statistical study of literary vocabulary, establishing with scientific accuracy that the author of the *Imitation of Christ* was writing about Christ. Evaluative critics, whatever their vagaries, are all held together by the common purpose of asking how good this or that work is. No such common purpose can be detected in the motley mass of their rivals.

The nearest to a generally acceptable description of their activities that I know of used to be 'helping the reader to a fuller understanding of literary works'. The term 'interpretation' was much used. The concept of interpretation here is not altogether clear. If interpretation means paraphrasing the author's work in dull prose, what is the point of it? And if the critic's prose is lively, what the reader gets is the critic's personality rather than the author's; or he gets the author at second or third hand, inextricably mixed up with the critic's personality. There need be no objection to this; criticism can be very entertaining. But it hardly seems compatible with the claim that it leads to greater understanding – if it is the author one is interested in, rather than the critic.

The notion of interpretation is more intelligible with regard to ancient works, or works in a different cultural tradition from the reader's. I should myself prefer to regard these scholarly activities as providing the means to criticism itself. But there is no need to quibble about terms. Without historical clarification it is difficult for the non-specialist reader to gain much access to some works. Their 'mode of projection' has to be grasped.

But what is the point of 'clarification' of a modern writer? The obscurity of authors like Joyce or Pound, Kafka or Beckett, is not due to purely contingent, historical reasons. It is intrinsic. The elucidating interpreter treats it as if it were an unfortunate accident, which can be removed by his ministrations. But this destroys the characteristic effect of their work. It is ironical that these interpreters claim to be doing a service to the author, respecting his intentions, when they explain his work with the aid of information about his reading, his sources, his private life. What they actually do, to the reader who takes all this in, is to prevent him from experiencing the author's work as the author meant him to experience it.

To remove what is problematic and mysterious in a writer, old or new, is to remove what makes him interesting. The corrective school may have gone wrong by stigmatising as faults what should rather be seen as characteristics. But at least they drew attention to roughness, inequalities. The tendency of 'interpretative' criticism is to make everything too bland. The interpreters fill up the gaps. They may believe themselves to be safeguarding the author from irrelevant (or irreverent) criticism. What they are actually doing is taking the life and character out of his work.

At the moment 'interpretation' has gone out of fashion. The new alternative is the attempt to make criticism an exact science. This is the explanation for the curious language, the 'structuralese' or 'sociologese', which the intelligent non-specialist interested in literature greets with bewilderment or derision. Is this sort of thing science? To ask what is or is not 'science' is to raise huge and difficult questions – and momentous ones, since the word 'science' is a word of potent suggestiveness in our culture. What is meant by science? Is history a science? (It seems to be one in France and Germany, not in Great Britain and the United States.) What the exponents of 'scientific criticism' seem to have in mind is the dissociation of criticism, not merely from taste, the personal equation, but from historical philology, literary history, cultural history generally, and its realignment with new sciences, or incipient sciences, such as psychology, linguistics, or anthropology – not to mention some with newer names.

If these new sciences can really do what their advocates claim for them, their contribution to literary study would be very relevant and welcome. Psychology is especially attractive. If anything is to be scientifically established about literary taste, it must surely be found through experimental investigation of people's psycho-physical reactions. Why did this line of poetry, rather than that, make A. E. Housman's hair bristle under the razor? Why is this book wonderful to reader A, and repellent nonsense to reader B? Why is it that Agatha Christie has conquered the world (in despite of the critics) and Thomas Love Peacock has not? There are, of course, commonsense answers to these questions, but they are merely intuitive, guesswork. It would be very interesting and instructive to have some facts and figures here.

Unfortunately there are none. This may be because of the practical difficulty (and financial expense) entailed by many of these inquiries. But I believe that there are difficulties of principle also. Some philosophers have suspected conceptual confusions in the nascent science of psychology – both 'individual' and 'social'. I cannot help thinking that the good clinician is as intuitive as the good literary critic – or the wise man generally.

But if there ever is a scientific psychology it would be very reasonable to turn to it for help. The same cannot be said for the enterprise of post-Chomsky linguistics. Without raising the question whether or not this discipline is just as confused about essentials as literary criticism, I must point out that it has no more obvious relevance to literary problems than any other study – nor has Chomsky ever claimed that it had.

And about incipient sciences in general it must be said that a critique which depends on them must be considered as a possible contribution to *them*, rather than to the solution of problems in criticism.

So criticism as a social science remains more an ideal than an actuality. But does this mean that no attempt should be made to attain this ideal? In a long chapter of his book *The Living Principle* (1975) the leading evaluative critic of our time, F. R. Leavis, made a heroic effort to rule it out of existence on *a priori* grounds. With the aid of a philosopher, Marjorie Grene, he tried to show that judgments of value enter inevitably into all statements of fact. I am not sure that Marjorie Grene actually does say this. But anyway I am sure it is wrong. 'Brighton has such-and-such an average annual rainfall' is one kind of statement, and 'Brighton has the best climate in the world' is quite another. What *is* true is that in most kinds of discourse fact and value are very much mixed up together. And this applies especially to criticism of the arts. Surely that must be conceded to Leavis's argument.

What I am not convinced of is that fact and value can never be separated, even in that domain. More than that, I think it is sometimes desirable to separate them. One of these occasions is the pedagogic. Younger students are apt to make premature value judgments, or – which is more likely – to take over as facts the assertions of some influential authority. For them to know a little of the history of opinion, what E. E. Kellett called 'the whirligig of taste', can be an enlightening experience. The judicial tradition of criticism tends to convey the impression that evaluations are fixed and final. *Paradise Lost* (say) stands in this or that comparative relation to other poems, now and for all time. This is Matthew Arnold's idea of a 'real' judgment, and it seems to me quite illusory.

There is also a psychological point to be considered. We are always told to approach a work without prejudice. But what if the idea of 'judging' is itself a prejudice? It is true that some people have a mania for rating and ranking, and this can result in fruitful criticism. But the clear description of actual features of literary works – what makes them function as the particular literary works that they are – must come before rating and ranking; and it may make rating and ranking unnecessary.

The most useful sort of non-evaluative criticism, as I see it, is what is traditionally called 'literary history'. Accounts of the careers of authors; the communities they lived in; their subject-matter; the ideas and imaginings that shaped their work – all these things can be relevant. More important still is the story of the development of some literary medium down to the moment when an individual writer felt the challenge of something new to be done. Literature in its own way, intuitive, or sensuous, or emotional, takes in the whole of human life; its matter is infinite. But the development of literary forms is determinate and can be displayed. Literature as an art can have its own history, like music or painting.

It is important that some histories should be non-teleological. We do not always want the story to be told in terms of the 'good guys', the authors we like already, or who influenced or 'led up

to' the authors we like. Even if we find some old work uninterest-
ing, we should not dismiss it if it can be shown that it once
pleased people. Contemporary taste should not be taken as an
absolute.

Still, unless the literary historian shares in some measure the
point of view of his own age, it is difficult for him to address it. He
too is a creature of history, transient. There is no way in which
he can eliminate the personal equation. And most literary
histories also contain critical estimates of the work of authors.
To use the words of Auden's headmaster in *The Orators*, we are
not only interested in 'What did it mean to them, there, then?'
We want to know 'What does it mean to us, here, now?'

So I come back to the original question: what is the status of
these reports? Clearly they are personal impressions. The word
'we', says Simone Weil, with characteristic overstatement, always
introduces a lie. The expression of sincere personal opinion is
always worth having. It retains its significance as testimony,
however we may disagree with the judgments that are made or
the criteria that are implied. But can evaluative criticism be more
than that? Can it appeal to common experience and reason?

I do not think criticism can be rational if it tries to draw a
line round 'poetry' or 'literature'. So we are brought back to the
old notion of criticism as moral, ideological, 'extrinsic'. I have
described it as corrective, censorious, prescriptive – Plato, Tolstoy,
Matthew Arnold. But does it have to be? Why cannot we respect
the author's right to his *donnée*, and his way of treating it, while
reserving our own right to bring general human values to bear
on his work? We must first understand what he is doing, and
this involves recognition that there are no artistic laws or rules.
But works of art can still be judged according to the immediate
pleasure and expansion of mind they give us.

The attempt of some critics to smuggle extra-literary values
into the discussion, under the pretext that they are literary
values, seems to me misguided. It is more honest to admit that
formal literary criteria, necessary as they are, are not our only
criteria. And we must concede to the unmaskers that the assumptions behind these evaluations are not self-evident, common
sense, transparently obvious to the disinterested eye. They have

ideological implications. Mostly, no doubt, these are unconscious. But then let us make them conscious. Some of our choices can be rationally defended, even if none can be proved to be right. If this or that work is praised or blamed by reference to this or that general value-criterion, it is always proper to ask: is this a relevant and useful criterion? Has it been fairly applied? Criticism is much criticised. But this logically establishes its title to exist. Criticism never decides anything. It is an argument. The argument goes on.

4
The Novel: a Critical Impasse?

The problem for discussion is this. There are two typical views, or theories, about the Novel – call them A and B. In theories of type A the Novel is given the high value, significance and importance which its admirers wish it to have. But when this view is spelt out explicitly it seems to be vitiated by an internal contradiction. A theory of type B is logically coherent; but it seems to deprive the Novel of serious interest. (I shall presently explain what these theories are.)

This problem only arises for those who claim a high standing for the Novel. Many, of course, do not read novels at all, and many more enjoy them only as light entertainment. But expressions like 'major fiction' are accepted. The publishers' advertisement for a reprint of Owen Wister's *The Virginian* (1902) speaks of its 'lasting appeal for readers of serious fiction as well as lovers of Western genre fiction'. The Novel is no longer an outlaw on Parnassus. However meagre may be the novelist's financial reward for his work, however unintelligently it may be treated by the 'irresponsible, indolent reviewers', he has at least the satisfaction (for what that is worth) of knowing that the art he practises has the support of a respected convention. This was not always so. The English novel began as a rather disreputable form of sub-literature, and there are still traces here and there of the old prejudices against fiction. But, academically speaking, the Novel has 'made the grade'. Today many university students, like readers in general, seem to take for granted that it is the main form of literature.

In the hectic world we live in there have been fears for the Novel's survival. Some influential voices, in the middle years of this century, have suggested that other forms, such as the Travelbook, held out greater artistic promise. More recently a few pundits, briefly in fashion, have declared that films and television were making the Novel obsolete, with its slow pace and its demand from the consumer of some mental activity. But it looks as if the predictions of Marshall McLuhan are unlikely to be fulfilled. Films and television are more and more being recognised as, for the most part, ephemeral. Only the written word counts in the end. So far from thinning the ranks of readers, adaptations of well-known novels by 'the media' seem to have the effect of increasing the readership of the books they are based on.

No doubt many novels are not very good, or not as good as they are cracked up to be. In every age much, perhaps most, prose fiction is no more than commercial entertainment. But few would deny that Europe, and America – and other parts of the world too – have produced novels which are an enrichment of life. It is true that some people who look at things from a radical point of view have maintained that, in the deepening 'crisis of capitalism', the Novel's great days are over. It was the creation of the European bourgeoisie in its heyday, and will never again reach the heights it achieved in the nineteenth century. For such people the classic novel has become a historical phenomenon. The present age may require something different, perhaps the 'disruptions' contrived by the new school of American novelists. However that may be, the masterpieces of the traditional novel are still read with pleasure. The Novel at its best challenges comparison with the best things in European poetry and drama.

Many enthusiasts for the Novel would regard this view as a commonplace. Some of them go even further, and claim that the Novel has taken over the resources of poetry and drama, which have now (at least as far as literature in English is concerned) become minor forms. This is the thesis of John Speirs's book *Poetry Towards Novel* (1971). His conception of the Novel as 'dramatic poem' was much favoured by the Cambridge critical journal *Scrutiny* (1932–53), which was dominated by F. R. and Q. D. Leavis. In a recent lively and provoking essay on 'The Englishness of the English Novel' (*New Universities Quarterly*, Spring 1981) Q. D. Leavis sketches, along similar lines, the historical development of prose fiction in English. She makes much of its debt to Shakespeare, whom she sees as the real founder of the English novel, and to other dramatists (Sheridan, for example). She shows what the novel owed to graphic art, such as the work of Hogarth. And she traces at some length the ways in which the classic English novel has been modified by the special features of English life and history, and how it has been moulded by, and has had a part in moulding, what used to be thought of as the English character and the English humane tradition.

In this article Mrs Leavis makes tremendous claims for the 'serious' novel. How are they to be justified? She refers to the Novel's incorporation of some of the qualities of drama and poetry. But if drama and poetry are what matter, why not recommend drama and poetry? What else has the Novel to offer? What is its special superiority to other forms? A theory of the 'A' type, warranting a high claim for the Novel, is surely under an obligation to say what are its distinctive excellences.

Everyday discussion of novels turns largely on Story (or Plot) and Characters. Both these are primitive, unanalysed notions. It is clear that an examination of the nature of fiction with any pretensions to rigour would have to draw subtler distinctions. The Russian formalist Viktor Shklovsky, for instance, distinguishes between Story (the mere chronological sequence of events in a novel) and Plot, which he sees as the particular way in which a novelist creates the interest, the mystery, the strangeness, the 'defamiliarisation' of his raw material. (See *On the Theory of Prose*, Moscow, 1925; discussed by Terence Hawkes in *Structuralism and Semiotics*, 1977.) Much can be learned by looking at Story, or Plot, in this way. But it is not clear that anything distinctive of the Novel would be discovered. Plays have plots as well as novels; indeed the Novel inherited the plot from the Drama. It may be that to have a story (if this is to be distinguished from a plot) is characteristic of the Novel. 'Yes, oh dear yes, the novel tells a story', said E. M. Forster. Even Virginia Woolf, who has been thought to do without a story, has one in *To the Lighthouse*. In the early part of this novel Mr Ramsay thinks about going to the lighthouse, and in the later part he goes to it. But it would obviously be quite wrong to make a story *distinctive* of the Novel. In the perspective of literary history the Novel is quite a recent arrival. The Story may be as old as humanity.

As for Character, this also is a rather vague abstraction. Discussions of whether or not Henry James or D. H. Lawrence could create 'character' have usually remained on the level of journalism, since no definite meaning has been given to the term. It would seem that many famous novelists have owed their fame to their ability to create a 'living world'. Most people, I suppose, remember type-figures from novels, rather than the plots. An emphasis on memorable characters, as a necessary condition of the best novels, has long been part of the stock-in-trade of the successful novelist turned critic, like J. B. Priestley, or Hugh Walpole, or Somerset Maugham. Perhaps that was why F. R. Leavis was inclined to be contemptuous of the notion of Character. He deprecated the common notion that 'the test of life' in a novelist's characters is that 'they go on living outside the book'. (See his article on *Hard Times*, in *Scrutiny* XIV, 3, 1947.) Yet one of the two novelists he came to regard as supreme said of the other: 'All his characters are my personal friends. I am constantly comparing them with living persons, and living persons with them.' This is Tolstoy on Dickens (see Sir Arthur Quiller-Couch, *Charles Dickens and other Victorians*, 1925).

In any case, without the notion of Character it is hard to see how novels could be discussed at all. Nor need thought about it be confined to the level of popular argument. There are historical questions which can be investigated. For instance, there is the question of the typology usable by an individual novelist at a particular time, the correlation of moral and physical qualities that was available to him, and intelligible and acceptable to the novel-readers of his day. There is also the question of what were the conventions that governed regional or class dialogue in the work of novelists of a particular epoch. And there are other matters relevant to the codes, or meaning-structures, through which 'character' is conveyed.

But Character cannot be regarded as a peculiar excellence of the Novel. Countless readers have found it in Homer's Achilles, or in the Bible's Joseph or David. It may be objected that this is an anachronism, since neither Homer nor the Bible had any conception of 'character' as we understand it. And this may be so. But considered as a contribution to the argument it is a *non sequitur*. If readers see some feature in a work, then they see it, whether or not the maker of the work thought of it as we think of it, or not. Homer and the Bible are perhaps special cases. But it is impossible not to see 'character' as an excellence of Dante's *Comedy*, or Chaucer's *Troilus and Criseyde*. (Indeed some critics have regarded Chaucer's poem as a forerunner of the Novel.) At one time academic opinion turned against the traditional view of Shakespeare as a great creator of characters. But it is becoming clear that, in some terminology or other, this is what should be said.

It may be that the Novel, for reasons to be mentioned presently, allows a greater fullness and inwardness in the treatment of Character than other forms. It may be that it is in novels that we meet the imaginary men and women we know best. But they have some competition from the records of people in real life: Plato's Socrates, Boswell's Johnson. What novelist has surpassed them?

Apart from the plot and characters of a novel, what else is there to discuss? There is a serious difficulty here. Plot and character may be primitive notions, but they seem to refer to something fairly definite. On the other hand, the author's 'style', or 'point of view', or 'sensibility', or 'quality of feeling', or his 'ideas' – unless we are content with the current cant of criticism, it is hard to know how to talk about them. What can be pointed to, what counts as evidence, when we discuss them?

This is not to say that they are not important. Indeed, I have little doubt that they are, in the end, the things that really count with readers. It may be that George Meredith lost popularity, and Wyndham Lewis never won it, because they could not tell a story well. And it may be that Virginia Woolf lacks the broad appeal of Jane Austen or George Eliot because she created few memorable characters. But there may be other reasons for the common judgment, of which the alleged failures in narrative or characterisation are merely symptomatic. In the end all a novelist, or any other imaginative writer, has to give us is himself, or herself. To the modern reader the novels of J. J. Rousseau seem astonishingly crude and sentimental. Yet they still have something of the 'grip' that they must once have had for innumerable readers. It has to do with the quality of feeling, the sensibility, which is that of the seducer – but of the soul rather than the body.

But once again the appeal of feeling can be found in many other forms. Perhaps today we do not immediately think of Rousseau as a novelist. He is to be ranked more with the 'personalities' who have influenced history and culture than with the creative artists. He has more in common with Hitler than with Mozart.

Nor is it easy to think of the novelist's 'ideas' as important. Of course the term 'ideas' is so vague that it needs a good deal of clarification before discussion can get any further. A novelist may have ideas in the sense in which a Pinero or an Ibsen have ideas: that is, they have 'a good idea for a play'. This is very important, probably essential. But it does not mean that Ibsen's ideas should be considered as on the same plane as, say, Hegel's. Perhaps they deserve to be; but if so, it is not because they are used effectively in plays. Ideas that, if expressed in general terms, would not be worth serious consideration can be used very powerfully by artists. As to 'ideas' in the other sense, the sense in which it can be said that Hegel had ideas, what do they amount to? We hear of the 'novel of ideas', but what interesting novel is *not* a novel of ideas? *Wuthering Heights* is not usually called a novel of ideas, but the passionate obsessions of Heathcliff and Catherine are certainly ideas in the artistic sense. Or are ideas only to be found in novels where there is a *raisonneur*, spouting about them as he paces up and down, as in D. H. Lawrence or Aldous Huxley? (There is an interesting discussion of this topic by a practising contemporary novelist in Mary McCarthy's *Ideas and the Novel*, 1981.)

We might distinguish two kinds of 'idea' here. One kind is the thematic material, the organising motifs, the central preoccupations of a literary work. These may be called its 'internal' ideas. The other kind is ideas that could be intelligibly expressed and discussed outside the novel, that have reference to things in the real world which have nothing to do with the particular 'world' of a particular novel. Thus some of Doris Lessing's novels mingle a treatment of the emotional problems of certain women with ponderings about the validity of Communism.

But in such cases the 'ideas' are unlikely to be very original or interesting. It is hard to think of a novelist (Tolstoy is the dubious exception) whose 'ideas' can be said to have made a difference in the world, as the ideas of Confucius, or Luther, or Marx have made a difference. Can it be claimed that the ideas of even the greatest novelists can stand comparison with them? And were they really competing with such people? No doubt many novelists have ideas. I am sure Angus Wilson has ideas, and I am sure he has expressed them in his novels. But would it be a fair adverse criticism of his novels to say that his ideas have made no impact in the world, compared with the ideas of Sir Isaac Newton, or Charles Darwin? Surely it would be absurdly unfair. I do not believe that the 'ideas' of the novelist, in the sense in which Confucius or Luther or Marx, or Newton or Darwin, may be said to have had ideas, are of much importance. I am sure they are not what he or she should be judged by.

It need hardly be added that prose fiction is not the characteristic medium for ideas in this sense. The essay, pamphlet, treatise are more obviously appropriate – an admirer of Bernard Shaw would add the theatre. And the novels in which 'ideas' are important, the novels of ideologues, have usually been judged negligible as novels. Winston S. Churchill's novel *Savrola*, full of interest as it is to students of Churchill, is not one of his major achievements. Newman's *Loss and Gain* is a poor novel. We come closer to the *differentia* of the Novel if we reflect on the name of the genre, and its implications. At first, no doubt, the word 'novel' merely signified that the work was a new work, an 'original', and not in any exalted sense; simply, it was not a translation from another work in a foreign language. But Ian Watt, in *The Rise of the Novel* (1957), finds a deep significance in this reference to novelty. For the first time in the history of literature there emerged a genre, if that is how we are to describe it, which made its primary criterion 'truth to individual experience', which is 'always unique and therefore new'. The plots of classical or Renaissance epics, in contrast, were based on ancient histories, or legends. The author's merits were judged by standards of literary decorum based on accepted models. But the first English novelists, such as Daniel Defoe or Samuel Richardson, presented their work as case-histories from real life. What we call their novels were offered by them as actual letters, or autobiographical records. And so there came about an astonishing literary revolution – astonishing, that is, to those who know something of the history of literary forms. It was not a matter of touches of realism, what Northrop Frye calls 'low mimesis'. That had been done before. What was new was the claim to present life as it is – the truth, the whole truth, and nothing but the truth. The convention was that no literary conventions were being used. The 'genre' was the absence of a recognisable genre. Other literature had dealt in norms and standards, moral and social types. The Novel dealt with people as they are, unique individuals: life, not art. This is what I have called Theory A.

It is here, I think, that the distinctive claim of the Novel must be located. The heart of the matter is that the Novel is thought to be the supreme form because it is closest to human realities. It is true to life, in some way in which other kinds of literature are not true to life. Authors have been divided into three categories: those who write to edify; those who write to perfect their art; and those who write to entertain, to 'give the public what it wants'. In short, they are prophets, priests, and purveyors. But, if Theory A is correct, there must now be added a fourth category: authors who write to tell the truth about life.

These categories have often been combined in a single author. (Dickens was all three, prophet, priest, and purveyor, in all his best work.) But in the realist theory the truth-telling aspect is the most important. Realists are apt to apply their theory to literature generally – even to an Edward Lear, even to a Thomas Lovell Beddoes. But the Novel is the realist genre *par excellence*. To investigate the claims of the Novel is to investigate the claims of literary realism: 'truthfulness to individual experience'.

What does that mean in practice? Would St Teresa's account of her interior castle be admissible? No. Is this because the Novel is rationalist and secular, Protestant and post-Protestant? Some would say so. But it seems an arbitrary restriction on the novelist's point of view. It might be fairer to say that 'individual experience', to qualify for the Novel, must be everyday experience. Historically speaking, the Novel emerged as a form of conscious resistance to any kind of romance or 'fantasy'. It was, as in *Don Quixote*, the mode whereby the old 'heroic' idealism, together with its marvels and impossibilities, was ridiculed. The English, and the Spanish, seem to have taken Romance more seriously than the French, and it put up a long struggle for survival, which some would say is not yet over, though knights and fair ladies, castles and dragons, enchanters and flying horses, may now appear in more up-to-date guises. But on the whole most of us assume that a novel deals with people more or less 'like us', in recognisable places and social settings, confronted with situations and problems that could happen in everyday life, and often do.

As the anti-realist C. S. Lewis says in his *Experiment in Criticism* (1961), it is difficult to find any explicit statement of this novelistic norm. But a short inspection of fiction reviews would show that it is widely taken for granted. Books which obviously do not comply with it, yet seem to have some merit, a realist is apt to bundle into the classification used by Owen Wister's publisher, in the description I have quoted: 'genre fiction'. The reviewer whose assumptions are 'realistic' will quite uninhibitedly and quite un-self-consciously use this term to express at one and the same time a distinction of kind and a judgment of value – which, as always, makes rational discussion difficult.

Let us separate realism from non-realism without this implied claim to superiority. What is being claimed? Some would say that it amounts to this. To any moral or aesthetic objection that is made to an element of his work, the realistic novelist has a complete answer if he can say with truth: 'This happens in real life.' Filth and obscenity are thus justified, because they 'establish a realistic atmosphere': everyone knows that there is plenty of filth and obscenity in real life. Much has been written in defence of this point of view by those who agree with the tenets of Continental European, and American, naturalism. So it has come about that some Continental European and American novels have become brutalised to a degree which makes it impossible for many people to read them. And they have had British imitators.

A more acceptable kind of realism may be found in the 'classic' novels. This may be called English realism. Appropriately, it involves a compromise. It accepts certain imaginative restrictions: no knights and fair ladies, castles and dragons, enchanters and flying horses. But, on the other hand, it avoids a too graphic naturalism, the seamy side of real life. And, though the experience it records must be credible, it is deliberately shaped by the novelist to point a moral lesson. Abundant examples can be found in English literature from Fanny Burney, and before her, to Rebecca West, and after her.

Samuel Johnson anticipated both the theory and the practice in his essay in *The Rambler* (31 March 1750), in which he saluted the new art of fiction as exhibiting 'life in its true state, diversified only by accidents that daily happen in the world, and influenced by passions and qualities which are really to be found in conversing with mankind'. The province of the Novel, he says, is 'to bring about natural events by easy means, and keep up curiosity without the help of wonder'. The novelist requires experience that cannot be learned from books, from 'solitary diligence', 'but must arise from general converse and accurate observation of the living world'. Since they deal with ordinary life, the ordinary reader is a fair judge of novels. 'They are engaged in portraits of which everyone knows the original, and can detect any deviation from exactness of resemblance.'

Johnson himself, as a novelist (in *Rasselas*) was not conspicuous for realism – if realism means mimicry. The characters all speak like Dr Johnson. The little fishes all talk like whales. But though Johnson was not good at mimicry, he approved of it, and thought it part of the novelist's art.

But his prescription of realism is qualified with a didactic recommendation. It is not, he says, 'a sufficient vindication of a character, that it is drawn as it appears; for many characters ought never to be drawn'. He urges the novelist to use the opportunity of fiction to display ideal types of human life. 'In narratives where historical veracity has no place, I cannot discover why there should not be exhibited the most perfect idea of virtue; of virtue not angelical, nor above probability, for what we cannot credit, we shall never imitate, but the highest and purest that humanity can reach.' 'Vice', he says, 'for vice is necessary to be shown, should always disgust.' Finally, 'it is to be steadily inculcated, that virtue is the highest proof of under-standing and the only solid basis of greatness'.

Johnson's theory of the novel has thus two aspects. One is realism. He is on the side of all those who talk of fiction as an 'adult' art, and who think fairytales should be left to the children. Indeed some modern educationalists who share his bias would even like to deny fairytales to children. G. H. Bantock, in *The Parochialism of the Present* (1981), disapproves of 'those ridiculous fantasies children indulge in' about Batman, or Superman, 'fantasies of a sort which make no contact with the realities of human life'. He disapproves of children who want to explore 'the pathological or the odd or the distant, the remote, the fantastic'. These youthful romantics are to be discouraged in favour of 'a concern for social meaning within a commonsense world'. Dreams and irrationality must yield to the sovereignty of the 'ordinary, the everyday'. That is what is 'true to life', what has the ontological prerogative.

It is not clear whether this view is adequate to some of the human realities that authors have wanted, or felt compelled, to deal with; whether it would make possible the rendering in art of a life like Johnson's own, with its dark side, his religious fears, his obsessions, and his neuroses. Perhaps it is too far from the edge of darkness. Yet, as the quotation from Bantock shows, it can appeal still to intelligent moderns, as one way of defining the Reality Principle.

The frank didacticism of Johnson may find fewer supporters today. But it seems in principle not very different from the 'humane tradition' advocated by Mrs Leavis in 'The Englishness of the English Novel'. Indeed she cites Johnson with approval. What needs correcting in his theory may be suggested by words of George Eliot which Mrs Leavis quotes, contrasting literary art as 'diagram' with literary art as 'picture'. The norms and ideals that the novelist ought to present have to be dramatised, given flesh and blood. They demand a contribution from the novelist's own capacity for suffering, and moral imagination, which Johnson's account of the novelist as an 'inculcator of virtue' fails to suggest. But the rejection both of indiscriminate realism, and of 'art for art's sake', is clear in all these writers. A novel may not have a lesson to teach, in a simple-minded sense, but it has a moral purpose.

This, then, is Theory A, in a characteristically English form: what may be called the moral–realistic theory. It has been held by many intelligent men and women, including both practitioners and non-practitioners of the art of fiction. It seems to fit many famous novels, though it fits some better than others. But is it correct?

The usual objection to it is that 'truth to life' implies that there is some general truth to life to be found, over and above the particular impressions, the 'reading of life', of an individual author. But every author, every artist, makes his own selection from the real world. And there is no more 'truth' in the hideous world of Nelson Algren than in the sunny world of Wee Mac-Gregor. Some selections may be thought wider, or deeper, but one cannot be more 'valid' than any other.

I think there is a lot in this objection. But it is not decisive – unless we are prepared to deny the existence of a common world altogether (as some of the wilder theoreticians of Paris seem prepared to do). There are such things as 'the facts of life' – and not only in the sexual sense. It seems to make sense to say that there are some writers who conform to these, and some who do not, and that it is reasonable to call the first kind of writers truer to life than the second kind.

The most serious objection to the realist theory goes deeper. On the face of it this theory, as summed up in Ian Watt's words, 'truth to individual experience', is illogical. It asks the novel to be at the same time fact and fiction. But that is impossible.

It is impossible, that is, given certain metaphysical presuppositions which I believe a rational person must accept. Any discussion of 'truth' and 'reality' must include an explicit statement of these, however brief and summary.

The presuppositions are these. There is something which is referred to, indifferently, as 'existence', or 'reality', or 'actuality'. This is an absolutely basic category, which is indefinable in simpler terms. It admits of no relativity, no degrees. Something cannot *almost* exist: it either exists or it does not. It is true that in Oliver Onions's story *Two Trifles* a ghost partially appears. If we allow for this possibility, this means that only part of the ghost exists. But the part that does exist, exists fully. There are no approximations to reality.

I am aware that this comes near to treating existence as a property, or quality. And I know of the (somewhat vague) philosophical thesis that 'existence is not a predicate'. 'The idea of existence, when conjoined with the idea of any object, makes no addition to it', says David Hume (*A Treatise of Human Nature*, i.ii.6). I find this hard to understand. It seems to me that my 'idea' of the Mafia, or of the God of Scholastic theology, would be different, and very importantly different, if I believed that they existed. But I agree that 'existent', if it can be called a property, or a quality, or a predicate, is a very peculiar sort of property, or quality, or predicate. I sympathise with the attempt of Bertrand Russell, in his theory of definite descriptions, to dispose of it by linguistic reformulations. Thus instead of saying 'Mr Pickwick did not exist', which can generate all the old puzzles (if Mr Pickwick did not exist, how can we be talking about him?), we should say ' "Mr Pickwick" is not the name of a real person.'

However this may be, it does not affect the fundamental division, in whatever terms this is to be described, between what is existent and what is not. But to accept the ultimacy of this division is not to commit oneself about just what things, or what categories of things, are to be found on which side of the fence. Do numbers exist? or other abstract entities, like 'the average Englishman'?

The immediately relevant point is the existential status of fictional characters, like Mr Pickwick. I will say dogmatically that fictional characters do not exist. They are not 'real in a world created by Charles Dickens'; they are not real at all. They are feigned to exist. But how then can they give us 'truth to life', if this means 'representation of matters of fact and reality'? It seems to make the novelist either mendacious or deluded.

The point may be made clearer if we compare the Novel to a documentary film. A documentary can be 'slanted' to prove the points the maker of the film wants to make. Or he may make a sincere and honest attempt simply to show the facts, without drawing a moral – while admitting that he is a human being, not God; he has to decide what he is to turn his camera to. Controversies between 'indiscriminate realists' and 'English realists' turn on this question of 'slanting'. But suppose it turns out that the people shown in the documentary were really actors, not the people they were supposed to be. Would not this put the claim to 'truth' in quite a different light? It would have to be 'truth of art', not 'truth of life'. But what *is* 'truth of art'?

'True to life', then, cannot be a valid claim for novels, if it is taken in a straightforward sense. I may have laboured the point. But in the work of very eminent critics such as Leavis, or Georg Lukács, you will find the word 'real' and the word 'reality' used over and over again of novelists' characters. No doubt they are using these words in a special sense. But they never say what that is. It seems worth labouring the point, because the champions of realism are all too apt to denigrate non-realistic genres, and bully those who like them, with the claim for the superior 'truth' of their favourites. It is clear that this claim to 'truth' is not to be taken literally; that it is, indeed, highly problematic.

In what sense, then, is the Novel true to life? The simplest way of asserting this claim is to point out that novels contain many facts. I have urged that something cannot be factual and fictional at the same time. But most novels mingle fiction and fact. As a whole a novel cannot claim veracity (to use Johnson's word): by definition, novels contain a fictitious element. But there is no law that says they have to be all fiction; and indeed a great many are not. A novel's characters can include real people. And the places it mentions are often real places, and what is said of these places is often meant to be true.

An August Sunday afternoon in the north side of Dublin. Epitome of all that is hot, arid, and empty. Tall brick houses, browbeating each other in gloomy respectability across the white streets; broad pavements, promenaded mainly by the nomadic cat; stifling squares, wherein the infant of unfashionable patronage is taken for the daily baking that is its substitute for the breezes and the press of perambulators on the Bray Esplanade or the Kingston pier. Few towns are duller out of the season than Dublin, but the dullness of its north side neither waxes nor wanes; it is immutable, unchangeable, fixed as the stars. So at least it appears to the observer whose impressions are only eye-deep, and are derived from the emptiness of the streets, the unvarying dirt of the window panes, and the almost forgotten type of ugliness of the window curtains.

That is the opening of *The Real Charlotte* (1894), the masterpiece of 'Somerville and Ross', and it is obviously typical of many novels. The story and the characters may be fictitious, but there is a factual basis to everything. The Novel has a 'special relationship' to facts. *The Real Charlotte* tells us things about Dublin that could be, or could have been, verified or falsified – at least in principle. Joyce's *Ulysses* notoriously tells us many more. References to things outside the world of the novel, things we could look at without the aid of the novelists' eyes, abound in traditional novels.

Novelists like Mary McCarthy and Elizabeth Bowen have testified to the irksomeness, to the imaginative writer, of this bondage of fact. Yet they consider it necessary. Their literary conscience requires it. Mary McCarthy rebukes Henry James for the elusiveness and, sometimes, the non-existence of his facts.

There is something touching about this literalism. It corresponds to what, in the real world, is sound logic and sound morality. We should always be suspicious of those who – usually with great eloquence – proclaim the irrelevance of fact to truth. ('Facts', says Ronald Knox's Bishop of Much Wenlock, 'are only the steam which obscure the mirror of truth.') In real-life situations we should be of the opinion of Anatole France, when he turned away from the circle round Maurice Barrès, with their rhetoric about 'organic, passionate truth', to insist upon the essential issue of the Dreyfus case: was it, or was it not, Captain Dreyfus whose handwriting was on the *bordereau*?

But none of this shows that the presence of literal fact improves fiction. On the contrary, it is often said of novels not set in recent periods – 'historical' novels – that they are lifeless just because the novelist, in trying to recreate the period, has put in too many of them. And even in books that do convince us that they give, in Walter Allen's words, 'a faithful picture of their times', it is difficult to sort out what is factual from what is fictitious. Nor is it clear that the things that seem most vivid are the things that were transcriptions of fact. Furthermore the word 'fact' here is not unequivocal. Many novelists have (implicitly) offered to convey the facts of their personal experience. But where matters of feeling, of sentiment, of impression are concerned, who is to be the judge of what is fact or not? Ought we to talk about 'facts' at all here?

In the later nineteenth century there grew up the notion of the novelist as a social investigator, patiently accumulating his facts. (No doubt this was influenced by a notion of the scientist which is equally outmoded.) Zola's theory required much collecting of facts. But novelists, including Zola, use their imaginations. They invent. Virginia Woolf was an adverse critic of the externality of naturalism, as she saw it (not, I think, justly) in the work of Arnold Bennett. Yet she seems to lend support to naturalist ways of thinking when she pictures the novelist speculating and guessing about the personality of 'Mrs Brown', the old lady in the railway carriage, the symbol of reality. But it appears that some great novelists, a Balzac or a Dickens, do not build up characters in this way. There is a certain demonism in these novelists. Their characters seem to 'come to' them. They are not carefully built up from this and that touch of observation, this and that shrewd insight. To use traditional language, they are 'created'. Of course the novelists do not literally create *ex nihilo*. But who is to say where their material comes from? 'I thought of Mr Pickwick', said Dickens. The two best characters in Virginia Woolf's work are Mr and Mrs Ramsay in *To the Lighthouse*, and it is true that they were based on real people. But the real people were her father and mother, people she knew in a very different way from 'Mrs Brown'.

The link between the Novel and real life is peculiarly close, closer than in some other literary forms. *Romans à clef* are common. Many novels have a firm basis in the author's early life – *Sons and Lovers*, *Portrait of the Artist as a Young Man*. Tolstoy's fiction is known to be very autobiographical. He used real-life models. Biographies have shown how much the 'world' of famous novelists was their own 'world': Ellmann on Joyce, Painter on Proust, Sherry on Conrad. There is a strong tradition of autobiographies in English that shade into novels, from

Bewick's *Memoirs*, or Miss Mitford's *Our Village*, down to Flora Thompson. Solzhenitsyn's novels have behind them the realities of *The Gulag Archipelago*.

But the fundamental distinction between the novelist and the historian remains. It can be put in ethical terms. The historian, as such, is not allowed to make up his facts. With the novelist it is quite different. It seems absurd to accuse a novelist of making up his facts. Why shouldn't he? But now 'facts' requires quotation marks.

In short, I do not think the 'truth' of the Novel rests upon literal veracity. If it did, it would be difficult to distinguish between the fictions of the novelist and straightforward lying. This is what F. W. Bateson, a critic who is hostile to the Novel, refuses to do when he calls the Novel 'fiction masquerading as fact', in his *jeu d'esprit* 'The Novel's Original Sin' (in *Essays in Critical Dissent*, 1972). But there is no 'masquerade' about it. Apart from a few border-line cases, like Defoe's *Memoirs of a Cavalier*, the novelist is not intending to deceive. A reader who mistakes a novel, a 'feigned history', for real history is in the same position as a very naive person, like Partridge in *Tom Jones*, who confuses stage characters with real people. He simply has not understood the convention, or 'language game', that is being used.

What then of realism, and the claim to truth? Although realists do not usually spell it out, I think what they have in mind is not literal truth but lifelikeness, verisimilitude. This is surface realism, what C. S. Lewis calls 'realism of presentation'. Many readers today, brought up on novels, find it hard to read anything that is without it. It is hard for most of us to detect any recognisable emotion, any human reality, in the noble Romans of Corneille, as they declaim endless well-polished couplets on the theme of love versus duty. (The actual human reality is of course the context of origin, the court of Louis XIV for whom Corneille composed these ideal attitudes.) In complete contrast are the novels of Jane Austen, or *The Diary of a Nobody*. In these books we find a 'world' that no one lives in now. But it is utterly convincing. We believe in the characters. They are not 'period' abstractions, but people we get to know.

This verisimilitude is characteristic of the Novel, and I need not give examples of it. Open a good novel almost anywhere and you will find it. It is not, indeed, distinctive of the Novel. It can be found in Homer, and in Dante – it was especially popular in medieval art. (E. Auerbach in his *Mimesis* (Princeton, N.J., 1953) discusses its philosophical and cultural origins.)

But verisimilitude is not a guarantee of truth: far from it. It is a well-known device of liars. Leslie Stephen compares the minute circumstantiality of the pioneer English novelist, Defoe, with the technique of the liar. Nor is it only a means used by realistic writers. Realistic touches may be a means to induce the reader to accept something very unrealistic. A familiar example is Swift's neat way of conveying to us the diminutive size of his Emperor of Blefuscu. 'His Majesty presented me. . .with his picture at full length, which I put immediately into one of my gloves, to keep it from being hurt.' ('A Voyage to Lilliput', chapter VIII.) Similarly the 'plain man' narrator is used to help us to accept something totally incredible (as with Captain Gulliver) or 'larger than life' (as with Dr Watson).

But what has this to do with truth? It is agreed by academic tradition that truth can be found in very non-realistic, stylised works: Greek or Japanese tragedy, Corneille and Racine. We do not usually look for this sort of truth in novels. But an example might be found in the work of Ivy Compton-Burnett. Her novels are deficient in surface realism. It is impossible to believe that butlers, or children, ever talked like that. Virginia Woolf, in *The Years*, seems much more faithful to the appearance of 'life as it is' – perhaps wearisomely so. Yet it is plausible to argue that in a deep sense Ivy Compton-Burnett is truer to life, in conveying the presence in the world of evil and greed, sinister forces which the art of Mrs Woolf does not adequately comprehend.

But at this point it is clear that artistic truth is neither identical with, nor dependent on, verisimilitude. And to be fair to the great realist critics, I do not believe that they ever thought it was. Tacitly, at least, they have accepted it as a means, rather than an end; they have condoned departures from it, as they have condoned departures from literal veracity, in the interest of a higher truth. We may call this higher truth 'verity'. I am worried when Leavis pronounces, in a discussion of *Anna Karenina* (*Cambridge Quarterly*, I.i, 1965) that 'a study of human nature is a study of social human nature, and the psychologist, sociologist and social historian aren't in it compared with the great novelists'. This raises the awkward question whether any real facts can be inferred from the mere appearance of facts. I doubt whether a novelist, even a Tolstoy, is really in the same business as a psychologist, sociologist and social historian. Leavis is on safer ground when he says: 'The greatness of *Anna Karenina* lies in the degree to which, along with its depth, it justifies the clear suggestion it conveys of a representative comprehensiveness.' It is this 'representative comprehensiveness' that I have in mind when I use the term 'verity'. The truth in it is not something there is an obvious way of checking, as we can check statements like 'My pen is on the table' or 'Water boils at 100 °C.' It is inconceivable that there should be any way of checking the truth of what is said in the fifty-first Psalm, or the words of the Chorus-leader in Aeschylus's *Agamemnon* (translated by Louis MacNeice):

> Ah the fortunes of men! When they go well
> A shadow sketch would match them, and in ill-fortune
> The dab of a wet sponge destroys the drawing.
> It is not myself but the life of man I pity.

The only test is intuition, experience, wisdom.

The sense that novels can contain verity of this kind is what deters me from adopting what I have called Theory B, the non-realist theory of the novel. It is stated eloquently by Vladimir Nabokov, in 'Good Readers and Bad Readers', from his *Lectures on Literature* (1980). 'Literature is invention. Fiction is fiction. To call a story a true story is an insult to both art and truth. Every great writer is a great inventor, but so is that arch-cheat Nature. Nature always deceives.'

This view, unlike the realist theory, seems consistent and logically coherent. And it seems difficult to deny that it is true. Fiction *is* make-believe. But some readers may think it is more than make-believe. And in the author of *Lolita* this view seems to go with a kind of ethical and human detachment they find too narrowly 'aesthetic'. Nabokov seems to pass too lightly over the problem of empathy. The worst thing a reader can do, he says, is to identify himself with a character in the book.

Some readers will reflect here that Nabokov differs from most of the great Russian novelists in his lack of moral passion. And an English reader will be reminded of Oscar Wilde (*The Decay of Lying*) and the controversies of the 1890s about 'art and morality'. But it must be remembered that Nabokov will have been familiar with similar Russian controversies at an earlier time, the 1850s and 60s, when the name of Nikolay Chernyshevsky (1828–89) was great in the land, with his demands for social 'commitment', which are in historical continuity with Socialist realism and the horrible barbarities of Zhdanov and Stalin. And I imagine that it is his very proper revulsion against that sort of thing that has led Nabokov into over-statement.

For that it is an over-statement seems clear. When he speaks, in the same series of lectures, about the Neckett children in *Bleak House*, he sounds a note of impassioned concern. 'I should not like to hear the charge of sentimentality made against this strain that runs through *Bleak House*. I want to submit that people who denounce the sentimental are generally unaware of what sentiment is.' He points out 'how different is this world of Dickens from the world of Homer or from the world of Cervantes'. He hears 'the very accent of profound pity in the words uttered'. This is the language of empathy. It does credit to Nabokov's humanity; but it creates difficulties for his aesthetic theory.

But this is an old problem: 'What's Hecuba to him, or he to Hecuba?' or St Augustine ashamed at weeping over the sorrows of Dido, rather than his own sins. It has nothing essentially to do with literary realism. We can be deeply moved by the story of Orpheus and Eurydice, or the *Alcestis*. Empathy remains a psychological, and perhaps a moral, problem. But, aesthetically speaking, it can be accommodated, just as easily as verisimilitude can, to a theory of the Novel as adult fantasy. (It is high time this term was rescued from the special, limited sense imposed on it by embarrassed realists trying to classify books like *A Voyage to Arcturus*.)

The novels of Tolstoy or George Eliot are quite as much adult fantasy as the work of George MacDonald, Lewis Carroll, William Morris, or J. R. R. Tolkien. Whether or not a book has a documentary look about it has nothing to do with its higher truth, its verity. The advantage of abandoning a realist theory is to repair the damage done to lyric poetry and poetic drama, to wisdom literature and what is called, rather unfortunately, 'imaginative prose'. It is to open the way to a juster criticism of romance, of satire, of the fantastic, the idyllic, the ingenious – all old forms of fiction, all constantly reappearing in new modes. A less restrictive theory would show up shortcomings in the realistic novel – its pedestrianism, its failure to intensify consciousness, its lack of unity of effect, compared not only with some poems or plays, but with some short stories, or the German *Novelle*, which stay in the mind as works of art, sending a ray of light over our turbid and confused everyday consciousness. How rarely the Novel does that!

But a non-realistic theory could also bring out the great virtues of the Novel. One of these is the 'envelopment' of the reader. He loses himself in it. (Older readers find it hard to do this.) For hours and hours, days and days, perhaps weeks and weeks, he is in the company of imaginary people. Sometimes he has the guidance of an over-arching intelligence, an 'omniscient narrator', as in the old-fashioned novels of Scott: 'tolerable horses and a civil driver'. More modern novels are more dramatic than narrative. But they too can envelop the reader. It all sounds like a holiday. But why not? Aren't holidays supposed to do us good?

This seems to concede that poetry and drama are higher forms. But we need not concede this. It is true that lack of poetry is a serious shortcoming in the Novel. Novel-lovers have claimed that this is made up for by effects similar to poetry – not only the use of 'symbolic' detail, but wider effects for which there is no accepted name, inventions of the novelist that have a greater significance, sound with a deeper resonance, than can be accounted for by their logical connection with the story. I am thinking of things like Melville's White Whale, or Dostoevsky's poem of the Grand Inquisitor, or Hardy's Egdon Heath, or

E. M. Forster's Marabar Caves. These, it will be said, are the Novel's equivalent to poetry. (I suggest the term 'evocative para-symbols'.)

Still, it is a pity to have to do without the real thing. Often the only flicker of poetry, in a modern novel, is in the title: *The Sun Also Rises,* or *Eyeless in Gaza,* a momentary incandescence from the language of the poet, before the relentless march of prosaic particulars begins. Matthew Arnold's 'touchstones' – short passages of verse, sometimes no more than single lines – have been much criticised, as a quick way of reminding ourselves what great poetry is like. Still, it was a practical suggestion, which might help. Anything like that is inconceivable in judging novels. In Johnson's phrase, they are for the most part 'level with life'. We might feel like inverting the realist theory, and wonder whether verity and higher truth can exist where there is no poetry. Is there not something in Arnold's characterisation of poetry as the most perfect speech of man, in which he comes nearest to uttering the truth?

5
The Sea Cook: a Study in the Art of Robert Louis Stevenson

Most readers agree with Henry James that *Treasure Island* is perfect of its kind; and they also agree that this is a kind quite different from any that James himself tried or wished to work in. What is more doubtful is in what way the book should be taken. Mr Robin Wood and M. François Truffaut have been accused of taking some of Alfred Hitchcock's films too seriously; and it would seem that R. L. Stevenson presents a similar critical problem. I know one critic who was rebuked for introducing *Treasure Island* into a literary discussion: 'we may leave Long John Silver and his wooden leg to our children and our childhood'. Is that all that needs to be said (even if Long John Silver had had a wooden leg)? Certainly the aesthetic satisfactoriness of *Treasure Island* is inseparable from the completeness with which Stevenson fulfilled his intention: to write in a particular genre of 'communicative' art – in this case, narrative fiction with an obvious point or purpose. His story has continued, through several generations, to attract voluntary readers of the sort he intended to attract. It has been called the best boys' book ever written. And I heard recently that in a very tough 'blackboard jungle' type of school it was eagerly devoured in preference to the present-day fiction about barrow boys in the East End which authority thought more suitable. There seems, then, some point in asking how Stevenson achieved this success.

Stevenson has given what, compared with most authors, is an unusually clear and full account of his intentions in writing *Treasure Island*. Writing of it as 'My First Book' in *The Idler*, August 1894, he says:

It was to be a story for boys; no need for psychology or fine writing; and I had a boy at hand to be a touchstone. Women were excluded. I was unable to handle a brig [which the *Hispaniola* should have been] but I thought I could make shift to sail her as a schooner without public shame. And then I had an idea for Long John Silver from which I promised myself funds of entertainment.

In the same essay Stevenson describes for us the personal circumstances, the setting in life, in which the story came to be written (with the map as the starting-point); and mentions his literary sources – *Robinson Crusoe*, Poe, Washington Irving, perhaps *Masterman Ready*, Johnson's *Buccaneers*, Kingsley. We need only add to this that *Treasure Island* first appeared, in slightly different form, as a serial in *Young Folks* (October 1881–January 1882): the author was stated to be 'Captain George North'. We may also note in passing that an inferior book, *The Black Arrow*, also appeared there, and comparison of the two lends support to the view that *Treasure Island*'s success is not *merely* due to its being 'a good story'.

Treasure Island was, as a matter of fact, by no means Stevenson's 'first book'. But he had good reason to write of it as if it had been. It was the first book of his to become widely known and popular. Looked at in the perspective of his whole career, it marks his emergence from the affectations of his earlier work. In *Treasure Island* Stevenson's work, for the first time, becomes truly 'adult' – in the sense in which that word is frequently used by critics, to mean sound and satisfying to adults. But, by an interesting paradox, his work first became 'adult' when he was able to recapture the point of view of a child. In this process, the self-conscious charm of his earlier work was replaced by genuine charm. We see for the first time the Stevenson who was to write *Kidnapped* and *A Child's Garden of Verses*. It is not clear, however, whether we can yet see in *Treasure Island* the first signs of Stevenson's later efforts, which Mr Leslie Fiedler has described, to exploit more deeply the universal meaning of his fables, while surrendering as little as possible of their structure and popular appeal as exciting stories. 'It was to be a story for boys.' And the 'story for boys', to Stevenson, is clearly a sub-division of the genre of romance which is characterised chiefly by *exclusion*. The elements of 'adult' complication, excluded in the manifest content of the tale, are as Stevenson indicates; what remains for critical investigation is what is excluded (and hence what is included) in the latent meaning; one point in particular: why does the *treasure* count so little, emotionally, in the tale?

The first chapter at once reveals a clear reason for *Treasure Island*'s enduring popularity: Stevenson's mastery of narrative. This is well brought out in David Daiches's fine study of the novelist (*Robert Louis Stevenson*, Glasgow, 1947). No more perfect example of storytelling exists. At once we see and hear

the brown old seaman with the sabre-cut. . .he came plodding to the inn door, his sea-chest following behind him in a hand-barrow; a tall, strong, heavy, nut-brown man; his tarry pigtail falling over the shoulders of his soiled blue coat; his hands ragged and scarred, with black, broken nails; and the sabre-cut across one cheek, a dirty, livid white. . .that old sea-song [to become a sinister *leit-motif* in the whole story] that he sang so often afterwards. . .in the high, old tottering voice. . .'This is a handy cove,' says he at length; 'and a pleasant sittyated grog-shop. Much company, mate?' My father told him no, very little company, the more was the pity. 'Well then,' said he, 'this is the berth for me.'

Billy Bones, the old 'captain', is primarily a technical device. He comes from the 'pre-story'; his character and actions point forward into the body of the story; and the memory of his time at the Admiral Benbow supplies elements of the 'post-story' – the grown Jim Hawkins looking back. Obviously he brings the note of the abnormal into the normal world of Jim, and provides a means for Jim (and hence for the reader) to enter the world of picturesque adventure. But Billy Bones also provides an example of Stevenson's skill in making necessary machinery of the story interesting in itself. His main function is to bring the world of Flint – the symbol of evil – into contact with the world of the Admiral Benbow. He brings danger, suspicion, mystery; but he also brings the colourful and the exciting. We have already a hint of the ambiguous meaning of 'evil' in this story. Looking back at Bones's coming from the point of view of the 'post-story', Jim reflects:

I really believe that his presence did us good. People were frightened at the time, but on looking back they rather liked it; it was a fine excitement in a quiet country life; and there was even a party of the younger men who pretended to admire him, calling him a 'true sea-dog', and a 'real old salt', and suchlike names, and saying there was the sort of man that made England terrible at sea.

In the last reflection we have an example of the confusion of imaginative and moral norms which was to preoccupy Stevenson, in more serious forms, throughout the rest of his writing life. All that we need note for the moment is that Bones is not an entirely unsympathetic character – for all his uncouthness and sinisterness and pirate background. Jim is 'less afraid' of him than most people are. He is even on terms of intimate confidence, almost affection, with him during Bones's last illness. And Bones's death, *in the telling*, seems to affect Jim more powerfully than his own father's death, which has occurred just before: 'It is a curious thing to understand, for I had certainly never liked the man, though of late I had begun to pity him, but as soon as I saw that he was dead, I burst into a flood of tears.' Stevenson announced that there was 'no need of psychology'; but it is difficult not to see Billy Bones as the first, though ludicrously unqualified, in a line of candidate foster-fathers who constitute Jim's social relationships in the story. At any rate, there are several touches of nature in the account of his last days. 'Once. . . to our extreme wonder, he piped up to a different air, a kind of country love-song, that he must have learned in his youth before he had begun to follow the sea.' We cannot imagine Black Dog or Pew as having had a 'youth'. The most moving touch is the 'five or six curious West Indian shells' that Jim and his mother find among Bones's possessions after his death. 'It has often set me thinking since,' says Jim from the 'post-story', 'that he should have carried about these shells with him in his wandering, guilty and hunted life.'

The incident which closes chapter I leaves us with our permanent picture of Bones as uncouth and menacing, yet pathetically ineffective in his clash with Doctor Livesey, here admirably introduced: '. . .the contrast the neat, bright doctor, with his powder as white as snow, and his bright, black eyes and pleasant manners, made with the coltish country folk, and above all, with that filthy, heavy, bleared scarecrow of a pirate of ours, sitting far gone in rum, with his arms on the table'. We may note in passing the economy of character-drawing (which Stevenson thought essential in a romance) whereby we are made so quickly to see, in this incident, Doctor Livesey's adult efficiency and gentlemanly authority, and the qualities that make him attractive to Jim and the reader. All that is really 'saved up' for later disclosure is the fact that compared to Long John or Captain Smollett he is a lightweight – as, in respect of the latter, he is in due course to recognise: ' "That man Smollett," he said once, "is a better man than I am. And when I say that it means a deal, Jim" ' (ch. XIX).

Meanwhile the pace of the story increases, and with it the involvement, and the isolation, of Jim. Stevenson follows the laws of the genre. Jim at first is just an ordinary boy, drawn into these events by chance; we feel him, in the Black Dog incident, carried along by forces he cannot control; with blind Pew, he has reached the point of no return. It is only much later that he is to emerge as a 'hero', capable of taking the initiative and controlling events. The visits of Black Dog, and of Pew, partake of the nightmare quality already suggested in Jim's accounts of his dreams of 'the seafaring man with one leg' whom Billy Bones was so afraid of.

How that personage haunted my dreams, I need scarcely tell you. On stormy nights, when the wind shook the four corners of the house, and the surf roared along the cove and up the cliffs, I would see him in a thousand forms, and with a thousand diabolical expressions. Now the leg would be cut off at the knee, now at the hip; now he was a monstrous kind of creature who had never had but the one leg, and that in a middle of his body. To see him leap and run and pursue me over hedge and ditch was the worst of nightmares.

One of the drawbacks of modern writers of boys' books, apart from their not being such good writers as Stevenson, is their inhibition from introducing so frankly such images as that of the castrated father raging for revenge; though here we are nearer to Captain Hook than to Captain Ahab. As far as Jim's waking life is concerned, Black Dog is a more sinister and unpleasant anti-father than Billy Bones was.

Once I stepped out myself into the road, but he [Black Dog] immedi-

83

ately called me back, and, as I did not obey quick enough for his fancy, a most horrible change came over his tallowy face, and he ordered me in, with an oath that made me jump. As soon as I was back again he returned to his former manner, half fawning, half sneering, patted me on the shoulder, told me I was a good boy, and he had taken quite a fancy to me. 'I have a son of my own,' said he, 'as like you as two blocks, and he's all the pride of my 'art. But the great thing for boys is discipline, sonny – discipline.'

The mounting unpleasantness of the anti-fathers seems to be related to the scale of their physical mutilation: Bones had a sabre-cut on his cheek, but Black Dog has lost two fingers, and the worst of the injuries is that suffered by the worst of the anti-fathers, a figure of horror: blind Pew. (It is noteworthy that his blindness, as we are told later, was caused by the same broadside which deprived Silver of his leg – see ch. XI.)

'I hear a voice,' said he, ' – a young voice. Will you give me your hand, my kind young friend, and lead me in?' I held out my hand, and the horrible, soft-spoken, eyeless creature gripped it in a moment like a vice.

The horror of Pew lies in the inhibition and reversal of the normal sympathetic reaction to a blind man; evinced here in the effective use of the word 'eyeless'.

Pew, as the point of no return for Jim, has also an important place in the structure of the book. Stevenson has now solved the technical problem of involving the hero effectively in the story. We may contrast, in a modern example, the inadequate motivation for this in *The Mask of Dimitrios* by Eric Ambler: what launches the hero into that story – his wish to investigate Dimitrios – is both too early and too improbable. We now see, as well, the hero's growing isolation.

No soul would consent to return with us to the Admiral Benbow. The more we told of our troubles, the more – man, woman and child – they clung to the shelter of their houses. The name of Captain Flint, though it was strange to me, was well enough known to some there, and carried a great weight of terror.

Pew, as a symbol of evil, can carry the evil of Flint effectively into the dramatic *present*. The return of Jim and his mother to the Admiral Benbow is of course necessitated for plot reasons. But it introduces a motif often important in popular fiction, and quite prominent in *Treasure Island*: the moral strengthening of an individual by adherence to a code. Here the courage of Jim's mother is inspired by the principle of getting her just dues. ' "If none of the rest of you dare," she said, "Jim and I dare. Back we will go, the way we came, and small thanks to you big, hulking, chicken-hearted men. We'll have that chest open, if we die for it." ' We see also here another element prominent in *Treasure Island* (though this is subordinate): discomfort at the behaviour of some-one we love. 'How I blamed my poor mother for her honesty and her greed, for her past foolhardiness and present weakness!' (This is after Jim's mother has collapsed on the road.)

But the prevailing mode hereabouts is 'romance'. The in-vasion of the Admiral Benbow, of which Jim is a helpless onlooker, is exciting, dramatic and very visualised.

The window of the captain's room was thrown open with a slam and a jingle of broken glass; and a man leaned out into the moonlight, head and shoulders, and addressed the blind beggar on the road below him.

The brawl that follows is given a romantic colour. The death of Pew is exciting, but we are dissociated from any concern for him as a human being; our attitude is epitomised by the exciseman Dance's 'I'm glad I trod on Master Pew's corns' and by Squire Trelawney's 'As for riding down that black, atrocious miscreant, I regard it as an act of virtue, sir, like stamping on a cockroach.' It seems doubtful, however, whether this exhausts the *total* significance of the Pew episode; we may note that Stevenson, to judge from a similar episode with an unpleasant blind man in *Kidnapped*, had not used up his 'Pew' material (although the episode in *Kidnapped* is much inferior).

Chapter VI, at the Hall, states the contrast between the world of comfort and domesticity, and the world of pirates and adven-ture, which we need to have before the journey to Treasure Island. This contrast had not been fully established earlier, since the Admiral Benbow itself is somewhat picturesque. For a con-trast, we might look at J. B. Priestley's affectionate tribute to the opening of *Treasure Island* in the first chapter of his *Faraway*, where the world of the 'hero' William Dursley is truly hum-drum. We are introduced to the Squire, and given a further touch of nature in the description of the Doctor, done with a boy's Dickensian freshness of vision: '. . .the doctor, as if to hear the better, had taken off his powdered wig, and sat there, looking very strange indeed with his own close-cropped, black poll'. In chapter VII, the scene at Bristol, Stevenson introduces a new kind of suspense, in what otherwise might have been a dull stretch. In this scene the reader is given significant information withheld from the main characters, the Squire with his unsuspiciousness, Jim with his inexperience. It is clear that Jim is no fool: he can-not accept the boyish Squire as an authority-figure: 'Doctor Livesey will not like that,' he says, reading the Squire's letter, 'the Squire has been talking after all', and is duly rebuked by the hierarchy-respecting gamekeeper: 'A pretty rum go if squire ain't to talk for Doctor Livesey, I should think.' Nor is Jim un-suspicious of Silver, after his glimpse of Black Dog at the Spy-Glass; but naturally Silver is too clever for him. We see through Jim's eyes his charm and interestingness, and his unexpectedness: he is not yet, either for Jim or the reader, a fully known quantity.

And then all of a sudden he stopped, and his jaw dropped as though he had remembered something. 'The score!' he burst out. 'Three goes o' rum! Why, shiver my timbers, if I hadn't forgotten my score!' And, falling on a bench, he laughed until the tears ran down his cheeks. I could not help joining; and we laughed together, peal after peal, until the tavern rang again.

The adult reader is reminded of a famous, and not fully explained, incident in Boswell's *Life of Johnson*. The piquancy is increased here by the reader's not quite understanding either, even if he understands more than Jim: 'though I did not see the joke as he did, I was again obliged to join him in his mirth'.

It is with the introduction of Silver that the serious interest of the book begins. He is described with a vividness that won the enthusiastic admiration of a French critic. 'His left leg was cut off close by the hip, and under the left shoulder he carried a crutch, which he managed with wonderful dexterity, hopping upon it like a bird. He was very tall and strong, with a face as big as a ham [this was the phrase the French critic particularly admired] – plain and pale, but intelligent and smiling.' He is differentiated by Jim both from the one-legged demon of nightmare and from the pirates he has encountered. 'I had seen the captain, and Black Dog, and the blind man Pew, and I thought I knew what a buccaneer was like – a very different creature, according to me, from this clean and pleasant-tempered landlord.' If Jim seems naive here, in his assumption that pirates are always dirty, we might recall that no less a poet than Baudelaire was accused, by no less a critic than Henry James, of a similar error about 'evil' in *Les Fleurs du Mal*!

But that Silver appears 'good' but is really 'evil' is only the most obvious aspect of his role in *Treasure Island*. In the sea cook, Stevenson has created something more complex: indeed with Jekyll and Hyde, Silver has escaped from the pages of a book into a public domain of legend, like Hänsel and Gretel, or Thor. Stevenson himself gave a simple explanation of the genesis of Silver: he had added the charm and strength of W. E. Henley to the black villainy of a fairytale pirate. We may wonder if this is how artists do in fact create archetypes, and whether this one is not rather what T. S. Eliot said of Falstaff, 'the offspring of deeper, less apprehensible feelings'. At any rate, we see the significance of Silver more fully when Captain Smollett ('I'll have no favourites on my ship') is introduced into the story. In the contrast of Silver and Smollett we have the beginnings of a subject which was more and more to reoccupy Stevenson: the unattractiveness of 'good' compared with the attractiveness of 'evil'. At the moment, everything remains on the plane of light comedy. We are not, like Jim, of the Squire's way of thinking, we do not hate the Captain *deeply*. But we already see a point that Stevenson was to be explicit about in the first of his *Fables*, written much later, when Silver and the Captain have a chat outside the pages of *Treasure Island*, and Silver says:

'What I know is this: if there is such a thing as an Author, I'm his favourite character. He does me fathoms better than he does you – fathoms, he does. And he likes doing me. He keeps me on deck mostly all the time, crutch and all; and he leaves you measling in the hold, where nobody can't see you, nor wants to, and you may lay to that! If there's an Author, by thunder, but he's on my side, and you may lay to it!' And Captain Smollett replies, sighing, 'I am a man that tries to do his duty, and makes a mess of it as often as not. I'm not a very popular man at home, Silver, I'm afraid.'

Stevenson here touches lightly (though not without a characteristic theological overtone) on a perennial problem of imaginative art: the superior fascination and vitality of 'evil'. Milton's Satan is the supreme example. In Stevenson's own *Weir of Hermiston*, we have a similar theme in the contrast between the good but unlovable Archie and the attractive seducer Frank Innes, and – more subtly – the contrast between the vital Scottish speech of the Lord Justice Clerk and the pallid English of his son.

The voyage (ch. X) is thus chiefly interesting because of the portrayal of Silver's attractions. '"He's no common man, Barbecue," said the coxswain to me. "He had good schooling in his young days, and can speak like a book when so minded; and brave – a lion's nothing alongside of Long John! I seen him grapple four, and knock their heads together – him unarmed." All the crew respected and even obeyed him.' We note also the renewed emphasis on his neatness and cleanness; we have been made to associate the pirates with dirt and disorder. Otherwise, the narrative interest is provided by suspense: we are waiting for the knowledge which will confirm our suspicions. (The incident of Mr Arrow, the secret-drinking mate, seems to have little point, except as an extra touch of mystery.) The similar episode in *Kidnapped* is much superior.

The apple-barrel scene (ch. XI) is crucial to the plot. In the narrative, it confirms the reader's suspicions, and puts Jim in possession of facts of which he and the reader were hitherto ignorant; while structurally it represents the re-establishment of Jim as an important agent in the story, and so prepares for his emergence as 'hero' in the full sense. At the time we enjoy, at Jim's expense, his reversal of feeling about Silver: 'You may imagine how I felt when I heard this abominable old rogue addressing another in the very same words of flattery as he had used to myself. I think, if I had been able, that I would have killed him through the barrel.'

Treasure Island itself, which we now reach, is not one of the great islands of fiction. It is much less 'there' for the reader in its own right than the islands in *Lord of the Flies* or *The Man Who Loved Islands*. It is skilfully described, but its geography is purely functional, mere stage-setting, like the island of *The Tempest*. Perhaps the significance of this particular exclusion may emerge more fully when we consider the similar want of resonance in the 'treasure' theme. For the moment, we note that Treasure Island exists mainly as a stage from which superfluous characters have been cleared, and we can enjoy the double vision that results from moving Jim between the Squire's party and Silver's. The ambiguous position of Silver is foreshadowed even before the mutiny. 'Mutiny, it was plain, hung over us like a thundercloud. "We've only one man to rely on." "And who is that?" asked the squire. "Silver, sir," returned the captain; "he's as anxious as you and I to smother things up." '

With chapter XIV – Silver's murder of the loyal seaman – we come, surely, to something serious. The fictive reality of this murder is of a different kind from many of the other deaths in *Treasure Island,* or in pirate stories generally. 'The sun beat full upon them. Silver had thrown his hat beside him on the ground, and his great smooth, blond face, all shining with heat, was lifted to the other man's in a kind of appeal.' What makes this scene powerful is our intimate closeness to Silver during the murder: he is referred to twice as 'John' – unusually for *Treasure Island*. There are some unforgettable touches. One, that a boy perhaps most notices, is Silver's whipping the crutch out of his armpit so that it strikes Tom between the shoulders and lays him low. The older reader may be more struck by the moment when Silver twice buries his knife in Tom's body, and Jim says, 'I could hear him pant aloud as he struck the blows.' Jim faints. The *obvious* force of this scene lies in Jim's identification with the victim; its less obvious force is the secret participation of Jim (because of his *closeness* to Silver) and hence of the reader.

This may be a good point to anticipate the objection that the story is now being taken too seriously. We recall Jim's remark about Billy Bones: 'People were frightened at the time, but on looking back they rather liked it' – this would be a perfect epigraph for an account of Hitchcock's intentions! Stevenson is committed to the conventions of romance; if we were in doubt of this during chapter XIV, we are brought back to the norms of the story in chapter XV, which introduces the maroon, Benn Gunn. Ben Gunn, unlike Silver, is a 'humour' (though he seems to have had enough archetypal existence to be borrowed by the writer of a 'sequel' to *Treasure Island*). The *realities* of such isolation, which we have in contemporary accounts of Alexander Selkirk after his rescue, are not, of course, touched on. This is not even the art of Defoe, let alone the art of Conrad. Doctor Livesey's question – 'Is this Benn Gunn a man?' – does have its incidental bearings on the serious moral question hinted at in *Treasure Island* (what *is* it to be a man?); but it is quickly dropped. Benn Gunn remains a merely comic figure. But, like Billy Bones, he is a technical device who is made interesting. He is to be the *deus ex machina*, who resolves the plot by his removal of the treasure. Structurally, he is valuable because he provides an element of the unexpected; otherwise, since we know as early as paragraph 1 of chapter I that the heroes escaped, the story might become too predictable. It is hard to over-praise this copybook craftsmanship.

The change of narrator in chapter XVI appears to have held Stevenson up in the actual writing of the story; but the reader feels no sense of hiatus, since Doctor Livesey's point of view is the same as Jim's. Apart from the plot-interest, this part of the books shows us, from the 'good' side, what we are later to see in different terms from the 'bad' side: the combination of a code with considerations of practical policy. Thus the Captain refuses to strike his colours in the stockade, partly out of 'stout, seamanly good feeling', but partly also to show the mutineers that the good party despise their cannonade. Similarly, he points out, when Redruth is killed, that rations are short and 'we're, perhaps, as well without that extra mouth'. Here we see adult recognition of necessity through adult eyes; and our view is later to be complemented by Jim's youthful view of Silver's equal efficiency in the enemy camp.

In the *Fable* conversation, Captain Smollett thought he had the best of the exchanges with Silver in chapter XX, 'Silver's Embassy'. The reader may indeed have the feeling that the author is redressing the balance here. But he is more likely to note a somewhat detached tone, towards the amusingly theatrical ('Them that die'll be the lucky ones!'), something which the characters themselves enjoy. 'And he filled a pipe and lighted it; and the two men sat silently smoking for quite a while, now looking each other in the face, now stopping their tobacco, now leaning forward to spit. It was as good as the play to see them.' One of the minor attractions of *Treasure Island* is Stevenson's ability to use this tone without spoiling the story for the younger reader – whereas, for example, the sophistication at the *expense* of the young reader damages parts of *The Wind in the Willows*.

But the main focus of interest is now Jim and his adventures. His sea adventure culminates in an episode of physical bravery: the seizure of the *Hispaniola* and the fight with Israel Hands. This is one of the parts of *Treasure Island* where the boyish interest may differ from the adult's. Jim, though he does not know it, is not only the active hero (who is all the same not too heroic for the boy reader to identify with). He is, to the adult eye, more experienced and psychologically secure in his handling of this new and grim anti-father. 'The eyes of the coxswain. . . followed me derisively about the deck. . .the odd smile that appeared continually on his face. . .had in it something both of pain and weakness – a haggard, old man's smile; but there was, besides that, a grain of derision, a shadow of treachery, in his expression as he craftily watched, and watched, and watched me at my work.' In so far as the book describes the 'growing up' of Jim, this is an important episode. Hands is an interesting character. Like Pew, he is purely a figure of evil, but he is seen in a more adult way. 'I never seen good come o' goodness yet. Him as strikes first is my fancy; dead men don't bite; them's my views – amen, so be it.' For Jim, the struggle with Hands is largely 'a boy's game' – this is, after all, a boy's book; he heaves the dead O'Brien, whom Hands has killed, overboard like a sack of bran; but for the adult reader, the dead men are seen somewhat differently:

He went in with a sounding plunge; the red cap came off, and remained floating on the surface; and as soon as the splash subsided,

I could see him and Israel lying side by side, both wavering with the tremulous movement of the water. O'Brien, though still quite a young man, was very bald. There he lay, with that bald head across the knees of the man who had killed him, and the quick fishes steering to and fro over both.

It is in such passages as this, in this early work, that we catch the glimpse of an explanation why Stevenson can be said to have 'developed' in his art as a Buchan or an A. E. W. Mason cannot. We might reflect on how such an art, both serious and popular, might close the communication gap that exists at present between the serious novel and ordinary readers. For the substance of the passage touches the serious moral subject, raised in quite different ways by an Israel Hands or a Ben Gunn: what is it to be a man? Jim is given words of simple faith. ' "You can kill the body, Mr Hands, but not the spirit; you must know that already," I replied. "O'Brien there is in another world, and maybe watching us." ' Stevenson does not dissociate himself; but he gives Israel a sardonic retort: ' "Ah!" says he. "Well, that's unfort'nate – appears as if killing parties was a waste of time." ' But what lingers in the memory, perhaps, is not so much that exchange as this picture: 'O'Brien, though still quite a young man, was very bald. There he lay, with that bald head across the knees of the man who had killed him, and the quick fishes steering to and fro over both.' We might be tempted to append here a bleak thought from another *Fable* of Stevenson's, *The Three Reformers*: ' "The first thing," said the third, "is to abolish mankind." '

But that note, of course, is no part of *Treasure Island*. At the same time, we might reflect that the deaths of these pirates are an exception to the rule that in pirate stories, Westerns, and so on, the deaths of 'baddies' don't count. The story now carries us, in part VI, to the enemy's camp. This is the crisis of the book, both for Jim and for Silver. For Jim, it is the place where he becomes a moral as well as a physical hero; when he refuses to break his word to Silver and go back with Doctor Livesey. 'You know right well you wouldn't do the thing yourself; neither you, nor squire, nor captain; and no more will I. Silver trusted me; I passed my word, and back I go.' It is dramatically right that in this scene Jim makes his boast – traditionally permitted in ancient epic to the brave man alone, or in peril – when he reveals to the mutineers that it was he throughout who ruined their plans. The adult reader's interest here is much the same as the boy's; but he may be more interested in Silver. A writer in the *Sunday Review* (8 December 1883) saw that Silver is the real hero of *Treasure Island*, and that the real centre of the book is the scene in which the pirate leader, by cunning and audacity, saves Jim's life in the conflict of wills between him and his followers. In so far as the book is about Jim's education, we can treat this scene as Jim's induction into *politics*, as he learns something of the arts of leadership, from the intellectual and moral supremacy of Silver over his followers, and his insight into the weaknesses of Dick, or George Merry. Our attitude to Silver shifts as Jim's does. The plot-interest resides in *how* they will escape, as well as in subordinate mysteries (why did the Squire's party desert the stockade? why did the Doctor give Silver the chart?). For those who maintain that this is the *main* interest, a reassuring way of reading the story is possible. They can maintain that Silver 'really' liked Jim Hawkins – apart from the essential need for retaining him as part of his plan of survival; so that we *know* that Jim will come to no harm from him. This is a popular way of reading the story, one vulgarised in the film. I think this reading misses something that Stevenson put into the story. When the treasure is in prospect, 'Silver hobbled, grunting, on his crutch; his nostrils stood out and quivered; he cursed like a madman when the flies settled on his hot and shiny countenance; he plucked furiously at the line that held me to him, and, from time to time, turned his eyes upon me with a deadly look'. The chief critical question about *Treasure Island* is raised here in a precise form: how *seriously* are we to take Silver's murderous intentions?

Then comes the discovery that the treasure has gone, and Silver, with immediate resourcefulness, performs his volte-face and passes Jim a pistol. Jim is understandably revolted. But what is *our* attitude? It is not quite Jim's; nor is it quite the same as the Doctor's: ' "Ah," said Silver, "it was fortunate for me that I had Hawkins here. You would have let old John be cut to bits, and never given it a thought, doctor." "Not a thought," replied

Doctor Livesey, cheerily.' But Silver has now resumed his earlier role, 'bland, polite, obsequious'.

What, then, is our feeling at the end of *Treasure Island*? The conventions of youthful romance are preserved. The good are rewarded and the evil punished. Silver's escape ingeniously solves a technical problem, and is in keeping with his ambiguous role throughout. (Ben Gunn, who engineers his escape, is once more used adroitly.) He is allowed to take away a *little* of the treasure.

But what *is* the treasure? Some might say that it is no more than a necessary ingredient of the plot, in itself morally neutral: good men as well as bad go in search of it. Others might feel, as Jim does, that it is contaminated by the blood that has been shed for it, and the evil of Flint who buried it there. Others again might feel that this is *innocent* gold, not like the gold of commerce, or of Balzac's novels. A pirate as the symbol of a scoundrel is a boyish, innocent imagining, and this is piratical gold. Personally, I do not think the treasure has much more of a symbolic role than the Maltese Falcon (in Hammett's story, not in the film). Like the Falcon, it is a token of greed rather than 'such stuff as dreams are made on'. It has little emotional significance. There is almost nothing of the inward, sensuous excitement we feel in Legrand and the Negro at the climax of Poe's *The Gold Bug* (to which Stevenson was admittedly indebted). The attainment of the treasure is almost an anti-climax. Part of it is even left behind (the bar *silver* – is this a mere coincidence?). At any rate, the book closes on a curiously *sad* note ('Oxen and wain-ropes would not bring me back again to the accursed island'). This makes me think that the book has a serious core, in Silver's relationship with Jim, and that 'real' elements – that is to say, elements of personal significance to Stevenson – went into the creation of that relationship.

There is an absence of emotional pressure in the winning of the treasure. Many readers may agree that Stevenson's first title, *The Sea Cook*, is better than the one he finally chose. We must respect his intuitive decision that he could not accommodate *two* such powerful archetypes as the sea cook and buried treasure. (There is more suggestion of a latent meaning in buried treasure

– the mother's body? – in the corresponding scene in *The Gold Bug*.) We might bear in mind some background considerations which, being psychological, are merely speculative. The avoidance of the 'treasure' theme of *Treasure Island* may have something to do with Stevenson's personal stabilisation at that time. After his marriage to a motherly type of woman, he had achieved a degree of resolution of his difficult relationship with his father (warm affection and passionate disagreement). *Treasure Island* was written with the enthusiastic collaboration of his father – himself a lover of romantic adventures – and of Stevenson's stepson, the boy Lloyd Osbourne. It was the first book in which he was really fulfilled as a writer. And yet there is that curious note of sadness at the end. There are some disturbing touches, like the marooning of the three pirates: 'Coming through the narrows, we had to lie very near the southern point, and there we saw all three of them kneeling together on a spit of sand, with their arms raised in supplication.' This seems very poignant for a boy's story. Where is the 'happy ending'?

I do not suggest that *Treasure Island* has anything of the emotional power of Stevenson's sombre *Fable*, 'The House of Eld', with its dark 'moral':

> Woodman, is your courage stout?
> Beware! the root is wrapped about
> Your mother's heart, your father's bones;
> And like the mandrake comes with groans.

But on its own plane it fulfils the primary purpose of all fiction: to provide the reader with imaginative understanding of human nature, in ideal conditions for the exercise of that understanding. Even by itself it suggests doubts about the view, still quite common, that Stevenson was not really a creative writer at all, but an essayist who occasionally graced the lighter forms of fiction with a characteristic touch. And taken in the context of Stevenson's developing art, we may see it as a preliminary sketch of his main theme: the theme, or insight, he indicates in these words from Dr Jekyll and Mr Hyde: 'I saw that of the two natures that contended in the field of my consciousness, if I could rightly be said to be either, it was only because I was radically both.' At a less profound level, we might conclude our revisiting of *Treasure Island* by remarking that it is the common-place and yet (to Stevenson) astounding co-presence of good and evil qualities in the same person – rather than the simpler human problem of reconciling personal liking with moral dis-approval – which gives a tinge of serious interest to this yarn about pirates.

6
On *Kidnapped*

Kidnapped is like *Treasure Island* in some ways and unlike it in others. To start with the likenesses. (1) Both of them are among those works – *Jekyll and Hyde* and *A Child's Garden of Verses* are others – which have suffered nothing from the disparagement or neglect by the critics of Stevenson's work in general. The common reader has taken them to his heart. (2) Both *Kidnapped* and *Treasure Island* are good boys' books. By that I do not mean that they are books for good boys. Nor do I wish to be taken as endorsing the tiresome and anti-literary custom of sorting out books on the basis of their supposed suitability to particular 'age-groups'. Literature is not like that. But authors' intentions – while not necessarily decisive for criticism – have to be taken into account, and there is no doubt that authors have intended to write such things. I would define a good boys' book as a book which the author meant to be a boys' book and which does in fact appeal to many boys. (It is not necessarily a book which adults think boys like; still less one they think boys ought to like.) Both *Kidnapped* and *Treasure Island* clearly satisfy that definition, and as far as *Kidnapped* is concerned Stevenson seems to have indicated his intention, at any rate as it was at the moment of completing the book, by calling it *Kidnapped* and publishing it in *Young Folks*. (3) *Kidnapped* is like *Treasure Island* in having obvious 'boys' book' qualities. Both have a youthful hero, who has exciting adventures. Neither has what film producers used to call a 'love interest' – for the people who use that term would not apply it to David's relations with Alan, or the author's passion for the countryside round Edinburgh. What is meant is that neither book has a heroine. The only important female character in *Kidnapped* is the fine lassie who helps David and Alan to cross the Forth. For a love interest in the Hollywood sense we have to wait for the sequel, *Catriona*. (4) Both *Kidnapped* and *Treasure Island*, though in varying degrees, convey signals to the reader that he is being invited to join the author in a game. As Henry James,[1] best of Stevenson's

97

critics, puts it: 'What he prizes most in the boy's ideal is the imaginative side of it, the capacity for successful make-believe.' No author has surpassed Stevenson in his power to recover this part of the secret joys and private poetry of childhood and youth. Remember his fable of *The Lantern-Bearers*.[2] He pictures a camp of small urchins who carry their smelly tin lanterns buttoned under their overcoats. He thinks how silly they must seem to an onlooker who does not understand their rapture, sheltering in the cold sand on a bleak sea-shore on a dark autumn night.

To miss the joy is to miss all. . .Hence the haunting and truly spectral unreality of realistic books. Hence, when we read the English realists, the incredulous wonder with which we observe the hero's constancy under the submerging tide of dulness, and how he bears up with his jibbing sweetheart, and endures the chatter of idiot girls, and stands by his whole unfeatured wilderness of an existence. . .Hence in the French, in that meat-market of middle-aged sensuality, the disgusted surprise with which we see the hero drift side-long, and practically quite untempted, into every description of misconduct and dishonour. In each, we miss the personal poetry, the enchanted atmosphere, that rainbow of fancy that clothes what is naked and seems to ennoble what is base; in each, life falls dead like dough, instead of soaring away like a balloon into the colours of the sunset; each is true, each inconceivable; for no man lives in the external truth, among salts and acids, but in the warm, phantasmagoric chamber of his brains, with the painted windows and the storied walls.

(5) Both *Kidnapped* and *Treasure Island* share to a superlative degree a quality without which few books are popular, something that looks so easy that we tend to take it for granted, and yet it is as rare as all good things are. Johnson[3] says in *The Rambler* (no. 122):

Of the various kinds of speaking and writing, which serve necessity or promote pleasure, none appears so artless or easy as simple narration; for what should make him that knows the whole order and progress of an affair unable to relate it? Yet we hourly find such an endeavour to entertain or instruct us by recitals, clouding the facts which they intend to illustrate, and losing themselves and their auditors in the wilds of digression, or the mazes of confusion.

Corresponding to this narrative fluency we have in Stevenson, what does not always go with it, the power to make a clear-cut plot-outline. Stevenson himself sets forth the outline of *Kidnapped* in his sub-title: 'being the adventures of David Balfour; how he was kidnapped and cast away; his sufferings in a desert isle; his journey in the West Highlands; his acquaintance with Alan Breck Stewart and other notorious Highland Jacobites; with all that he suffered at the hands of his uncle, Ebenezer Balfour of Shaws, falsely so-called; written by himself, and now set forth by Robert Louis Stevenson'. Well, that *is* what *Kidnapped* is about. But imagine having to write an equivalent summary of *The Way We Live Now,* or *Little Dorrit!* (6) Finally, both *Kidnapped* and *Treasure Island* offer many satisfactions to the reader who is not only interested in what is said, but also in how it is said. The boy who likes *Kidnapped* better than some ordinary adventure tale is not interested in 'style'; but perhaps he intuitively appreciates that his preference for *Kidnapped* lies in Stevenson's superior ability to make the things happen that we are to understand to have happened. And once he has become conscious of that, he has learned what 'style' means.

About half way down, the wind sprang up in a clap and shook the tower, and died again; the rain followed; and before I had reached the ground level it fell in buckets. I put out my head into the storm, and looked along towards the kitchen. The door, which I had shut behind me when I left, now stood open, and shed a little glimmer of light; and I thought I could see a figure standing in the rain, quite still, like a man hearkening. And then there came a blinding flash, which showed me my uncle plainly, just where I had fancied him to stand; and hard upon the heels of it, a great tow-row of thunder.

(chapter 4)

It came all of a sudden when it did, with a rush of feet and a roar, and then a shout from Alan, and a sound of blows and someone crying out as if hurt. I looked back over my shoulder, and saw Mr Shuan in the doorway, crossing blades with Alan.

'That's him that killed the boy!' I cried.

'Look to your window!' said Alan; and as I turned back to my place, I saw him pass his sword through the mate's body.

(chapter 10)

The mountains on either side were high, rough and barren, very black

99

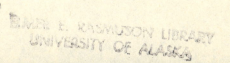

and gloomy in the shadow of the clouds, but all silver-laced with
little watercourses where the sun shone upon them. It seemed a hard
country, this of Appin, for people to care about as much as Alan did.

(chapter 17)

...the sun shone upon a little moving clump of scarlet close in along
the waterside to the north. It was much of the same red as soldiers'
coats; every now and then, too, there came little sparks and light-
nings, as though the sun had struck upon bright steel.

(chapter 17)

Where are the frills and mannerisms of which Stevenson has
been so often accused?

' "Look to your window!" said Alan; and as I turned back to
my place, I saw him pass his sword through the mate's body.' If
we are to talk about literary influences at all, it is the plain style
of Defoe that comes to mind. But it is the plain style of Defoe
handled by a sensuous artist. The same could be said of *Treasure
Island.*

So much for the likenesses between the two books. Now for
the unlikenesses. First, *Kidnapped* is a real travel book. The
topography is carefully worked out. You can follow the actual
route of David and Alan, either literally, or on a map – prefer-
ably an eighteenth-century map – as you can trace the whole
Scottish journey of Johnson and Boswell, twenty-two years after;
which Frank Morley does in his *Literary Britain*. Morley sets it
all out in all the detail Stevenson carefully provided; how the
brig *Covenant*, bearing Alan Breck and David Balfour, having
cleared Iona, struck and was lost on the Torran rocks (Stevenson,
it seems, puts them closer to Mull than the map shows); so that
they were castaways in a land of Alan's hereditary foes, the
Campbells. From then on the route of the travellers may be
traced from Glen Coe eastward across the Rannoch Moor, south
from Ben Alder to the Braes of Balquhidder – Scott country,
The Lady of the Lake and parts of *Rob Roy* – and so to the final
stage of the fugitives' journey, when Alan and David, having
bypassed Stirling, make their way along the north shore of the
Firth of Forth, which they are enabled to cross by the help of the
lass from whom they bought bread and cheese, and, landing near

Carriden, are in just the right place for the dénouement at the House of Shaws, placed by Stevenson in the countryside he knew from his boyhood holidays. For the parting with Alan, David walked with him towards Edinburgh as far as the hill of Corstorphine, and there was the halting-place bearing the same name as the halting-place Dr Johnson had noticed at Glen Crose: Rest-and-be-Thankful. It marked Johnson's farewell to his Scottish peregrinations; and what better end for an adventure story than Rest-and-be-Thankful?

Kidnapped, then, unlike *Treasure Island*, is bound up with real geography, and this element of reality is part of its essence. But there is a deeper difference. *Treasure Island* may or may not have a high place in literature (I myself would rank it very high) but no one could dispute its outstanding quality as a work of what is called 'genre fiction'. It is a pirate story – surely the best pirate story ever written? But *Kidnapped* is less self-evident generically. Is it a travel book, or an adventure story, or a historical novel? It seems to be all these things, and yet not precisely any of them. The same sort of problem arises in the discussion of *Huckleberry Finn*, and it suggests that there are some occasions when the guidance we get from the concept of 'genre fiction' ceases to be helpful. Stevenson knew exactly what he was doing in *Treasure Island*. He was writing in the genre 'pirate story', but improving it. But what about *Kidnapped*? Stevenson wrote to Watts-Dunton that it was originally conceived as another *Treasure Island*, but when he saw how to use his historical material the novel developed in an unexpected direction. His interest in the Appin murder may well be the genetic explanation for the difference between the two books. But reference to these antecedents, to the author's original intentions, does not help us much to understand the meaning of *Kidnapped*. For, as Stevenson tells us, in this book and in this book only, 'the characters took the bit between their teeth; all at once they became detached from the flat paper, they turned their backs on me bodily; and from that time my task was stenographic; it was they who spoke, it was they who wrote the remainder of the story'. There are other famous examples of this kind of thing in the history of literature, and Stevenson's account of the writing of *Kidnapped* suggests that I have not begged the question in speaking of its 'meaning'. It has a meaning in a sense in which *St. Ives*, for example, has not. *St. Ives* is full of author's intentions, the formulas of romantic adventure, but critical examination suggests that in carrying them out the author's deeper imagination was not involved.

Stevenson does not tell us at what precise point the characters took the bit between their teeth. But the fact that this occurred at all suggests that it is the structure of *Kidnapped* that provides the clue to its interpretation. Let us look into the structure. *Kidnapped* obviously consists of two stories, David Balfour's and Alan Breck's. Their stories begin to interweave when in a night of thick weather the *Covenant* ran down a boat and Alan Breck leaped from the stern and clutched the brig's bowsprit. And their destinies become inseparably interwoven with the Appin murder. Clearly the murder of Red Colin is pivotal. It leads to complications which are not cleared up in *Kidnapped*, and had to wait some years till Stevenson wrote a sequel, *Catriona*. This feature of the book has been adversely criticised. '*Kidnapped*', says Ernest Baker,[4] 'is only a congeries of events...The Appin murder is only a mechanical centre, not an organic motive;...it has nothing to do with David or Alan.' So this critic finds *Kidnapped*, like *Catriona*, just a miscellany of adventure, though admirably pieced together. And Baker thinks this typical of Stevenson. 'He seems not to have visualized his novels as complete wholes, but to have built them up from one episode to the next.' 'Except *Treasure Island*, story rather than novel, and *Weir of Hermiston*, Stevenson's masterpieces in fiction are in the briefer and more concentrated genre.' Other critics (Frank Swinnerton, for example) have concurred in finding that Sevenson's real gift was for the short story. Let us then look more closely at the construction of *Kidnapped* and see whether analysis can disclose an essential unifying theme.

The narrative seems to me to fall into five movements. Chapters 1 to 6 are concerned with David and his uncle; this movement ends with the kidnapping. Chapters 7 to 13 tell the story of David on board the *Covenant*, and culminate with the loss of the brig. The third movement, chapters 14 to the middle of 17, recounts David's adventures without Alan. This movement is spectacularly cut short by the Appin murder, which David witnesses. The fourth movement, from the middle of chapter 17 to the end of chapter 25, is about David on the run with Alan: it includes the famous flight in the heather. Chapter 26, the crossing of the Forth, may be seen as something of an intermezzo, leading to the final movement, chapters 27 to 30, which tell of David's return to Shaws and the recovery of his inheritance.

The first movement is full of conscious and affectionate references to the tradition of romance, ballad, folktale – genre-signals, so to speak:

> there came up into my mind (quite unbidden by me and even discouraged) a story like some ballad I had heard folks singing, of a poor lad that was a rightful heir and a wicked kinsman that tried to keep him from his own.
>
> (chapter 4)

When David on the *Covenant* tells Riach his story, 'he declared it was like a ballad'. This generic indication is given literary expression in the final movement by the cultivated Rankeillor, who humorously speculates on what kind of book David and he are going to be in.

> This is a great epic, a great Odyssey of yours. You must tell it, sir, in a sound Latinity when your scholarship is riper; or in English if you please, though for my part I prefer the stronger tongue. You have rolled much; *quae regio in terris* – what parish in Scotland (to make a homely translation) has not been filled with your wanderings? You have shown, besides, a singular aptitude for getting into false positions; and yet, upon the whole, for behaving well in them.
>
> (chapter 27)

This generic reference is rounded off by David himself in chapter 29:

> So the beggar in the ballad had come home; and when I lay down that night on the kitchen chests, I was a man of means and had a name in the country.

This way of looking at *Kidnapped* seems to offer the only explanation of the otherwise inexplicable incident of Jennet

Clouston. She is introduced with strong emphasis, as a Meg
Merrilies figure calling down doom on Uncle Ebenezer and the
House of Shaws:

tell him that this makes the twelve hunner and nineteen time that
Jennet Clouston has called down the curse on him and his house,
byre and stable, man, guest, and master, wife, miss, or bairn – black,
black, be their fall!

(chapter 2)

She is mentioned again in chapter 6, when the landlord of the
Hawes Inn says of Ebenezer: 'He's a wicked auld man, and
there's many would like to see him girning in a tow [rope]:
Jennet Clouston and mony mair that he has harried out of house
and hame'. . .ringing it out like a Scots alliterative poem. But
after that we hear no more of Jennet Clouston. Why is this?
Stevenson, a master of narrative if ever there was one, must have
known that to introduce so colourful a character, with so strong
an emphasis, must leave the reader in pleasurable suspense. But
he never resolves it. The only commonsense, 'external', explanation I can think of is that Stevenson changed his design. But if
this explanation is rejected as unverifiable, the alternative must
be that Jennet Clouston is a genre-signal: a sort of musical
quotation from the old kind of romance.

It might be said that Uncle Ebenezer himself belongs entirely
to that world. I wish I had time to look at the different facets of
Uncle Ebenezer, that 'man of principles' as he calls himself, the
most disagreeable figure in Stevenson's gallery of bad Lowlanders.
(He is not, indeed, totally unsympathetic, but then no one in
Stevenson is totally unsympathetic.) His introduction is masterly.

I was in two minds whether to run away; but anger got the upper
hand, and I began instead to rain kicks and buffets on the door, and
to shout aloud for Mr. Balfour. I was in full career, when I heard the
cough right overhead, and jumping back and looking up, beheld a
man's head in a tall nightcap, and the bell mouth of a blunderbuss at
one of the first-storey windows.
'It's loaded,' said a voice.

(chapter 2)

David's introduction to him reminds me a little of Becky Sharp's introduction to Sir Pitt Crawley in *Vanity Fair*. Edwin M. Eigner,[5] perhaps more to the point, has recalled Lockwood's reception at Wuthering Heights. At any rate, it is storybook stuff. Even the dismayed David, as well as the reader, finds a kind of artistic pleasure in contemplating Ebenezer.

> He fetched another cup from the shelf; and then, to my great surprise, instead of drawing more beer, he poured an accurate half from one cup to the other. There was a kind of nobleness in this that took my breath away; if my uncle was certainly a miser, he was one of that thorough breed that goes near to make the vice respectable.
>
> (chapter 2)

Henry James,[6] however, was a little unhappy about him. 'The cruel and miserly uncle...is rather in the tone of superseded tradition, and the tricks he plays upon his ingenuous nephew are a little like those of country conjurers; in these pages we feel that Mr Stevenson is thinking too much of what a "boys' paper" is expected to contain.' Perhaps so; but to connoisseurs of that tradition the first movement of *Kidnapped* offers superb examples of the revitalising of its formulas. One of its characteristic devices is what Aristotle calls the *anagnorisis*, or moment of recognition; there is no better example of it in literature than what happened on the stair at Shaws:

> as I advanced, it seemed to me the stair grew airier and a thought more lightsome; and I was wondering what might be the cause of this change, when a second blink of the summer lightning came and went. If I did not cry out, it was because fear had me by the throat; and if I did not fall, it was more by Heaven's mercy than by my own strength. It was not only that the flash shone in on every side through breaches in the wall, so that I seemed to be clambering aloft upon an open scaffold, but the same passing brightness showed me the steps were of unequal length, and that one of my feet rested that moment within two inches of the well.
>
> (chapter 4)

Another 'recognition' device is the use of the pre-story, the explanation in the final movement of how Uncle Ebenezer came to be what he was. There is again some likeness to *Wuthering Heights*, which Rankeillor explains:

'. . .the matter hinges on a love affair.'
'Truly,' said I, 'I cannot well join that notion with my uncle.'
'But your uncle, Mr. David, was not always ugly. He had a fine, gallant air. . .'
'It sounds like a dream,' said I.
'Ay, ay,' said the lawyer, 'that is how it is with youth and age.'

———

'. . .The one man took the lady, the other the estate.'
'. . .this piece of Quixotry on your father's part, as it was unjust in itself, has brought forth a monstrous family of injustices. . .'

(chapter 28)

Stevenson was to make this kind of story the centre of interest in *The Master of Ballantrae*. But here it must be judged, in Jamesian language, to belong to the treatment rather than the essence of the story: it is another genre-signal.

Once David is on board the *Covenant* Henry James has no further objections – until the end of the book; 'The remaining five-sixths. . .deserve to stand by *Henry Esmond*, as a fictive autobiography in archaic form.' Yet the second movement of *Kidnapped* can be still seen as conforming to Stevenson's theory of romance. This can be summarised as the placing of an unromantic hero in a romantic situation, and so as the opposite of some of the great works of realist fiction: *Madame Bovary*, for example, is the tragedy of a romantic person in an unromantic situation. We may see also in *Kidnapped* other features of Stevensonian romance: the comparative 'transparency' of the hero; the absence of the omniscient author (and hence of psychological analysis of the characters); the stress on striking incident. We note the kinship with folktales and fairytales which John Buchan[7] saw in the great Victorian novelists: the 'good story'; the characters recognisable as 'real types'; the method of reproducing reality not as an inventory of details, but by 'judicious selection'; the storyteller's primary interest in the events he has to tell of, and not in his own reactions to them: he does not obtrude his moods.

But Buchan lays equal emphasis on another aspect of this tradition: the moral aspect. The storyteller passes moral judgments on his characters; he regards some as definitely good and

106

some as definitely bad. And finally 'he has a dominant purpose,
a lesson, if you like, to teach, a creed to suggest'. This brings us
to the question of the morality, the *ethos*, of Stevensonian
romance. To discuss this is to go to the heart of *Kidnapped*. It is
surprising that F. R. Leavis excluded Stevenson from his 'great
tradition'. Leavis seems to require from a great novelist a profound concern with moral problems. But was there ever an
author more concerned with moral problems than Stevenson? —
not to speak of theological problems? We are never far away
from the Scottish Catechism in Stevenson, with its awe-inspiring
first question: 'What is the whole duty of man?'

But perhaps Leavis would not have found Stevenson's treatment of moral problems profound enough. Now certainly the
morality of romance is simple. It belongs to what Gilbert Ryle,[8]
in his essay on Jane Austen, calls the 'Calvinist', as opposed to
the 'Aristotelian' pattern.

In the eighteenth century, and in other centuries too, moralists tended
to belong to one of two camps...the Calvinist camp...thinks, like a
criminal lawyer, of human beings as...Saved or Damned, Elect or
Reject, children of Vice, heading for Heaven or heading for Hell,
White or Black, Innocent or Guilty, Saints or Sinners...The Calvinist's moral psychology is correspondingly bi-polar. People are dragged
upwards by Soul or Spirit or Reason or Conscience; but they are
dragged down by Body or Flesh or Passion or Pleasure or Inclination.
A man is an unhappy combination of a white angelic part and a black
satanic part. At the best, the angelic part has the satanic part cowed
and starved and subjugated now, and can hope to be released altogether from it in the future. Man's life here is either a life of Sin or
it is a life of self-extrication from Sin...the seducer in The *Vicar of
Wakefield*...is wickedness incarnate...[like] Fanny Burney's bad
characters. Johnson in The *Rambler*...persons who are all black...
no Tuesday morning attributes.

In contrast is the Aristotelian pattern of ethical ideas.

People differ from each other in degree and not in kind, not in respect
just of a single generic Sunday attribute, but a whole spectrum of
specific weekday attributes...A is a bit more irritable and ambitious
than B, less indolent and less sentimental. C is meaner and quicker-
witted than D, and D is greedier and more athletic than C. A person

is not black and white, but iridescent with all the colours of the rainbow. . .not a flat plane, but a highly irregular solid. . .better than most in one respect, about level with the average in another respect, and a bit, perhaps a big bit, deficient in a third respect. In fact he is like people we really know, in a way in which we do not know and could not know any people who are just Bad or else just Good.

Ryle's argument is that Jane Austen's moral ideas are, with certain exceptions, ideas of the Aristotelian and not of the Calvinist pattern. 'Much as she had learned from Johnson, this she had not learned from him.'

How then is Stevenson's morality, in his fiction, to be classified – Calvinist or Aristotelian? On the face of it, it is Calvinist. There is no doubt that Uncle Ebenezer is bad. What about the captain and crew of the *Covenant*? They are mixed. But they are seen as black-and-white mixtures, not 'iridescent'. The poor crazy boy Ransome thinks Captain Hoseason wholly bad, but David discovers that 'he was neither so good as I supposed him, nor quite so bad as Ransome did; for, in fact, he was two men, and left the better one behind as soon as he set foot on board his vessel'. He is, in fact, a case of Jekyll and Hyde, not in the subtle sense that Stevenson had in mind in that story, but in the popular interpretation of it. He is a cold-blooded villain – literally:

'Captain Hoseason,' returned my uncle, 'you keep your room unco hot.'
'It's a habit I have, Mr. Balfour,' said the skipper, 'I'm a cold-rife man in my nature; I have a cold blood, sir. There's neither fur nor flannel – no, sir, nor hot rum will warm up what they call the temperature. Sir, it's the same with most men that have been carbonadoed, as they call it, in the south seas.'
'Well, well,' replied my uncle, 'we must all be in the way we're made.'

(chapter 6)

Yet he says, 'I am a true-blue Protestant, and I thank God for it.' 'It was,' says David, 'the first word of any religion I had ever heard from him, but I learnt afterwards that he was a great church-goer while on shore.' He loves his mother.

I heard a gun fire, and supposed the storm had proved too strong for us, and we were firing signals of distress. . .Yet it was no such matter; but (as I was afterwards told) a common habit of the captain's. . .We were then passing, it appeared, within some miles of Dysart, where the brig was built, and where old Mrs. Hoseason, the captain's mother, had come some years before to live; and whether outward or inward bound, the *Covenant* was never suffered to go by that place by day, without a gun fired and colours shown.

(chapter 7)

David learns to see similar dualities in the crew of the *Covenant*.

. . .I found there was a strange peculiarity about our two mates: that Mr. Riach was sullen, unkind, and harsh when he was sober, and Mr. Shuan would not hurt a fly except when he was drinking. I asked about the captain; but I was told drink made no difference upon that man of iron.

(chapter 7)

David has to learn that human nature is strangely mixed. But there is no doubt about the ingredients of the mixture: good and evil. We have terrifying glimpses of pure evil.

. . .two seamen appeared in the scuttle, carrying Ransome in their arms; and the ship at that moment giving a great sheer into the sea, and the lantern swinging, the light fell direct on the boy's face. It was as white as wax, and had a look upon it like a dreadful smile.

(chapter 8)

'Sit down!' roars the captain. 'Ye sot and swine, do ye know what ye've done? Ye've murdered the boy!'
Mr. Shuan seemed to understand; for he sat down again, and put up his hand to his brow.
'Well,' he said, 'he brought me a dirty pannikin!'

(chapter 8)

What makes it so terrible is what Hannah Arendt calls the 'banality of evil': appalling crimes are committed by ordinary, helpless human beings.

Hoseason walked up to his chief officer, took him by the shoulder, led him across to his bunk, and bade him lie down and go to sleep, as you might speak to a bad child. The murderer cried a little, but he took off his sea-boots and obeyed.

(chapter 8)

'You may think it strange,' says David, 'but for all the horror I had, I was still sorry for him. He was a married man, with a wife in Leith; but whether or no he had a family, I have now forgotten; I hope not.'
(chapter 8)

In this second movement, then, we are still in a 'Calvinist' moral world. It culminates in the defeat of the bad characters in the fight in the roundhouse, and the loss of the brig.

The third movement, when David and Alan are parted, shows in comparison a slackening of intensity. Here, if anywhere, *Kidnapped* is open to the charge of being merely episodic. The incidents in this part of the book seem mainly designed to show the disturbed state of the Highlands in the 1750s. But they may also be put in deliberately to relieve tension. The comic note is prominent. David's 'marooning' on Earraid is due not to a malign fate, but to his own folly and ignorance, as he himself ruefully recognises. Mr Henderland is introduced to sound the note of positive goodness and to remind us of David's piety. But he is also a semi-comic character, with his roundabout way of gratifying his passion for snuff while having ascetically renounced it. In short, the novel becomes rather picaresque hereabouts, and some of the incidents show a lack of inspiration. It has often been remarked that the sinister blind catechist is much inferior, in thrilling suggestiveness, to blind Pew in *Treasure Island*.

The tension mounts again with the Appin murder. It is interesting to contrast this with the murder of Ransome:

just as he turned there came the shot of a firelock from higher up the hill; and with the very sound of it Glenure fell upon the road.
'O, I am dead!' he cried, several times over.
The lawyer had caught him up and held him in his arms, the servant standing over and clasping his hands. (chapter 17)

The effect is quite different. The murder of Red Colin happens so suddenly. We have not yet learned to care about him as we care about Ransome. And it is a different kind of murder: a political assassination, not an act of drunken cruelty. For David, however – and this is the important point – there is no difference, morally speaking. Murder is murder.

Morally speaking – but not psychologically. For this murder David, because of his love for Alan, is involved in. He experiences 'a new kind of terror'.

> It is one thing to stand the danger of your life, and quite another to run the peril of both life and character. The thing, besides, had come so suddenly, like thunder out of a clear sky, that I was all amazed and helpless. (chapter 17)

This, then, is the psychological turning-point of *Kidnapped*. We pass from the timeless world of folktale, with its appropriate black-and-white morality, to a historical world, with a problematic, relative, regionally and culturally conditioned morality. Aristotle presides, not Calvin. With the coming together again of David and Alan both the genre and the ethos of *Kidnapped* have changed. Generically, it becomes a pursuit story – and one with a historical background. The Appin murder is something that really happened. I am not concerned here with who really was the murderer. (It seems, as a matter of fact, that there was a conspiracy of the gentry of Appin.) I am only concerned with the murder as Stevenson presents it. And one thing he is clear about: Alan was not the murderer. He is prepared to swear this, to David, on his holy dirk. David accepts it, and so must we. But this does not bridge the moral chasm between David and Alan. Alan does not think the killing of a Campbell is wrong. And he equivocates about his knowledge of the murderer's identity. What does a Campbell matter? There are plenty of others. The Campbells will take their revenge by the judicial murder of a Stewart. And Alan does not think they would be wrong to do that. The Duke of Argyll, the head of the clan, knows that if circumstances were reversed, a Stewart would do the same thing to a Campbell. In short, Alan recognises only a tribal morality. He gives voice naively to what Prestongrange in *Catriona* is to defend with all his formidable and sophisticated intellectual resources. His morals, says David helplessly, are 'tail-first'.

This is the beginning of David's moral ordeal. Hitherto his ordeal had been mainly physical. And it is to go on being physical: we are never allowed to forget that David, hero of romance as he may be, is constantly fainting because of his bad feet. And there is no more sustained evocation of a physical ordeal in literature than the flight in the heather: Stevenson was justly proud of it, arguing against Henry James that something an author has not in fact lived through can be more imaginatively stimulating than something he has lived through. But from now on it is to be a moral and psychological ordeal as well. First, the moral ordeal. The law, in *Kidnapped*, as in much imaginative literature, is the symbol of civilisation, order, the good. But what happens to a country in a time of troubles, when the law can be all too plausibly seen as an instrument of oppression of one faction by another? You cannot expect people who are persecuted by the law to respect it. But what happens is not that a better law replaces it, but that clan loyalty becomes all in all – or even more self-centred ideologies: it is clear that much of Alan Breck's 'code' consists of little more than personal vanity.

The general political and social implications of this lawlessness are explored more fully in *Catriona*. In *Kidnapped* the focus is more individual. The moral interest centres on the relationship between a civilised man and a primitive – as does the most memorable part of *Huckleberry Finn*. Eigner points out that Stevenson read *Huckleberry Finn* in 1885, and it was at this time that he dropped his plans for a highwayman novel and wrote *Kidnapped* instead. And many suggestive parallels can be drawn between Stevenson and Mark Twain, notably the 'eternal boy' theme which has figured so much in the criticism of both of them. But whether or not Stevenson was influenced by *Huckleberry Finn*, David is like Huck with Nigger Jim in having to undergo a conflict of imperatives. He is caught between his love for Alan and his reprobation of Alan's morality. It is another case of what Leslie Fiedler[9] has called the 'theme of the Beloved Scoundrel', adumbrated in the relation of Jim Hawkins to John Silver in *Treasure Island*: the moral ambiguity that results from a character's being both admired and condemned. (Was Achilles in the *Iliad* the first of these in literature?) We must remember that – to use a distinction of Ronald Knox's – David is a 'pathetic' rather than a 'drastic' character. On the whole, things happen to him, while the Beloved Scoundrel is the one who does things.

The moral contrast between David and Alan has already appeared in the second movement, in the fight in the round-house. David's feelings are those of the civilised man:

what with the long suspense of the waiting, and the scurry and strain of our two spirts of fighting, and more than all, the horror I had of some of my own share in it, the thing was no sooner over than I was glad to stagger to a seat. There was that tightness of my chest that I could hardly breathe; the thought of the two men I had shot sat upon me like a nightmare. . .

(chapter 10)

Alan's reactions are those of the child, the primitive.

Thereupon he turned to the four enemies, passed his sword clean through each of them, and tumbled them out of doors one after the other. As he did so, he kept humming, and singing, and whistling to himself, like a man trying to recall an air; only what *he* was trying was to make one. All the while, the flush was in his face, and his eyes were as bright as a five-year-old child's with a new toy. And presently he sat down upon the table, sword in hand; the air that he was making all the time began to run a little clearer, and then clearer still; and then out he burst with a great voice into a Gaelic song.

———

He came up to me with open arms. 'Come to my arms!' he cried, and embraced and kissed me hard upon both cheeks. 'David,' said he, 'I love you like a brother. And O, man,' he cried in a kind of ecstasy, 'am I no a bonny fighter?'

(chapter 10)

But at this stage there is no moral *problem*, because Alan is on the side of good. In the central part of *Kidnapped* it is no longer clear what is good or what is bad. Is Alan good or bad? Is he even a mixture of good and bad? He is going to present St Peter with a problem. Not that David ever gives up his 'Calvinist' moral views. It is this above all that adds a special quality of pathos to the great scene which is the climax of *Kidnapped*, the quarrel between David and Alan. We have seen it coming, of course, from the beginning, and the scene in which Alan gambles away David's money only brings matters to a head. What follows has been justly praised by Henry James for its psychological truth, its humour, and its pathos.

Alan had behaved like a child, and (what is worse) a treacherous child...

'I will only say this to ye, David,' said Alan, very quietly, 'that I have long been owing ye my life, and now I owe ye money. Ye should try to make that burden light for me.'

He had just called me 'Whig'. I stopped.

'Mr. Stewart...you are older than I am, and should know your manners. Do you think it either very wise or very witty to cast my politics in my teeth? I thought, where folk differed, it was the part of gentlemen to differ civilly; and if I did not, I may tell you I could find a better taunt than some of yours.'

He began to whistle a Jacobite air. . .made in mockery of General Cope's defeat at Prestonpans...'Why do ye take that air, Mr. Stewart?...Is that to remind me you have been beaten on both sides?'

[Alan] drew his sword. But before I could touch his blade with mine, he had thrown it from him and fallen to the ground. 'Na, na,' he kept saying, 'na, na – I cannae, I cannae.'

'Alan,' cried I, 'what makes ye so good to me? What makes ye care for such a thankless fellow?'

'Deed, and I don't know,' said Alan. 'For just precisely what I thought I liked about ye, was that ye never quarrelled; and now I like ye better!'

(chapter 24)

It is a fine example of one kind of love (what C. S. Lewis in his *Four Loves* calls *philia*) rising for a moment to another, which he calls *agape*. There is a little coda, both comic and touching, in which Alan tries to stay at the level of 1 Corinthians and sacrifice his vanity.

'My poor man, will ye no be better on my back?'

'Oh, Alan,' says I, 'and me a good twelve inches taller.'

'Ye're no such a thing,' cried Alan with a start. 'There may be a trifling matter of an inch or two; I'm no saying I'm just exactly what ye would call a tall man, whatever; and I dare say,' he added, his voice tailing off in a laughable manner, 'now when I come to think of it, I dare say ye'll be just about right. Ay, it'll be a foot, or near hand; or may be even mair!' (chapter 24)

Humour, imaginative insight, moral delicacy. But above all pathos: what makes this episode especially pathetic is that the moral impasse between them, momentarily forgotten in this upsurge of love, remains complete.

It is notable how much emphasis there is in this part of *Kidnapped* on the state of mind which David calls 'horror'. 'I was conscious of no particular nightmare, only of a general, black, abiding horror' (ch. 23). Of course David has been in a pretty sullen, glowering frame of mind for most of *Kidnapped*: this is one of the reasons why *Kidnapped* is a 'good boys' book'; that feeling that the world is against you, that sulky rage against existence in general, which filmed or dramatised versions of the book never manage to convey. And of course David has plenty of dramatically adequate reason for it, in what has happened to him: the boy reader may enjoy David's adventures, but David himself did not. But I am not sure that his ill-treatment and sufferings are entirely sufficient to explain his mood. He has passed from being an innocent castaway to being a hunted criminal. He is on the wrong side: the representative of civilisation is at odds with it. From being the 'good' romance-hero, he has become merely a member of a particular faction – a Lowland Whig, incongruously and fortuitously thrown into the power of a Highland Jacobite.

So is it that the fourth movement of *Kidnapped* develops many paradoxes. We have already seen the child Alan contrasted with the man David, yet in years David is the child and Alan the man. We have seen, of course, the contrast of the Lowlander with the Highlander, and what may be called the Lowland view of things with the Highland view of things. This contrast obviously has its basis in history and observation. But Stevenson does not seem to be primarily concerned with it, as Scott was, in either historical or picturesque terms. It is as if for him 'Lowland' and 'Highland' stand for two possibilities of man, possibilities that might ideally be realised in the same individual. And what David unwittingly seems to register is that the individual who does not realise them both is lacking in something. I suspect that the true moral of *Jekyll and Hyde* is to be found here, not in the popular reading.

115

The essential story of *Kidnapped* could have been told as a beast-fable: the story of a wolf hunted by dogs. But to complicate matters many of the other wolves are on the side of the dogs, while the wolf is accompanied on his flight by a dog. Stevenson tells us in *Travels with a Donkey* that he feared dogs more than wolves. We might think of the contrast between Silver and the other pirates in *Treasure Island*: Silver is a 'dog', disciplined, self-controlled, prudent, who has gone to the bad. This, according to Stevenson, is the most dangerous kind of human being. The Lowland villain is more to be feared than the Highland villain; an ordered wickedness more to be feared than a wild wickedness. If, as Machiavelli says, the ideal ruler must combine the lion and the fox, we may say that for Stevenson the ideal man must combine the wolf and the dog – but only in their virtues.

With the crossing of the Forth we return to the key of romance. There is another fine example of a romance-device, what Aristotle calls the *peripeteia*, in David's defeat of his uncle. (Though it is noteworthy that even here the effective agent is Alan; David merely waits in the darkness, 'pathetic' rather than 'drastic' to the last.) The hero has come home from his ordeal with the savages, through which Alan has been his savage guide. Civilisation at last!

...a very good house on the landward side, a house with beautiful clear glass windows, flowering knots upon the sills, the walls new-harled [newly rough-cast], and a chase-dog sitting yawning on the step like one that was at home.   (chapter 27)

Yet the ending seems almost an anti-climax. This is what Henry James thought the other 'weak spot' in *Kidnapped*. He gave an external explanation for it: Stevenson's health. Stevenson was physically unable to complete more than one of the three stories he had started, so he wound up the story of David's inheritance, leaving the fate of Alan and James of the Glens undecided.

This may indeed have been the true state of affairs, and it accounts for the very subdued way *Kidnapped* ends. But it does not completely account for the *sadness* with which it ends. There is a similar sadness at the end of *Treasure Island*, but this sadness

116

seems deeper. Jim's sadness can be explained as his realisation that the adventures are over (though I think there is more in it than that – perhaps an intuition that his childhood is over). But why does David feel 'something like remorse' at the end of *Kidnapped*? He is worried about Alan, of course, and James of the Glens. But their plight was not his fault. I think the use of the word 'remorse' suggests that we are here at the level of deep imagination. Without Silver, Jim is without something that he needs psychologically, but must reprobate morally. But that story is over. What is needed to complete *Kidnapped*? It might have been the beginning of a series like *The Three Musketeers* of Stevenson's favourite Dumas (Alan may perhaps be inspired by D'Artagnan). He can have further adventures, because he is an adventurer: David is settled. Settled, but sad. How can there be a psychologically satisfying solution as far as David is concerned?

What is needed is some way in which to show concretely the ideal convergence of Highland and Lowland virtues. But it would be hard to follow this out in terms of the relation of David and Alan. They are not homosexuals. Whatever might have been the case in real life, their love in the book is that of *philia* only: *eros* plays no part. It could be, then, that in the sequel Catriona is a surrogate for Alan, and that Stevenson intended some symbolic significance in the marriage of David to Catriona, the union of Jacobite and Covenanter, the wild girl of Alban with the Westminster Confession. This might have a meaning in regard to the unity of sundered Scotland. It might have a more important meaning in the reconciliation of contrasting and conflicting impulses in the individual human soul.

However that may be, I do not think *Catriona* a complete artistic success. It contains some fine things. But Stevenson is only at his best in treating adult problems and pressures when he works behind the mask of a boys' story. Kipling may be a parallel here; and perhaps, again, Mark Twain. But, as Kipling would say, that is another story. *Kidnapped*, unlike *Catriona*, seems to me a complete and unified artistic success, and the sad ending is an essential part of it. Stevenson has not attempted to impose false unity on a dualism which haunted him to the end of his life.

NOTES

1 Henry James, 'Robert Louis Stevenson', in *The House of Fiction*, ed. Leon Edel (London 1957), p. 119.

2 In *Works of Robert Louis Stevenson* (Edinburgh 1894), Miscellanies, vol. I, pp. 353–5.

3 In *Works of Samuel Johnson* (Yale University Press 1969), vol. IV, p. 287.

4 Ernest Baker, *History of the English Novel*, vol. IX (London 1938), p. 315.

5 Edwin M. Eigner, *Robert Louis Stevenson and the Romantic Tradition* (Princeton 1966).

6 *Ibid.*, p. 136.

7 John Buchan, *The Novel and the Fairy Tale*, English Association pamphlet no. 79, 1931.

8 Gilbert Ryle, 'Jane Austen and the Moralists', in *Collected Papers*, vol. I (London 1971), pp. 284–5.

9 Leslie Fiedler, *No! In Thunder* (London 1960).

On *The Wind in the Willows*

Many people think of Kenneth Grahame's *The Wind in the Willows* as a children's book, and it certainly begins like one: indeed the first sentence sounds as if the book is going to be addressed to very young children.

The Mole had been working very hard all the morning, spring-cleaning his little home.

We are not far from the world of Beatrix Potter (*Peter Rabbit*, 1904; *Wind in the Willows*, 1908). But even in the first few sentences we are aware of a larger rhythm, something on a greater scale than her tiny world. The novel begins with a dramatic gesture of revolt, like *Vanity Fair*:

But, lo! and just as the coach drove off, Miss Sharp put her pale face out of the window and actually flung the book back into the garden.

or *Antic Hay*:

He picked up his pen and denounced.

Mole responds to the first 'imperious summons' of the book. There are to be more; but none more elemental.

Spring was moving in the air above and in the earth below and around him, penetrating even his dark and lowly little house with its spirit of divine discontent and longing. It was small wonder, then, that he suddenly flung down his brush on the floor, said 'Bother!' and 'O blow!' and also 'Hang spring-cleaning!' and bolted out of the house without even waiting to put on his coat. Something up above was calling him imperiously, and he made for the steep little tunnel which answered in his case to the gravelled carriage-drive owned by animals whose residences are nearer to the sun and air.

The irruption of Mole is made to seem as natural and inevitable as the transition to the dream world at the opening of *Alice's Adventures in Wonderland*. But otherwise the effect is very different. In Alice's case there is no 'imperious summons'; going *down* the rabbit-hole, descending into an inner world, involves no effort of will, but a passive, matter-of-fact acceptance of things happening to one, in all their bizarre inconsequence.

The rabbit-hole went straight on like a tunnel for some way, and then dipped suddenly down, so suddenly that Alice had not a moment to think about stopping herself before she found herself falling down a very deep well.
 Down, down, down. . .
 Down, down, down. . .

The progress of Mole is very different: determined, purposeful, heading for the sun and air.

So he scraped and scratched and scrabbled and scrooged, and then he scrooged again and scrabbled and scratched and scraped, working busily with his little paws and muttering to himself. 'Up we go! Up we go!' till at last, pop! his snout came out into the sunlight, and he found himself rolling in the warm grass of a great meadow.
'This is fine!' he said to himself. 'This is better than whitewashing!'

So we enter *The Wind in the Willows* with the Mole, the first of the three inward centres from which the book works. What does Mole bring with him? First, the holiday spirit, frank and joyous escapism.

It all seemed too good to be true. . .instead of having an uneasy conscience pricking him and whispering 'Whitewash!' he somehow could only feel how jolly it was to be the only idle dog among all these busy citizens. After all, the best part of a holiday is perhaps not so much to be resting yourself, as to see all the other fellows working.

But Mole also brings in something else. It is through him that we are introduced to the River Bank, the constitutive symbol around which the whole book turns; and the spirit in which he himself is introduced to the River helps to shape the reader's response.

Never in his life had he seen a river before. . .The Mole was bewitched, entranced, fascinated. By the side of the river he trotted as one trots, when very small, by the side of a man who holds one spellbound with exciting stories. . .

This is a note of childishness. But is the book childish? The childishness here, I think, is confined to Mole. His attitude here is one of total acceptance. So when he meets the Water Rat, and they immediately strike up a friendship, we accept without question that this is how it would happen:

'Hello Mole!'
'Hello Rat!'

Now Rat takes the lead: he is dominant here, Mole recessive.

The Rat sculled smartly across and made fast. Then he held up his fore-paw as the Mole stepped gingerly down. 'Lean on that!' he said, 'Now then, step lively!' and the Mole to his surprise and rapture found himself actually seated in the stern of a real boat.

There is nothing particularly childish about Rat and his pleasures. We see them as the token of a whole new world into which the Mole is being initiated. Its *ethos* is epitomised when Rat says:

Believe me, my young friend, there is *nothing* – absolutely nothing – half so much worth doing as simply messing about in boats.

He explains why.

Nothing seems really to matter, that's the charm of it. Whether you get away, or whether you don't; whether you arrive at your destination or whether you reach somewhere else or whether you never get anywhere at all, you're always busy, and you never do anything in particular. . .

It is the paradox of a busy-ness that is not business, the secret of a game that is really a game and nothing but a game, the secret of art as Immanuel Kant defined it: 'purposeful purposelessness'. To the Mole this is something he has never encountered before: it makes his day.

The Mole waggled his toes from sheer happiness, spread his chest with a sigh of full contentment, and leaned back blissfully into the soft cushions. '*What* a day I'm having!' he said.

And there is still a final touch of magic to come, something very important in *The Wind in the Willows*: creature comforts.

'Shove that under your feet. . .'
'What's inside it?'
'There's cold chicken inside it,' replied the Rat briefly; 'cold tonguecoldhamcoldbeefpickledgherkinsaladfrenchrollscress sandwidgespottedmeatgingerbeerlemonadesodawater. . .'
'O stop, stop,' cried the Mole in ecstasies: 'this is too much!'

We may stop to make two notes here, while Rat rows Mole towards the backwater picnic. (1) Does *The Wind in the Willows* 'sing us a song of social significance'? How much stress do we put on the possible *class* implications of the Mole's '*Up* we go!'? Is the leisured community he is being introduced to 'above' him socially as well as physically? There is no class tension between Rat and Mole; they accept each other as equals. Yet the Rat is certainly a gentleman. And the Badger is an aristocrat: nothing else can account for the invisible authority he wields over the River Bank, as well as the Wild Wood. About Toad I fancy there is a hint of *nouveau riche*: not, of course, that we can imagine Toad himself making money, but Toad Hall has not always belonged to his family, and the Badger refers to Toad's father, whom he knew well, as 'a very worthy animal'. But this is to anticipate. For the moment let us merely note that the principal River Bank figures are all leisured. Work is as absent from their lives as sex, illness, ageing, or death. (2) So far the story is essentially about two boys, from different backgrounds and, as we shall see, of very different temperaments, striking up a holiday friendship. Why, then, does the author make them animals? and remind us from time to time that they are animals?

'I like your clothes awfully, old chap,' says Rat to Mole. 'I'm going to get a black velvet smoking suit myself some day, as soon as I can afford it.'

The handling of the animal-as-human, human-as-animal convention in *The Wind in the Willows* has come in for some comment. If it is to be categorised as a beast-fable, it sits a good deal more loosely to the beast-fable mode than some other famous examples. It obviously breaks many of the rules enforced so sternly today by the young ladies in the editorial departments of publishers of children's books, who condemn such transgressions with the severity of the Académie française coming down on Corneille. It is full of inconsistencies, which children notice. What size are the characters? How are we to imagine them? When Toad is disguised as a washerwoman he seems to be washerwoman size, but when the bargewoman detects him he is toad size (she picks him up by the leg and throws him into the river). Any reader of the book will be able to think of dozens of other examples. Children notice these things.

Children notice; but do they mind? In the view of one critic of authority, they do not.

Kenneth Grahame says:

It is the special charm of the child's point of view that the dual nature of these characters does not present the slightest difficulty to them. It is only the old fogies who are apt to begin 'Well, but...' and so on. To the child it is all entirely natural and as it should be.

But whether children mind or not, the question why the characters have this 'dual nature' still remains.

One very simple answer is that the author loved these little animals in real life. Some men who have a streak of misanthropy in them find a warmth and tenderness in writing about animals that is not evident when they are writing about human beings. (Another famous beast-fable, George Orwell's *Animal Farm*, is an example.) No one who did not love these creatures could have written *The Wind in the Willows*. But we must not make the book too realistic. As the *Times* reviewer said, it is negligible as a contribution to natural history. Nor is it a book like Gavin Maxwell's *Ring of Bright Water* (1960). And, for all it seems to owe to Richard Jefferies, it avoids Jefferies's realism. Jefferies wrote about the real-life enemies of the River Bank: the men who were slaughtering its inhabitants wholesale. Nor is there anything of Nature's own cruelty in *The Wind in the Willows*.

This is not meant as an adverse criticism. Books should be judged by the standards which are appropriate to them. The author's love of nature is plainly an important motive in the book. The pageant of the seasons is given to us in many beautiful pages. No book is richer in its evocation of the times of year, and of weather – early spring in 'The River Bank', high summer in 'The Piper at the Gates of Dawn', October in 'Wayfarers All', Christmas in 'Dulce Domum'. I am sure all this is an important part, if perhaps not the most important part, of the book's deep appeal. But all this could have been done without the animal-device. Jefferies did without it.

A better explanation of the animal-device, at least as far as

the older child or adult reader is concerned, is that it cuts off the
possibility of the book's being read other than symbolically.
Everyone knows that toads do not ride on horses or bargain with
gipsies. And the author does not really pretend that they do.
Rather, he pretends that he pretends that they do; so that the
child being read to, the adult reading, and the author, are all
joined in a friendly conspiracy. This artful artlessness can then
be used by the author for more serious purposes or, I should say,
purposes that lie nearer his heart than Toad's farcical adventures.

Grahame's *Dream Days* and *The Golden Age*, which do not
employ the animal-device, are essentially the work of an essayist.
Their mode is discursive. Now there is plenty of essay-like writing in *The Wind in the Willows* also, and in its weaker places it
becomes the sort of essay writing typical of the period, something
that Edward Thomas, speaking of Hudson, called 'Norfolk
jacket writing'. Thomas wrote a good deal of it himself in his
prose works, though his best writing, like Hudson's, is free of it.
But no one remembers this sort of thing in *The Wind in the
Willows*, prose masquerading as poetry. What *is* remembered is
the poetry; and it is poetry that works by means of symbol, or
implication, not statement. The four great characters of the book
– Mole, Rat, Toad, and Badger – are given to us in essence by the
use of the animal-device. They embody keen psychological and
social observation. But they are presences, not analyses. We feel
that we know Toad as we know Falstaff, or Micawber, or Long
John Silver. But we have got to know him by other means than
those of the realistic writer.

But all this could be said of some quite different fictional
device, which preserved the fully human quality of the characters. Why, then, is it disguised? It hardly needs saying that
some of the characterisation depends upon a kind of bestiary-like
appropriateness. I need not dwell on the importance of the Mole
and the Badger being underground creatures (this is one of the
reasons why they get on so well together); of the Water Rat
(more accurately, the Water Vole) living in his hole by the
River; of the expression which human beings can't help seeing
in the face of a real toad, at one irresistibly comic and pathetic.
You have only to make the experiment of trying to imagine the

four great characters as some other kinds of animal to see that they are unified in conception. The anthropomorphised animal qualities are inseparable from their identity. Yet they cannot be visualised. Ernest Shepard's illustrations are charming, and for some readers they are as much part of the book as Tenniel's are of the *Alice* books. But they pin down the characters in a way the book does not. In the book, there is constant fluctuation between the characters' 'human' aspect and their 'animal' aspect. This cannot be represented pictorially, or put on the stage.

Perhaps the best explanation for the animal-device is this. The contradiction which the child notices may be the cover for a deeper contradiction which he does not notice. The characters belong to the timeless ideal world of children, freed from adult cares and responsibilities. Yet they have the independence of adults. The indispensable ingredient of 'messing about in boats', and the whole River Bank way of life, is freedom. *The Wind in the Willows* is an artistic expression of the human longing to 'have it both ways', to break down the antithesis of the Grecian Urn, to take the coldness out of the 'cold pastoral'. Its success can be measured by the corresponding failure in *Peter Pan* to achieve a similar resolution in human terms.

So let us go back to Rat and Mole – two men in a boat? two boys in a boat? two animals in a boat. With the Mole we are now inducted, given the freedom of the River Bank. All this is the magic of the book. (By 'magic' I mean something ultimate, unanalysable.) Other meanings of 'magic' are not there. The book does not deal in the marvellous or *outré*. 'The Piper at the Gates of Dawn' may be a partial exception. But the 'Piper' chapter is a special case, different in tone and atmosphere from the rest of the book. And in any case the emphasis there falls on religious awe, not on wizardry or witchcraft. There is no fantastic 'machinery', none of the devices used by Edith Nesbit, for example, to move between different planes of fictional 'reality'. Nor is the book particularly dream-like – I mean, suggestive of the night dream – as the *Alice* books are, now and then (and *Sylvie and Bruno* almost continuously). The one exception is Toad's incarceration, with its bizarre changes of style, pastiche of Harrison Ainsworth, and so on. But this is the exception that proves the rule. The whole episode is nightmarish. We have a sense that it is not really happening on the usual plane of the book. The authorial or editorial voice itself seems to have gone slightly crazy. We are witnessing a nightmare in which Toad is a hallucinated participant. The usual mode of dreaming in *The Wind in the Willows* – as both those who like and those who dislike the book would probably agree – is the day-dream. And in a day-dream we retain something of the spectator's role; our participation is voluntary, and can be withdrawn if we wish.

The 'magic' is conveyed most effectively in *The Wind in the Willows*, not by the purple passages, which belong with an element in the book which has somewhat dated, but in the simplest possible words.

'I beg your pardon,' said the Mole, pulling himself together with some effort. 'You must think me very rude; but this is all so new to me. So – this – is – a – River!'
'*The* River,' corrected the Rat.

And there, essentially, the thing is done. The first chapter, 'The River Bank', introduces all the main characters of the book, touches on all its leading themes, and lays down the lines of its geography – physical, political, and moral. What is the River? It is many things, but, most importantly, it is a frontier.

'What lies over *there*?' asked the Mole. . .
'That? O, that's just the Wild Wood,' said Rat shortly. 'We don't go there very much, we river-bankers.'

The Wild Wood represents the external threat to the River Bank. Yet, as we are to see, the real dangers to the River Bank are internal; it is only through the weakness of character of one of the River-Bankers that the Wild Wood secures any foothold at all. Toad breaks the code of the River Bank, the severe discipline which the leisured community imposes upon itself. Again and again it is rubbed in that Toad is the fellow who let the side down; he has made the River Bank vulnerable to its enemies. Here we are in touch with the political allegory in *The Wind in the Willows*, so ably expounded by Peter Green in his book on Kenneth Grahame: the squirearchy, representing an idealised rural England, defending itself against the incursion of the un-principled radical *canaille.*

But the Mole knows nothing about the Wild Wood. He is to have painful personal experience of it later. But at this stage, like the reader, he has to pick up what clues he can from the Rat's compelled reluctant venture into the explicit (great stress is laid on the requirement of animal etiquette to refrain from spelling things out).

'Aren't they – aren't they very *nice* people there?' said the Mole... 'Well, of course there are others,' explained the Rat in a hesitating sort of way. 'Weasels – and stoats – and foxes – and so on. They're all right in a way – I'm very good friends with them – pass the time of day when we meet, and all that – but they break out sometimes, there's no denying it, and then – well, you can't really trust them, and that's the fact.'

The Mole realises that it is

against animal etiquette to dwell on possible trouble ahead, or even allude to it.

And what is beyond the Wild Wood? There is an interesting moment here. Generally speaking, after his joyous self-liberation, the Mole is Sancho Panza, Dr Watson to Rat's Sherlock Holmes (remember the episode of Badger's door-scraper). Rat is the romantic, the poet. Yet for the moment it is Mole's language that is tinged with longing for the far horizon.

'And beyond the Wild Wood again?' he asked. 'Where it's all blue and dim, and one sees what may be hills or perhaps they mayn't, and something like the smoke of towns, or perhaps it's only cloud-drift?'

But Rat's romanticism, at this point, is the domestic, Words-worthian kind, 'true to the kindred points of Heaven and Home'. We feel that the poetry he writes would be 'Georgian' poetry. He rejects the far horizon.

'Beyond the Wild Wood comes the Wide World,' said the Rat. 'And that's something that doesn't matter either to you or me. I've never been there, and I'm never going, nor you either, if you've got any sense at all. Don't ever refer to it again, please.'

But in this momentary contrast between Rat and Mole we have an anticipation of the deeper threat to the River Bank, an anticipation of 'Wayfarers All'; a deeper threat, because it is a temptation in the heart of Rat himself, the embodiment of River Bank values; a threat of treachery to the country of his heart. Mole had already innocently adumbrated it, when he asked the question that must trouble any artist or imaginative person attempting to form the image of Arcadia, or Heaven: the question of Mephistopheles: 'But isn't it a bit dull at times?' Rat, of course, has his answer ready; there is plenty of bustle, he explains: too much for a fellow who has business of his own to attend to! But that innocent question of Mole's is to reverberate. At this stage it is a question which the authorial voice is intent on obviating. And it is remarkable what solid substantiation that voice is able to give to the paradise of the River Bank – considering how little, in fact, we are told about its day-to-day life. We feel we understand, from within, Mole's happiness in his changed environment, though we are told little more than that 'he learned to swim and row, and entered into the joy of running water'. The sort of detail an author like Arthur Ransome enters into would be out of place; the magic works better without it.

What remains more tentative is the mystical dimension. 'With his ear to the reed-stems he caught, at intervals, something of what the wind was whispering so constantly among them.' This aspect of *The Wind in the Willows* has been adversely criticised. Even some of those who like the book are, I suspect, apt to ignore it as mere decoration; they put up with it for the sake of the comedy and character-drawing. Arnold Bennett admired the urbane irony of the book, but I cannot imagine him doing what Mole does, putting his ear to the reed-stems. (The child Edward Elgar apparently did, and even tried to write down the music.) But Bennett was a realist, and from the realist point of view the trouble about wind in the willows, and all the other things that Nature says, is that Nature says whatever you want her to say. There is an element of vagueness in the 'wind in the willows' motif, and a literary historian will recognise modes of the period. The book was to have been entitled *The Wind in the Reeds*, but Yeats had already published *The Wind among the Reeds* (1899).

Of course Grahame meant something different. For Yeats the voice of the wind among the reeds seems to be that of the spirits of the past, laying a desolating spell on the living. For Grahame it echoes the pipes of Pan. But when this becomes more than a motif, and Pan himself is introduced, 'the piper at the gates of dawn', and the mystique of Nature is given full statement and apotheosis, some readers feel that the author has gone beyond his range and that this chapter doesn't belong to the essential book at all.

There are some distinctions to be drawn here. First, it has to be conceded that there is some would-be evocative writing in the book which doesn't work for the reader who appreciates the best parts of it: writing that is too suggestive of a mode of the period that is not to our taste. Dr Watson on one occasion succumbed to it.

'The Haven is the name of Mr. Josiah Amberley's house,' I explained. 'I think it would interest you, Holmes. It is like some penurious patrician who has sunk into the company of his inferiors. You know that particular quarter, the monotonous brick streets, the weary suburban highways. Right in the middle of them, a little island of culture and comfort, lies this old home, surrounded by a high sun-baked wall mottled with lichens and topped with moss, the sort of wall...'

'Cut out the poetry, Watson,' said Holmes severely. 'I note that it was a high brick wall.'

('The Retired Colourman')

Other authors, however, did not cut out the poetry.

...in the pauses of our talk, the river, playing round the boat, prattled strange old tales and secrets, sings low the old child's song that it has sung so many thousand years – will sing so many thousand years to come, before its voice grows harsh and old – a song that we, who have learnt to love its changing face, who have so often nestled on its yielding bosom, think, somehow, we understand, though we could not tell you in mere words the story that we listen to.

That 'somehow' is suspicious, and so is the whole passage. It comes, actually, not from *The Wind in the Willows* but from *Three Men in a Boat* (1889), and admirers of Grahame's book

129

will protest at its being assimilated to Jerome's book, and especially to Jerome's book on its weaker side. Yet it seems to me that some of the incantatory prose passages in *The Wind in the Willows*, if they are different from this, are not different enough.

But the 'Piper' chapter cannot be assimilated to that kind of thing. For good or ill, it is much more ambitious; it is not, like the passage from *Three Men in a Boat*, simply a lapse into sentiment, from which we are soon to be rescued by the voice of Harris, or an episode of genial farce. The 'Piper' is a sustained poem in prose, which raises the River Bank to the arch of dawn and the summit of heaven. Like the other thematic chapter, 'Wayfarers All', it has none of the atmosphere of the children's book. There is no comedy. The mood of the chapter is strongly influenced by Rat's and Mole's concern for the missing baby otter and his father. It is notable that elsewhere in *The Wind in the Willows* Otter is cheerful, extrovert, rather a *Three Men in a Boat* sort of character; here he is very different.

'So Otter goes there every night and watches – on the chance, you know, just on the chance!'
They were silent for a time, both thinking of the same thing – the lonely, heart-sore animal, crouched by the ford, watching and waiting, the long night through – on the chance.

But the mood is also influenced by the heavy, restless summer night, a curious mixture of longing and foreboding. Before this, the contrast between Mole's domestic stolidity and Rat's reveries was touched on in a minor, humorous way. Here all is serious, exalted.

'O Mole! the beauty of it! The merry bubble and joy, the thin, clear, happy call of the distant piping! Such music I never dreamed of, and the call in it is stronger than the music is sweet! Row on, Mole, row! For the music and the call must be for us.'

Is this the Rat we have known in the earlier chapters?

'This is the place of my song-dream, the place the music played to me,' whispered the Rat, as if in a trance. 'Here in this holy place, here if anywhere, surely we shall find him!'

The Mole remains in character.

'I hear nothing myself,' he said, 'but the wind playing in the reeds and rushes and osiers.'

The crucial importance of Mole in this episode is that he too experiences what Rudolf Otto calls *das Heilige*.

'Rat!' he found breath to whisper, shaking. 'Are you afraid?'
'Afraid?' murmured the Rat, his eyes shining with unutterable love.
'Afraid? Of *Him*? O, never, never! And yet – and yet – O Mole, I am afraid!'

Why is this theophany disliked so much? How is it that critics otherwise sympathetic to the book find a note of falsity here, an author trying to work on the reader's feelings for a god he didn't himself believe in? Again, there are distinctions to be drawn. It may have been an artistic mistake to introduce the actual figure of Pan himself, though the description of him is brief and rather unspecific. Illustrators of the book fail here, and it may be that their failure insensibly colours critics' judgments. But I think we must beware of supposing that we ourselves have a clear-cut, definite standard of knowledge here that we can bring to bear on a poet's striving to express what must in the nature of the case be elusive. Critics, however, have seized on this presentation of Pan to discredit or limit the reader's response to this chapter. Now Pan is a frequent visitor to Edwardian literature, and sometimes in a rather embarrassing form. And critics have not been slow to point out how this Pan is desexualised, quite contrary to his mythological character (he was a fertility god). And there may be one or two 'period' sentimentalities which weaken the effect, things reminiscent of Grahame's own *Pagan Papers*.

But I am afraid I must put down the hostility which this chapter arouses in some readers to anti-religious bias. And if they say that for them there is nothing in religion, then I must reply that in that case they are not qualified to say whether the religious element in the book is the real thing or not. But this is not an occasion for argument, but for testimony. I find 'The Piper at the Gates of Dawn' moving and convincing as a religious poem. The writing in general shows a sensitive awareness on the author's part that what he is saying is difficult to say. It may be that the impulse behind this chapter would have found better expression in music. But Walter Pater has told us that all art aspires to the condition of music, and I would point to this part of *The Wind in the Willows* as an example of one of the things he may have meant.

Whether the chapter can be wholly harmonised into the total experience of the book is another question, and a more difficult one. I think it can. Historically speaking it was, we have reason to think, an afterthought on the author's part; artistically, it is the reason for which the whole book exists. It is the contradiction of the political allegory to which in other places the metaphor of the River Bank runs the risk of being subordinated. Anyone who could read this chapter and imagine that the author was thinking about politics goes beyond my comprehension.

What perhaps may be said more justly against the 'Piper' chapter, even by those who admire it, is that if you respond to it deeply the rest of the book is rather anti-climactic. Such readers feel rather like the Mole, whose state of soul is conveyed in a simile Homer might have used.

As one wakened suddenly from a beautiful dream who struggles to recall it, and can recapture nothing but a dim sense of the beauty of it, the beauty! Till that, too, fades away in its turn, and the dreamer bitterly accepts the hard, cold waking and all its penalties. . .

Just as awe never again appears in *The Wind in the Willows*, the element of beauty also is greatly reduced. The plot predominates, in the adventures of Toad; and while the comedy and homeliness of the River Bank remain, its poetry has gone. There are no more whisperings among the reeds. Yet might not this itself be part of the artistic effect? the return to the light of common day?

But many readers, I expect, are happier with the simpler and homelier ways in which the River Bank is made desirable. The artistic problem was to make it interesting, after the first chapter. And this was achieved by constantly taking us away from it, and so making it something to be regretted and looked back to: a familiar paradox. In 'The Open Road' a rival Utopia is proposed; the method here is not poetic or fantastic, but a comedy of manners. Our curiosity about Toad has already been whetted by Otter:

'Such a good fellow, too,' remarked the Otter reflectively. 'But no stability – especially in a boat!'

Otter's 'no stability' introduces the central feature of Toad's character and the threat he poses to the River Bank. But we do not yet know the measure of Toad's instability. Our point of view here is Mole's, and he is rather taken with Toad. What we first hear of him from Rat is attractive, and it is never gone back on.

'It's never the wrong time to call on Toad. Early or late he's always the same fellow. Always good-tempered, always glad to see you, always sorry when you leave!'

But Rat's fuller judgment is cautionary; it is couched in the form of compliment sometimes called an 'Oxford sandwich': you begin by praise, then say something quite lethal, and round it off with praise again.

'He is indeed the best of animals. . .So simple, so good-natured, and so affectionate. Perhaps he's not very clever – we can't all be geniuses; and it may be that he is both boastful and conceited. But he has got some great qualities, has Toady.'

But for the moment we are still looking through Mole's eyes: at Toad Hall:

. . .a handsome, dignified house of mellowed red brick, with well-kept lawns reaching down to the water's edge. . .
'That's the banqueting-hall you're looking at now – very old, that is. Toad is rather rich, you know, and this is really one of the nicest houses in these parts, though we never admit as much to Toad.'

And when we actually meet Toad we are aware of a challenge to the River Bank – coming from 'real life', 'the far horizon'.

'There you are!' cried the Toad, straddling and expanding himself. 'There's real life, for you, embodied in that little cart. The open road, the dusty highway, the heath, the common, the hedgerow, the rolling downs! Camps, villages, towns, cities! Here to-day, up and off to somewhere else to-morrow! The whole world before you, and a horizon that's always changing!'

133

Rat is challenged.

'You surely don't mean to stick to your dull fusty old river all your
life, and just live in a hole in a bank, and *boat*? I want to show you
the world; I'm going to make an *animal* of you, my boy!'

Rat remains loyal, and turns to Mole to support him.

'I don't care,' said the Rat doggedly. 'I'm not coming, and that's flat.
And I *am* going to stick to my old river, *and* boat, as I've always done.
And what's more, Mole's going to stick to me and do as I do, aren't
you, Mole?'

Mole, as always, is loyal, but their friendship is put to a test: he
is tempted:

'Of course I am. I'll always stick to you, Rat, and what you say is to
be – has got to be. All the same, it sounds as if it might have been –
well, rather fun, you know!'

The Rat's goodness forbids him to take a stronger line.

He hated disappointing people, and he was fond of the Mole, and
would do almost anything to oblige him. Toad was watching both of
them closely.
    'Come along in and have some lunch,' he said diplomatically, 'and
we'll talk it over. We needn't decide anything in a hurry. Of course,
I don't really care. I only want to give pleasure to you fellows. "Live
for others!" That's my motto in life.'

Rat acquiesces, whatever his misgivings; but his deeper loyalty
is unaffected.

Toad, kicking out his legs, sleepily said: 'Well, good night, you
fellows! This is the real life for a gentleman! Talk about your old
river!'
'I *don't* talk about my river,' replied the patient Rat.
'You *know* I don't, Toad. But I *think* about it,' he added pathetically,
in a lower tone: 'I think about it all the time!'

    Of course Mole's eyes, and ours, are soon opened to the realities
of Toad's character. The incident of the motor-car is the point at
which Toad's harmless fads turn into a dangerous mania. He in
turn becomes the victim of 'an imperious summons'.

'Police-station! Complaint!' murmured Toad dreamily. 'Me *complain* of that beautiful, that heavenly vision that has been vouchsafed me? *Mend* the *cart*? I've done with carts for ever, I never want to see the cart, or to hear of it, again. O, Ratty! You can't think how obliged I am to you for consenting to come on this trip! I wouldn't have gone without you, and then I might never have seen that – that swan, that sunbeam, that thunderbolt!. . .I owe it all to you, my best of friends!'

From this point on Toad becomes for many readers the main character of the book. But the Rat–Mole friendship continues to be the basis for some of the finest and most sensitively observed things in *The Wind in the Willows*, such as Mole's adventure in the Wild Wood, and the story of how he came at last to make the acquaintance of the mysterious Mr Badger. And there is the 'Dulce Domum' chapter, with its mingling of poignancy, comedy, and cosiness in the story of how the suddenly homesick Mole is persuaded by the tactful Rat to give a Christmas party in his old home. The theme of this chapter is the antithesis to the Open Road: nostalgia. It is a very old theme of literature. Here, the old wine is poured into new bottles. Animal instinct and human longing fuse together at one magic word.

Home! That was what they meant, those caressing appeals, those soft touches wafted through the air, those invisible little hands pulling and tugging, all one way! Why, it must be quite close to him at that moment, his old home that he had hurriedly forsaken and never sought again, that day when he first found the river!

So a new slant is given to the vision of the River Bank. We are being reminded of something the 'emancipated' Mole had almost forgotten: the River Bank is not his home. His state of mind is exquisitely rendered: the homesickness itself; the sense of guilt at the violation of animal etiquette entailed in inflicting one's personal emotions on someone else; the pressure put on his loyalty to a friend.

I know it's a shabby, dingy little place. . .not like – your cosy quarters – or Toad's beautiful hall – or Badger's great house – but it was my own little home – and I was fond of it – and I went away and forgot all about it – and then smelt it suddenly – on the road, when I called and you wouldn't listen, Rat – ...and I had to leave it, though I was smelling it all the time – I thought my heart would break – We might have just gone and had one look at it, Ratty –, only one look – it was close by – but you wouldn't turn back, Ratty, you wouldn't turn back!

It is the mixture of need to reproach a friend, and anguish at reproaching a friend, that wrings the heart. This emotional depth extends our knowledge of Mole. But what follows extends our knowledge of Rat also. It is the finest possible advertisement for the River Bank at its best, more than the pages which describe its natural beauty. What is evoked is the beauty that can exist in human relations. It is, above all, a matter of *manners*. Manners, as we know from Restoration comedy and much else, are not enough, can even be sinister, or chilling, in isolation from other virtues. But in 'Dulce Domum' manners rest upon moral values. It is a moral fineness in Rat that enables him to cheer Mole up and make him feel at home again in his old house. The effect on Mole is summed up in the editorial *moralitas* at the end of this wonderful episode.

[Mole] was now in just the frame of mind that the tactful Rat had quietly worked to bring about in him. He saw clearly how plain and simple – how narrow, even – it all was; but clearly, too, how much it all meant to him, and the special value of some such anchor in one's existence. He did not at all want to abandon the new life and its splendid spaces, to turn his back on sun and air and all they offered him and creep home and stay there; the upper world was all too strong; it called to him still, and he knew he must return to the larger stage. But it was good to think that he had this to come back to, this place which was all his own, these things which were so glad to see him again and could always be counted upon for the same simple welcome.

It sums up Mole's achievement of balance. From now on he has the 'stability' Toad will never achieve – whatever the author tells us at the end. And he is to be there, in 'Wayfarers All', to provide moral and spiritual support for Rat himself when he too experiences an 'imperious longing' which tempts him into treachery to the River Bank.

Meanwhile Toad's adventures continue in, as it were, a different order of time – the clock-time of ordinary life, not the rhythmic time of the seasons. Toad has passed, unlike the other characters, into the public domain: he is an archetypal figure. He has claims to be the real hero of the book. Historically speaking, it began with him; *The Wind in the Willows*, like the *Pooh* books and *The Hobbit*, grew out of a father's stories for his son. And it is in the chapters centred on Toad that the book is most like a children's book, though no doubt adults enjoy them just as much as children do. They are not so subtle and fine as the Mole–Rat chapters. But they are very amusing. And it is good to have a contrast and change of mood from the perhaps over-charged atmosphere of 'The Piper at the Gates of Dawn' and 'Wayfarers All'. It is good to have a scherzo in the symphony.

All the same, the author is less deeply engaged than in the other chapters. The Mole–Rat scenes, like 'Dulce Domum' are unique and irreplaceable, whereas we feel that the author could have thought of other adventures for Toad. They provide the plot and an exciting climax to the book, but that is all.

Most readers, I think, are content to enjoy themselves as Toad, a forerunner of Walter Mitty. With some part of their minds they acquiesce in the politico-moral allegory. But they like Toad too much to care greatly about it.

Mr. Toad, arrayed in goggles, cap, gaiters, and enormous overcoat, came swaggering down the steps, drawing on his gauntleted gloves.
'Hullo! come on, you fellows!' he cried cheerfully on catching sight of them. 'You're just in time to come with me for a jolly – for a – er – jolly –'

Toad never seems more than a naughty child. His escapades do glance at real social history; he can be seen as having a rather disreputable place in the long descent of the country gentleman from Sir Roger de Coverley to Sir Malcolm Campbell. But do we really identify wholeheartedly with the *senes severiores*, the father-figures, the reality principle?

'You knew it must come to this, sooner or later, Toad,' the Badger explained severely. 'You've disregarded all the warnings we've given you, you've gone on squandering the money your father left you, and you're getting us animals a bad name by your furious driving and your smashes and your rows with the police. Independence is all

very well, but we animals never allow our friends to make fools of
themselves beyond a certain limit; and that limit you've reached...'

Yet it is after Badger's sermon that Toad attains his greatest
moment.

There was a long, long pause. Toad looked desperately this way and
that, while the other animals waited in grave silence. At last he
spoke.
'No!' he said a little sullenly but stoutly; 'I'm *not* sorry. And it
wasn't folly at all! It was simply glorious!'

If only Toad could have lived up to this! Then there would have
been a real challenge to the paternalism of the River Bank;
inciting us to question how far this image of the Golden Age
requires a child-like submissiveness which must, in the end, be
unacceptable.

But from now on Toad, though he remains very sympathetic,
ceases to be an independent moral centre. He is now a 'case',
close to the psychopathic personality. He is another victim of
'the imperious demand', but the effect on him is to make him
more and more neurotic. He has strange seizures. Is this what
has happened to the missing sexuality of *The Wind in the
Willows*?

When his violent paroxysms possessed him he would arrange bed-
room chairs in rude resemblance of a motor-car and would crouch on
the foremost of them, bent forward and staring fixedly ahead, making
uncouth and ghastly noises, till the climax was reached, when, turning a complete somersault, he would lie prostrate among the ruins of
the chairs, apparently completely satisfied for the moment.

The observation of Toad's obsession is acute.

The 'poop-poop' drew nearer and nearer, the car could be heard to
turn into the inn-yard and come to a stop, and Toad had to hold on
to the leg of the table to conceal his overmastering emotion.

And the moral insight is irreproachable. The 'imperious demand'
which brought Mole into the happy life of the River Bank made
him a fuller and richer person; the 'imperious demand' to which
Toad surrenders only feeds his egotism.

As if in a dream he found himself, somehow, seated in the driver's seat; as if in a dream, he pulled the lever and swung the car round the yard and out through the archway; and, as if in a dream, all sense of right and wrong, all fear of obvious consequences, seemed temporarily suspended.

. . .he was only conscious that he was Toad once more, Toad at his best and highest, Toad the terror, the traffic-queller, the Lord of the lone trail, before whom all must give way or be smitten into nothingness and everlasting night.

I suppose we don't take all this very seriously. There is plenty of children's book atmosphere to allow us to take Toad's misdeeds lightly. Still, he is *us*, a vivid evocation of a psychological malady, a weakness of the super-ego, which in the real world can take sinister forms.

What follows Toad's stealing of the motor-car is, I feel, unsatisfactory. The trial and punishment of Toad are burlesqued. We know that he is not the 'incorrigible rogue and hardened ruffian' that authority finds him. This is too like Serjeant Buzfuz on Mr Pickwick's 'revolting heartlessness and systematic villainy'. The book's attitude to authority hereabouts is so uncertain that we lose our bearings. It may be right for us, the readers, to be uncertain whether Toad has done anything bad or not, but the author should not be uncertain. Similarly in the nightmare pursuit on the railway line the point of all the surrealism is not clear.

'They are gaining on us fast!' cried the engine-driver. 'And the engine is crowded with the queerest lot of people! Men like ancient warders, waving halberds; policemen in their helmets, waving truncheons; and shabbily dressed men in pot-hats, obvious and unmistakable plain-clothes detectives even at this distance, waving revolvers and walking-sticks; all waving, and all shouting the same thing – "Stop, stop, stop!"'

Whose side are we supposed to be on? Surely not the side of authority, if this gang represents it. Here Toad seems to stand for progress against reaction. And the author is on the side of progress. How can this be fitted in? Progress means the motor-car; and we all know what progress will do to the River Bank (rural traditionalism). Of course we can say that all this shows how complex a figure Toad is, that he stands for something which, however deplorable to traditionalists, is needed for life to go on. I don't believe this. The author certainly loves Toad as much as most of us do, but I think he saw the kind of progress Toad stands for, in so far as he stands for anything, as an evil. In short, I suspect that what we have here is not complexity but confusion.

Otherwise Toad's adventures are wholeheartedly enjoyable. My favourite is the scene of Toad selling the bargewoman's horse to the gipsy, a hilarious parody of *Lavengro*, as Peter Green has pointed out. ('He's a blood horse, he is, partly; not the part you see, of course – another part.') But essentially these chapters offer more of the same thing, rather than a new development. The real challenge to the author was to make us believe in a chastened Toad. But he cannot do it. We do believe it when he unexpectedly turns the tables on Rat and Mole at the banquet by an unexpected show of modesty.

At intervals he stole a glance at the Badger and the Rat, and always when he looked they were staring at each other with their mouths open; and this gave him the greatest satisfaction...

But do we believe it when the author goes on to add: 'He was indeed an altered Toad!'?

The result is that the end of *The Wind in the Willows* is one of those occasions when we feel that an artist has not quite succeeded, without being able to suggest what he should have done instead.

The most psychologically interesting chapter is, however, 'Wayfarers All'. Here at last is the really powerful challenge to the River Bank – Rat's restlessness and boredom reinforced by the seductive, the hypnotic influence of the Sea Rat. I suspect that this is a very personal chapter indeed – all the exotic places the Sea Rat mentions were places where Grahame himself had actually been. And – to note only one interesting detail – it is from 'the little grey sea town' of Fowey, where Grahame was married, that the Adventurer plans to set out again on another of his voyages. ('Family troubles, as usual, began it', he says of his wandering life.) Here at last is revealed the likeness between

Rat and Toad which the author's art has kept partly concealed. This is 'stability' under the greatest of stresses. 'Take the Adventure, hear the call, now ere the irrevocable moment passes!'

As with the other poet of The Wind in the Willows – Toad – the 'imperious demand' has a strange, even pathological effect, and as with Toad the representative of the River Bank (now it is Mole) resorts to coercion – for the patient's own good, of course.

He pressed resolutely forward, still without haste, but with dogged fixity of purpose; but the Mole, now thoroughly alarmed, placed himself in front of him, and looking into his eyes saw that they were glazed and set and turned a streaked and shifting grey – not his friend's eyes, but the eyes of some other animal! Grappling with him strongly he dragged him inside, threw him down, and held him.

The cure for Rat's malady is first of all the re-creation of the River Bank in the imagination:

. . .the Mole turned his talk to the harvest that was being gathered in. . .towering wagons and their straining teams. . .growing ricks. . . the large moon rising over bare acres dotted with sheaves. . .reddening apples. . .browning nuts. . .jams. . .preserves. . .distilling of cordials . .by easy stages. . .he reached midwinter, its hearty joys and its snug home life, and then he became almost lyrical.

And '. . .the Rat began to sit up and join in'. But it has essentially to be a self-therapy, and one that brings back an aspect of Rat we had almost forgotten.

. . .the tactful Mole. . .returned with a pencil and a few half-sheets of paper. . .'It's quite a long time since you did any poetry,' he remarked. 'You might have a try at it this evening, instead of – well, brooding over things so much. I've an idea that you'll feel a lot better when you've got something jotted down. . .'

And, slowly and painfully, the therapy works.

The Rat pushed the paper away from him wearily, but the discreet Mole took occasion to leave the room, and when he peeped in later, the Rat was absorbed and deaf to the world; alternately scribbling and sucking the top of his pencil. It is true that he sucked a good deal more than he scribbled: but it was joy to the Mole to know that the cure had at least begun.

In all this we feel that Rat is more intimately close to the author than any of the other characters. It would not be a surprise to learn that this beautiful work, *The Wind in the Willows*, grew out of frustration and sorrow; nor that, in closing this chapter with the picture of Rat 'sucking and scribbling' Kenneth Grahame was tacitly recognising that his River Bank could never be anything more than a country of the heart.

Of the Badger I have said little. We are not so close to him as to Mole, Rat, or Toad. It was surely a fine artistic stroke to draw him only from the outside. It reinforces our impression of his shyness, his dislike of society and its ways. Only the Wild Wood's threat to the River Bank forces him out of his cosy retirement. I think the remoteness of the Badger is due to his high rank. It has been suggested that the character was inspired by Jefferies's Alexander Iden in *Amaryllis at the Fair* (1886), Jefferies's portrait of his own father, one of the most memorable portraits of a countryman in English literature. And Badger is like Iden in his alternation of educated and common speech, and in its mixture of gruffness and kindness. But Iden is a tragic figure, a great human force wasted, a village Hampden. *The Wind in the Willows* has its moments of sadness, but it is not a tragic book. Badger's life is cosy and serene. He is alone, but he is not lonely. He exercises natural authority. He is an aristocrat.

Badger is not drawn from within. But Mole, Rat, and Toad all are, and even Toad, the simplest of them, cannot be summed up in a formula; he too has unexpected moments. *The Wind in the Willows* is unusual among English novels in working from as many as three centres (not counting the authorial voice). Many novels, of course, have a large cast of characters; but in how many of them can it be said that there are more than one or two characters who are both drawn from within, and at the same level of probability? And I hope I have shown that these centres, and the relations between them, develop and vary subtly in their relation to the authorial norm and the reader's sympathies. In short, *The Wind in the Willows*, for all its obvious unrealism of presentation, seems to me more essentially like a novel than any of the books which derive from it. And I hope my discussion has conveyed my view that considerations of genre here are confusing, and anyway secondary and subordinate, and apt to focus attention on the form or matter of the work, rather than on what it really does.

What finally can be said about the place of *The Wind in the Willows* in English literature? It is very popular. There are more than one hundred editions; more than 80,000 copies are sold every year. Nor is there any sign that its appeal is diminishing. It appears more and more of its period; yet this seems to do nothing to weaken its hold. Indeed, its 'period' quality may actually strengthen it. Yet its place in the literary canon is uncertain. This may be partly because of the dominant critical orthodoxy, according to which only what is manifestly a novel of manners can claim major status. It may also be partly due to the uncertainty about whether or not the book is children's literature. (My answer to that is no – unless you mean by children's literature one of those books which are ineffective unless the child in the reader responds to the child in the author.)

But perhaps a more fundamental reason for the critics' uncertainty is their suspicion of Arcadias. Many modern critics, unlike ordinary readers, seem to dislike the idyllic. Certainly *The Wind in the Willows* is not universally popular. Cyril Connolly dismissed it as a whimsy. Frank Kermode could see nothing in it. Raymond Williams's brief reference to it in his interesting book *The Country and the City* does not suggest that he cares for it. Perhaps the mere thought of Toad Hall fills people like Raymond Williams with anger. At any rate, *The Country and the City* shows much more sympathy with anti-Arcadias than with Arcadias. As regards this book his case is, from his own point of view, unanswerable. *The Wind in the Willows* is escapist. It does ignore the realities of country life – the oppression, the exploitation. It ignores sex and death. It is open to the criticism of radicals: it does idealise the country gentleman. It does protest against urbanisation. (Though we should remember that in this respect it cuts across party lines: William Morris and Robert Blatchford, who were certainly radicals, detested urbanisation.) Considered as a political allegory, *The Wind in the Willows* is reactionary – or, at least, very conservative.

But I don't think it is primarily a political book at all. It is one man's private dream, his vision of the paradisal. And surely only an individual is capable of happiness or misery. What business are radicals, or for that matter revolutionaries, supposed to be in? Don't they want the Kingdom of Heaven? But if they do want the Kingdom of Heaven, as a real thing, not a propagandist abstraction, they might learn something from *The Wind in the Willows*, in its own way and on its own scale, about what the Kingdom of Heaven might be like.

8
The Present Value of Tennyson

I think many of those who care about literature share my misgivings about the present-day vogue for enormously detailed biographies of writers. It is not only because they minister to a taste for gossip, which for many readers is more attractive than all those tiresome lines of verse. Too often they diminish the author's work by restoring it to its context of origin, the outgrowing of which is what makes it poetry. They force on the reader particularities which the author, with good reason, may have wanted to leave out. They sometimes make it impossible for us to experience the text. They turn poems into documents. I agree with Alfred Tennyson in yearning for the days 'Before the Love of Letters, overdone / Had swamped the sacred poets with themselves.' The ideal condition for a reader is that of a child listening to a story, who cares everything about what is in the story, and nothing about who wrote it.

But in the adult world things cannot be as simple as that. Often we cannot help having an image of the author behind the page. Sometimes this is part of our pleasure. Some authors, we feel, are our friends. But sometimes the image of the author influences what we read to the detriment of the work. For that image can be grossly misleading, the product of myths and unreliable anecdotes and baseless prejudices. That is why Sir Charles Tennyson's life of the poet Tennyson is so valuable, because it is so frank, because it lets in air and light. We like and respect him all the more because we realise what his personal problems were. He is clearer to us as a human being. But what gives Sir Charles's memoir its special virtue is that on every page it is guided by the recognition that the only reason why we should want to know about Tennyson is because we care for his poetry.

I want to speak about how Tennyson's poetry looks today. But at once we are confronted by the problem of critical judgment. This is an age when subjectivism is rampant everywhere – in moral philosophy, in political theory, in religious thought.

Nowhere is it so notoriously powerful as in the arts. It is often taken for granted that 'beauty is in the eye of the beholder', that if you think, or profess to think, that a pile of rubbish is more beautiful than Chartres Cathedral, you can't be wrong, because there are no rights and wrongs in the matter. This general question about value is of course much too large for me to go into here. This is a moment for testimony, not discussion. All I will say is that I regard subjectivism as wrong, and that I think its influence in every sphere of life has been poisonous.

But, as Spinoza says, it is better to try to understand one's enemy than to hate him. And where the arts are concerned the attraction of subjectivism is very understandable. In poetry, for example, the art with which we are concerned here, variations of taste and fluctuations of opinion are obvious. Quite apart from the contemporary chaos, one age ridicules the idols of another. Yesterday's fashions look absurd. Poets' reputations go up and down. Opinions vary from person to person. More than that, our own opinions change from one time of our lives to another. When I was a boy I loved the poems of Tennyson which I read in Arthur Mee's encyclopedias, such as 'The Lady of Shalott' and the lyric in *The Brook* and 'Flower in the crannied wall'. I would have been amazed to discover that anyone did not consider Tennyson a very great poet. When I was an undergraduate I took it for granted that Tennyson was a very outmoded and dated author, one who did not speak to my condition at all. And once again I assumed that all thinking people agreed with me. Today I have returned to my first opinion. I dare say many others could report similar fluctuations. But then how can there be anything objective about this, anything on a par with the statement that Tennyson was born in 1809 and died in 1892? Isn't it all just a matter of personal taste? and don't we all know that *de gustibus non est disputandum*?

I can't hope in a few pages to convert those of you who hold that view. I will only ask you to suspend it for a moment and try and look at the matter as the literary objectivist sees it. First of all, the objectivist is not fond of the word 'value', which carries an irremovable suggestion of subjectivity. He prefers to talk about goodness, or beauty, or truthfulness. And if he has to use an even more general term, he prefers to talk about 'quality', or 'virtue', or 'excellence', which suggests things that exist out there, irrespective of what you or I personally happen to think about them. But how then does the objectivist cope with the notorious variations of taste I have referred to, the ups and downs of the literary stock-market? His first step is to get people to admit that there can be many kinds of excellence. And some kinds are more admired by some people than by others. And some kinds are more popular at some periods than at others. This is apt to be forgotten in times of literary revolutions, like the twentieth century. Literary revolutions occur when some hitherto neglected or underrated kinds of excellence are recognised again in new writers. At such times the authors of the past who exhibit them, or are thought to exhibit them, are hailed as the forerunners of the moderns. They become the 'good guys' of the history of literature and art. The authors who do not exhibit this excellence, who may have been previously admired for other excellences, are abused, or dropped from the canon, perhaps for a time, perhaps indefinitely. Now it is certainly possible to write the history of art and literature in this way. And it may be psychologically necessary for a new age to remodel the past to suit its own needs. All the same, to follow the crowd in these revolutions is not only to commit the sin of injustice, it is to miss a great deal of pleasure. There are unfashionable kinds of excellence as well as fashionable ones. And to be out of step with our ancestors is not always a good thing. It is parochial and – what may be a more cogent objection for some people – it is undemocratic; as Chesterton said, tradition is the democracy of the dead, a refusal to commit everything to the judgment of the minority of people who merely happen to be walking about.

Nowhere is this parochial tendency more obvious than in the habit there once was of treating the mid-Victorian age as a very odd period. All those tabus on the physical side of sex, for example, how ludicrous! Now I do not deny that there were ways in which – as the late-Victorian H. G. Wells put it – mid-Victorian literature was 'clipped and limited'. But the people who took that line did not always remember that later ages have their inhibitions and shallownesses too, and that in some respects the great mid-Victorian writers can be seen as more 'normal', more in harmony with what has always been recognised as great in Western literature, than our own age. Let me take one or two examples especially pertinent to Tennyson. The first is what the poet Thomas Gray – not a Victorian – called 'the sacred source of sympathetic tears'. Can it be denied that in our uncomfortableness about this it is we, and not the mid-Victorians, who are out of step? All the great heroes of epic and romance wept copiously, and were thought more, not less, manly for doing so. Shakespeare is full of pathos. But how often is a writer today praised for his command of pathos? We can still laugh with Dickens, as the Victorians did; but are we prepared to admit that we weep with him as the Victorians did? Let me remind you of a poem which you will all know. It is taken from Tennyson's *The Princess*.

> Tears, idle tears, I know not what they mean.
> Tears from the depth of some divine despair
> Rise in the heart, and gather to the eyes
> In looking on the happy Autumn-fields,
> And thinking of the days that are no more.
>
> Fresh as the first beam glittering on a sail
> That brings our friends up from the underworld,
> Sad as the last which reddens over one
> That sinks with all we love below the verge;
> So sad, so fresh, the days that are no more.
>
> Ah, sad and strange as in dark summer dawns
> The earliest pipe of half-awakened birds
> To dying ears, when unto dying eyes
> The casement slowly grows a glimmering square;
> So sad, so strange, the days that are no more.
>
> Dear as remembered kisses after death,
> And sweet as those by hopeless fancy feigned
> On lips that are for others; deep as love,
> Deep as first love, and wild with all regret;
> O Death in life, the days that are no more.

This poem has been greatly admired and loved. But I have read modern accounts of it which are strongly hostile. Others respect its sincerity of feeling, but obviously react to it much as Tennyson's Princess, that sturdy progressive, reacts to it in its context.

> If indeed there haunt
> About the mouldered lodges of the Past
> So sweet a voice and vague, fatal to men,
> Well needs be we should cram our ears with wool
> And so pace by...
> [She asks the singer for a song]
> Not such as moans about the retrospect,
> But deals with the other distance and the hues
> Of promise; not a death's head at the wine.

F. R. Leavis, while acknowledging the distinction of 'Tears, idle tears', contrasts it unfavourably with D. H. Lawrence's 'Piano', in which the poet fights against his wish to weep. (I am reminded also of the moment in George Eliot's *Middlemarch* when the heroine Dorothea says that organ-music makes her sob, and her uncle Mr Brooke says 'That kind of thing is not healthy, my dear.') I think we find it difficult to deal with such poems today. Either we condemn them, or allot them to a minor category because there is no critical or ironic element in them to counterbalance the pathos. Or, if we admire them, we try to show that the counterbalancing element is there. We are somehow reluctant to take pathos straight, to admit that something in us answers directly to the timeless poignancy of 'Break, break, break':

> And the stately ships go on
> To their haven under the hill;
> But O for the touch of a vanished hand,
> And the sound of a voice that is still!

The twentieth century has a horror of sentimentality, though no one seems able to say exactly what sentimentality is. So far as I can see, it means the appeal by an author to a mood which for some reason we do not want to feel at the moment. But sometimes nowadays it seems to mean the expression of any distinctively human emotion whatever. I think this dread of sentimentality has been one of the most crippling limitations on writers at the present time. A writer who is afraid of sentimentality can never write anything emotionally full-blooded, just as a writer who fears melodrama can never write a tragedy.

Another excellence that has been devalued today, a quality in which Tennyson especially excels, is one for which there is now no acceptable positive word. The best I can suggest is 'pomp' in the sense in which Shakespeare means it when he makes Othello speak of the 'pride, pomp and circumstance of glorious war'. It is significant that we cannot use this word without explaining that we do not mean it pejoratively. And its adjective, 'pompous', is exclusively pejorative. This is another indication of the constrictions of modern literature in the age of irony. Everything has to be, as Auden put it, 'ironic, *sotto voce*, monochrome', and Auden thought that for a sincere poet today this must be so. Farewell to the grand style. Tennyson could write his ode on the death of Wellington:

> Bury the Great Duke
> With an empire's lamentation.
> Let us bury the Great Duke
> To the noise of the mourning of a mighty nation.

But so far as I know no modern poet has succeeded in writing a single memorable line, let alone a good poem, on the deaths of Winston Churchill or John F. Kennedy. We have a word for pomp in the wrong place: pomposity. But where is our word for pomp in the right place? It may be said that we don't believe in 'great men' as the Victorians did. Similarly, when it is observed that no modern poet since Kipling – Tennyson's disciple – has written a great hymn, it will be said that this is because we don't believe in God any more: ours is not an age of faith. But Tennyson himself, as he was well aware, did not live in an age of faith, and yet he could write a great hymn:

> Strong Son of God, immortal Love,
> Whom we that have not seen thy face
> By faith, and faith alone, embrace,
> Believing where we cannot prove.

The greatness of *In Memoriam* is that it destroys any simple contrast between 'faith' and 'doubt'; agnostics can have religious feelings, and Tennyson is the devotional poet of agnosticism.

Many other kinds of excellence that are not characteristic of present-day writing could be illustrated from Tennyson. Besides rising to these grand occasions he is the poet of private celebration and commemoration, as few moderns are. I think for instance of his capacity for a happy blend of dignity and informality, as in 'The Daisy', or 'To the Rev. F. D. Maurice', or 'To Mary Boyle'; and his power to join the touchingly personal to the impersonally grand, as in 'To E. Fitzgerald'. All sorts of things are scattered about the margins of Tennyson's work, which if they were better known would quite transform the simplified picture of him that some people still have. There is a frequent critical habit of splitting up Tennyson into the morbid mystic and the celebrant of Victorian domesticities, the gruff Lincolnshire pipe-smoker and the exquisite dreamer, the angry young man and the ancient sage, and then declaring one's bafflement at how to put him together again. The fact is, as Christopher Ricks pointed out, that Tennyson was all those things, and other things too: 'he was many things'.

So far I have been discussing excellences that are excellences *sometimes*. They may be more valued in one period than in another. And they may sometimes be out of place. One of the things that once attracted readers to Tennyson, and may now put them off, is his passion for the minute description of nature. Who could deny that this is an excellence? 'A million emeralds break from the ruby-budded lime. . .' Who could look at a lime-tree again without relishing that? *In Memoriam* alone is full of single lines which have that quality.

> Unloved, the sun-flower, shining fair
> Ray round with flames her disk of seed. . .

Everyone can think of places like this in Tennyson where we are delighted to recognise what we may have seen for ourselves, but put into words with more delicate precision than we could ever find. But I suspect that these things were more admired by Victorian critics than they are today, and that many of us find that our own response to them, while it may be admiring, is cool. Tennyson's lines on the sun-flower

> . . .shining fair,
> Ray round with flames her disk of seed

would help the police to an identification better than Blake's:

> Ah, Sunflower, weary of time,
> Who countest the steps of the sun. . .

But what Blake gives us is not so much a recognition of what we already know, but something that flashes on us as a new insight, something that takes us beyond a beautiful transient phenomenon to a glimpse of the eternal; not what the sun-flower looks like, but what it 'is', what it 'means', in the world of the spirit. Please understand that I am not reproaching Tennyson for not writing like Blake. That would be quite contrary to the principles I recommend. Every poet is entitled to his own singularity. What I am trying to do is to specify a quality in Tennyson's verse which is sometimes an excellence but sometimes not. When the May Queen says

> The building rook'll call from the windy tall elm-tree,
> And the tufted plover pipe along the fallow lea

it detracts from that poem to have to think of her as a keen amateur naturalist. When Burns said his love was like a red, red rose he would have weakened the poem by mentioning the species of rose, as I fear Tennyson might have done. It is one of Tennyson's faults as a poet that he was sometimes betrayed into over-elaboration. In this respect he is Hellenistic, not classical.

Some excellences, then, can be out of place. But the literary objectivist is committed to the view that there are some excellences which are never out of place. No work of art can be called great without them. Poignancy and unambiguous feeling, pomp and stateliness, minute description and felicity of observation – all these are excellences, and all can be found in Tennyson's work. But they are not excellences always or all the time. What we must be concerned with, if we are to substantiate the claim of Tennyson to a place among the great poets, are those excellences that are always excellences – what might be called the 'marks' or, to use Newman's word, the 'notes', of great poetry, and great art in general. These permanent excellences may be many. I propose to select four of them, and see how far they apply to Tennyson.

The first essential excellence, something that is always a virtue in a poet, is effectiveness of communication. It might be objected that this seems an almost tautologous requirement. If, to use an expressive vulgarism, the poet cannot 'get his stuff across', we can hardly call him a poet at all. Yet, especially in modern times, the communicative aspect of poetry has not been much stressed by some poets and critics who write about poetry. Some have even pooh-poohed it as a rather banal conception. Leave that sort of thing to the people who write singing commercials. It was a commonplace in the early modernist period that the poet's only duty is to find the unique expression for the unique thing he wants to say. As Eliot put it, he may be talking to himself, or to no one. It is a matter of good luck if the reader's point of view happens to coincide sufficiently with the poet's for him to be able to understand what the poet is saying. And the poet should not be expected to do anything about this – at any rate, to do anything deliberate about it. I. A. Richards said that poets who can be suspected of paying conscious attention to communication will probably be found to be of a lower order. There are historical and cultural reasons for the rise of this doctrine which I must not go into now. All I will say is that it has not been universally shared. Some critics have attached paramount importance to communication. For Tolstoy it was the sole criterion of art. Stern moralist as he was, he was prepared to allow the title of 'art' to works which even, as he thought, promoted immorality. Communicative efficacy was enough. Thus his objection to the French symbolist poets was not that they were bad men communicating bad things. His objection was that they were bad men communicating nothing at all. I think Tolstoy was fundamentally right. My only criticism of him is that – influenced like the rest of us by his own tastes and training – he was too ready to proclaim the communicative inefficacy of what he didn't like without finding out whether it was so for other readers. Tolstoy was convinced that the symbolists were completely unintelligible, and a critic like Georges Ohnet was quite representative of his kind when he urged Mallarmé, the most obscure of the symbolist poets, to give up that sort of thing and write comprehensibly like the immensely popular authors of the time. But today Georges Ohnet and the immensely popular authors of the time are forgotten and Mallarmé has thousands of readers. One should not be too ready to say in advance what will or will not communicate.

The case of Tennyson, of course, is precisely the opposite. He has been blamed for not being obscure enough. It would be as rare to find him accused of obscurity as it would be to find him accused of bawdiness. As a matter of fact some of the reflective passages of *In Memoriam* are very difficult, and Tennyson is by no means always as sweetly pellucid as he is commonly held to be. And in his early work, when he was still a coterie poet, he was often ridiculed by reviewers for his obscurity. But no one will deny that Tennyson in many of his poems did eventually come home to the business and bosoms of his mid-Victorian public. It is not only that some of his poems were popular and his volumes sold well, that he represented poetry for the Victorians as Lord Roberts represented soldiering or W. G. Grace cricket. The evidence is in the very fabric of the language, all those familiar quotations that put Tennyson beside Shakespeare and Pope and Kipling as a source of literary ornaments and clichés. It is almost a test of knowledge of the English language to recognise Nature red in tooth and claw, and the little rift within the lute, and kind hearts are more than coronets, and 'Tis better to have loved and lost than never to have loved at all', and all the rest of them. Tennyson's lines and phrases are quoted and misquoted, his best-known short poems parodied, his aphorisms cited for approval or mockery, as much today as they were in the nineteenth century. I am not saying that these things are Tennyson's best lines, or that the test of a poet is whether he supplies quotations for Victorian calendars. Quotability and memorability are not, it seems, thought specially important virtues nowadays. I have found that admirers of a new poet who were recommending him to me were somewhat put out by my request that they should quote a line or two of his. Certainly to have become a poetic father-figure is not a proof of permanent excellence. But it is a proof of communicative efficacy.

However, what I had in mind in suggesting this as the first criterion for permanent excellence is not so much this sort of communal communication as a capacity which only the individual reader can judge: the power to make us feel that what the poet says 'finds' us at once, immediately and finally. This is something that cannot be talked about, only indicated. We can only say that this or that poem hits the mark, does what it does so perfectly that there is nothing the critic needs to say. Here is an example.

> Come not, when I am dead,
>   To drop thy foolish tears upon my grave,
> To trample round my fallen head,
>   And vex the unhappy dust thou wouldst not save.
> There let the wind sweep and the plover cry;
>   But thou, go by.
>
> Child, if it were thine error or thy crime
>   I care no longer, being all unblest:
> Wed whom thou wilt, but I am sick of Time,
>   And I desire to rest.
> Pass on, weak heart, and leave me where I lie:
>   Go by, go by.

But communicative efficacy will not take us very far as a criterion. It has often been pointed out that bad poems can have it as well as good. There are poems that stick obstinately in my mind that I would not dream of calling good, including some by Tennyson. I loathe 'The Lord of Burleigh', for example.

> In her ear he whispers gaily,
>   'If my heart by signs can tell,
> Maiden, I have watched thee daily,
>   And I think thou lov'st me well.'

I find the whole poem distasteful, and if there is one word that particularly makes me want to retch, it is 'gaily'. So often in inferior Tennyson what we flinch from is not any clumsiness or bathos, but some kind of false, specious glitter. But I cannot deny that 'The Lord of Burleigh' has had many admirers, along with other poems of that kind that I don't like, such as 'Lady Clara

Vere de Vere'. So communicative efficacy may be a necessary condition of good poetry, but it is not a sufficient condition.

We come nearer to a sufficient condition – indeed some have held that we have a complete definition of poetry – in the second of the all-time goods I am going to mention. This is what I will call 'abundant felicity of expression'. Now here again we are in danger of tautology. Croce, as is well known, held that art *was* expression. At any rate no one will deny that it is impossible to talk about literature without it. Any poem, any literary work whatsoever, must be held to be in some degree expressive. Nor can the expression be thought of as something superadded. If you change the expression, you change the poem.

All the same, everyone will surely admit that there are some authors – and I mean good authors, not bad authors – in whom it is possible to imagine the expression bettered. Take the case of Anthony Trollope. There are good reasons for calling Trollope the best Victorian novelist, with his range of character, his comic genius, his wonderful gift for convincing dialogue – surely unsurpassed in the language – his profound tolerance, his moral sense that is all the more convincing because it works without the aid of self-importance and evangelical exhortations. And it could be said that, conservative as he was in temperament and literary habit, he really did more than some noisier authors to tackle unpopular and disturbing subjects and to change public opinion and not merely amplify it. But if we hesitate to call Trollope the best Victorian novelist, it may well be because of his undistinguished style. It is adequate, no doubt, for his purposes, but again and again we feel that Trollope has made no particular effort to find the right word. The result is a sort of greyness and drabness about the writing. No doubt if it had been livelier Trollope's novels would have been different. But it seems to me that they need not have been *radically* different. We could imagine a Trollope who wrote better, while still retaining the qualities for which we value him.

I am suggesting, then, that it is possible to separate, to some degree, what delights us in a writer's power of expression from the general pleasure and interest his work has to offer us. And it is in incidental felicities of expression that Tennyson is peculiarly strong. I could fill pages with the passages that come into my mind at this point. Is there a greater technical master in the language? I can illustrate only one aspect of this felicitousness, something rather neglected in poetry today, the emotional suggestiveness of sound-effect. It is by the use of this that through the elaborate syntactical patterns what I would like to call the essential *cry* of Tennyson comes through.

> So all day long the noise of battle roll'd
> Among the mountains by the winter sea. . .
>   . . .the many knotted waterflags
> That whistled dry and stiff about the mere. . .
> 'I heard the ripple washing in the reeds,
> And the wild water lapping on the crag.'
> ****
>
> Dry clash'd his armour in the icy caves
> And barren chasms, and all to left and right
> The bare black cliff clang'd round him as he based
> His feet on juts of slippery crag that rang
> Sharp-smitten with the dint of armed heels. . .
> ****
>   And from them rose
> A cry that shivered to the tingling stars,
> And, as it were one voice, an agony
> Of lamentation, like a wind that shrills
> All night in a waste land, where no one comes
> Or has come, since the making of the world. . .
> And on the mere the wailing died away. (*Morte d'Arthur*)
> ****
>   And all at once
> With twelve great shocks of sound, the shameless noon
> Was clash'd and hammer'd from a hundred towers,
> One after one. . .   (*Godiva*)
> ****
> The splendour falls on castle walls
> And snowy summits old in story,
> The long light shakes across the lakes,
> And the wild cataract leaps in glory.
> Blow, bugle, blow, set the wild echoes flying;
> Blow, bugle; answer echoes, dying, dying, dying.
> ****   (*The Princess*)

Then, ere that last weird battle in the west
There came on Arthur sleeping, Gawain kill'd
In Lancelot's war, the ghost of Gawain blown
Along a wandering wind, and past his ear
Went shrilling, 'Hollow, hollow all delight!
Hail, King! to-morrow thou shalt pass away,
Farewell! there is an isle of rest for thee,
And I am blown along a wandering wind,
And hollow, hollow, hollow all delight.'

(The Passing of Arthur)

But it is unnecessary to go on with these examples. Even Tennyson's detractors have always conceded his skill in this kind of effect. Indeed the judicious admirer of Tennyson may well feel that he delighted too much in what Whitman, in a remark Christopher Ricks quotes, called his 'finest verbalism'. I feel that I share the poet's own delight in this little bit from *Maud*:

> ...The snowy-banded, dilettante,
> Delicate-handed priest intone

where, as a critic has said, Tennyson is turning double and treble somersaults. But I am slightly uneasy about whether this is quite in place in a tragic romance like *Maud*. I have the same sort of reservation even about a wonderful lyric like this from *The Princess*, which conveys the essential 'message' of the whole work better than the poem as a whole manages to do.

Come down, O maid, from yonder mountain height:
What pleasure lives in height (the shepherd sang)
In height and cold, the splendour of the hills?
But cease to move so near the Heavens, and cease
To glide a sunbeam by the blasted Pine,
To sit a star upon the sparkling spire;
And come, for Love is of the valley, come,
For Love is of the valley, come thou down
And find him; by the happy threshold, he,
Or hand in hand with Plenty in the maize,
Or red with spirted purple of the vats,
Or foxlike in the vine; nor cares to walk
With Death and Morning on the silver horns,
Nor wilt thou snare him in the white ravine,

Nor find him dropt upon the firths of ice,
That huddling slant in furrow-cloven falls
To roll the torrent out of dusky doors:
But follow; let the torrent dance thee down
To find him in the valley; let the wild
Lean-headed Eagles yelp alone, and leave
The monstrous ledges there to slope, and spill
Their thousand wreaths of dangling water-smoke,
That like a broken purpose waste in air:
So waste not thou; but come; for all the vales
Await thee; azure pillars of the hearth
Arise to thee; the children call, and I
Thy shepherd pipe, and sweet is every sound,
Sweeter thy voice, but every sound is sweet;
Myriads of rivulets hurrying through the lawn,
The moan of doves in immemorial elms,
And murmuring of innumerable bees.

The poet here is like a dancer who moves from point to point with never an ugly movement. But there is a saying that *ars est celare artem*, and for me the poem does not conceal its art quite enough. For that reason 'And murmuring of innumerable bees' strikes me as less effective than Keats's: 'The murmurous haunt of flies on summer eves'. Perhaps Tennyson was over-fond of echoic verse. I say echoic verse rather than onomatopoeia, for onomatopoeia, the mysterious matching of sound to sense, is a more general quality of poetry. I would call

> Music that gentlier on the spirit lies
> Than tired eyelids upon tired eyes

(from 'The Lotos-Eaters') onomatopoeic, for it is the soothing effect of music, not the actual sound, that is imitated. Homer and Virgil, of course, did use echoic verse now and then, but they used it more sparingly than Tennyson. It is the kind of thing that can help to make poetry more attractive to literary beginners, but more experienced readers are less impressed by it.

This over-doing of directly imitative verse is closely related to something that Gerard Manley Hopkins, when he began to 'doubt' Tennyson, called Tennyson's Parnassianism. I hesitate to call this a fault, as Hopkins hesitated when he drew attention to

the passage I am going to quote. It comes from *Enoch Arden*.
I do not think *Enoch Arden* is one of Tennyson's best poems, but
I am quite awed by the brilliance of the description of the ship-
wrecked Enoch's desert island.

> The mountain wooded to the peak, the lawns
> And winding glades high up like ways to Heaven,
> The slender coco's drooping crown of plumes,
> The lightning flash of insect and of bird,
> The lustre of the long convolvuluses
> That coiled around the stately stems, and ran
> Even to the limit of the land, the glows
> And glories of the broad belt of the world,
> All these he saw; but what he fain had seen
> He could not see, the kindly human face,
> Nor ever hear a kindly voice, but heard
> The myriad shriek of wheeling ocean-fowl,
> The league-long roller thundering on the reef,
> The moving whisper of huge trees that branched
> And blossomed in the zenith, or the sweep
> Of some precipitous rivulet to the wave,
> As down the shore he ranged, or all day long
> Sat often in the seaward-gazing gorge,
> A shipwrecked sailor, waiting for a sail;
> No sail from day to day, but every day
> The sunrise broken into scarlet shafts
> Among the palms and ferns and precipices;
> The blaze upon the waters to the east;
> The blaze upon his island overhead;
> The blaze upon the waters to the west;
> Then the great stars that globed themselves in Heaven,
> The hollower-bellowing ocean, and again
> The scarlet shafts of sunrise – but no sail.

It is magnificent – but I see what Hopkins meant by calling it
Parnassian. Tennyson is writing too much within himself. He is
giving us 'Tennysonian', though of the very best quality.

Abundant felicity of expression, then, is one mark of the great
poet; but it should not, I think, be the one on which advocates
of the present value of Tennyson should lay most stress. Indeed
to lay stress on it might be to concede too much to the view that

at one time I was inclined to hold, that Tennyson is only at his best in lines and passages, not in complete poems. The decoration is splendid, but there is a kind of hollow at the centre. This was Matthew Arnold's view, though we must remember that Arnold was a rival poet and a bit tinged with artist's jealousy. Here, I have come, of course, to another sempiternal excellence, and one which Tennyson has often been accused of lacking. Again there is no agreed term today for what I have in mind. Matthew Arnold used the term 'architectonic power', but this may too much suggest Victorian classicism. Perhaps Clive Bell's 'significant form' is better; or perhaps one might speak of 'self-evident internal coherence'. Put more simply, it is a question of how well the poet's clothes fit him. Now it seems to me that some poems of Tennyson do suffer from structural weakness. In 'The Palace of Art', for example, the allegory does not really come alive, and 'A Dream of Fair Women' exists in the memory only as a series of cameos. But there are many of Tennyson's shorter poems in which no one has found any structural fault. It would be difficult to imagine how 'Mariana' or 'The Lady of Shalott', 'The Lotos-Eaters' or 'Ulysses', could be improved in this respect. But this perfect fittingness has often been denied to Tennyson's four most ambitious poetic creations, *The Princess*, *In Memoriam*, *Maud*, and the *Idylls of the King*. Was Tennyson capable of poetic creation on a large scale? This may not be an essential characteristic of the great poet, but it has been very marked in the poets whom posterity has agreed to number among the greatest. And I think the feeling that Tennyson did lack this capacity is often behind the modern view that the Victorians were wrong to think him a great poet. So this question is one that should be looked into.

The Princess does not give grounds for saying yes to it. Tennyson might be thought implicitly to have conceded the point by subtitling it 'a medley'. It contains some of Tennyson's most delightful and some of his most irritating work. For me, despite some beautiful passages, especially at the end, *The Princess* remains interesting Victoriana rather than engrossing reading for its own sake. The exception that proves the rule is the blank verse lyrics it contains, such as 'Tears, idle tears' and 'Now sleeps the crimson petal, now the white', and the rhymed songs that were inserted into it later. And I am afraid that for me the *Idylls of the King* falls into the same category as *The Princess*. It is a remarkable document rather than a remarkable poem. As an epic it seems factitious. It should be said in Tennyson's defence that no English writing has succeeded in making a whole epic out of the Arthurian material. From *Sir Gawain and the Green Knight* onwards the best things that have been done with it have always been particular episodes or adventures. The Arthurian material still awaits its Virgil. Tennyson came nearer to being that than any other writer. But for me the *Idylls* lives only in episodes and fragments, though a few of them contain some of Tennyson's finest poetry. They are not convincing evidence of his architectonic powers.

So we are left with *In Memoriam* and *Maud*. I will speak of *Maud* first, though it was published later. It is the most problematic of Tennyson's poems. The reader who tries to sum up his impressions of it finds himself pulled in different directions. It seems an extraordinary farrago. First of all it can be read for the story, which is not very clearly told and rather melodramatic, about a young man who has been ruined by the old 'Lord of the Hall', falls in love with the lord's beautiful daughter, kills her brother in a duel and escapes to France, has a mental breakdown and is finally cured by responding to the call of his country at war and (as I interpret the end of the poem) is killed in battle. Here Tennyson is offering entertainment in competition with popular novelists and dramatists of the time. But *Maud* can also be read as a denunciation of the manners and morals of the day, like the earlier 'Locksley Hall'. And here Tennyson seems to be speaking through his unbalanced mouthpiece as the sage–poet and moralist in an angry mood. Finally, to the reader who has read Sir Charles Tennyson's life, and R. W. Rader's fascinating study of the poem, *Maud* looks like an autobiographical document. Behind it must lie Tennyson's relationship with his strange father, the 'black blood' of the Tennysons, the fear of madness and mental disorientation which clouded Tennyson's life down to the 1850s and sent him after those endless 'water-cures'. It is all very remote from the pillar of the Victorian household he was to become. Behind *Maud* also is the rage against his snobbish relatives the D'Eyncourts, and his rejection, because of his poverty, by the girl he loved, Rosa Baring, at the prompting of her well-to-do family. And his relations with other women, Sophy Rawnsley and Emily Sellwood, are also shadowed there. And there is the whole complex of his love for Hallam, and his feeling, in the troubled years after Hallam's death, that he had lost the pivot of his life. What with the stagey plot, the denunciations of the age, and the constant pressure of personal material, it is no wonder that many readers both in the poet's own time and in ours have found the poem perplexing and chaotic. For some it is saved only, if at all, by its wonderful craftsmanship and exquisite lyric passages. And these it certainly has. Whatever we may think of *Maud* as a whole, it is surely impossible not to be moved by one part of it.

> Oh! that 'twere possible
>   After long grief and pain,
> To find the arms of my true-love
>   Round me once again!
> . . .
> A shadow flits before me –
>   Not thou, but like to thee,
> Ah God! that it were possible
>   For one short hour to see
> The souls we loved, that they might tell us
>   What and where they be.
>
> . . .
> Then I rise: the eave-drops fall
>   And the yellow-vapours choke
>   The great city sounding wide;
> The day comes – a dull red ball,
>   Wrapt in drifts of lurid smoke
>   On the misty-river-side.
> Through the hubbub of the market
>   I steal, a wasted frame;
> . . .
> Then the broad light glares and beats,
>   And the sunk eye flits and fleets,
> And will not let me be.

I loathe the squares and streets,
And the faces that one meets,
    Hearts with no love for me;
Always I long to creep
To some still cavern deep,
And to weep, and weep, and weep
    My whole soul out to thee.

If it is possible to say that any one passage takes us to the heart
of the poem, it is surely this. But I believe that *Maud* is more
than a few exquisite lyrics. There is a clue to the maze, and if we
miss it we shall miss something essential that Tennyson has to
give us. It is the presence of this clue that explains why, as Rader
says, 'of all his poems *Maud* was peculiarly dear to Tennyson'.

Throughout his long later life, it was the poem he loved best to read
aloud and the one he read most often and most powerfully. It was,
above all, the one he most wished others to feel and understand.
Shortly after the poem was published, for instance, a perplexed and
annoyed Mrs. Carlyle watched Tennyson going about at Lady
Ashburton's 'asking everybody if they had liked his *Maud* – and
reading *Maud* aloud, and endlessly talking Maud, Maud, Maud'.
Earlier, in Chelsea, he had forced her to approve the poem by reading
it to her three times in insistent succession; so that now, used as she
was to his crotchets, she thought his actions odd indeed. 'He was
strangely excited about Maud,' she said, 'as sensitive to criticisms as
if they were imputations on her honour'. . .Rossetti describes a reading in which the poet shed tears and felt obviously strong emotion,
and we hear of another occasion on which he read the poem 'with
such intensity of feeling that he seized and kept quite unconsciously
twisting in his powerful hands a large brocaded cushion which was
lying at his side'. 'There was a peculiar freshness and passion in his
reading of *Maud*', his son writes, 'giving the impression that he had
just written the poem, and that the emotion which created it was
fresh in him. This had an extraordinary influence on the listener,
who felt that the reader had been *present* at the scenes he described,
and that he still felt their bliss or agony.'
    (R. W. Rader, *Tennyson's Maud: The Biographical Genesis* (1963),
                                                            pp. 1–2)

What then is this clue to *Maud*? I believe that the American
writer Henry Van Dyke realised what it was when he heard the

old Tennyson, shortly before his death, read the poem. Van Dyke
found himself

> amazed at the intensity with which the poet had felt, and the tenacity
> with which he pursued, the moral meaning of the poem. It was love,
> but not love in itself alone, as an emotion, an inward experience, a
> selfish possession, that he was revealing. It was love as a vital force,
> love as a part of life, love as an influence – nay, the influence which
> rescues the soul from prison or the madhouse, of self, and leads it
> into the larger, saner existence. This was the theme of *Maud*. And
> the poet's voice brought it out, and rang the changes on it, so that it
> was unmistakable and unforgettable.   (Quoted by Rader, *ibid.*, p. 98)

I think it is what Van Dyke calls the 'theme' of *Maud* that
makes an emotional unity out of the poem and makes it a convincing example, if a strange one, of Tennyson's power to create
order out of turbulence; even though the 'love' he speaks of may
seem to the modern reader less a liberation than a strange
neurotic obsession.

In Memoriam does not seem to me to have an equivalent
principle of unity. There is a better case than with *Maud* for
regarding it as a collection of separate poems, held together by
the uniform metre which Tennyson made his own and by
recurrent similarities of thought and mood. However it may
have been for the Victorians, the intellectual framework of the
poem's debate is not now a living one for us. And despite the
efforts of A. C. Bradley and others, I cannot see in the form of
the poem a manifest inevitability of structure. Yet I believe it to
be the greatest of Tennyson's poems, and for a reason which
brings me to the last of those marks or notes of the great poet
that I want to mention. Once again our modern critical vocabulary fails to supply an adequate term. What I have in mind is
what the ancient writer known as Longinus called 'the echo of a
great soul'. Unlike the eighteenth century, or the Victorians, we
find such words, or words like 'sublime' or 'noble', slightly
embarrassing. Perhaps I can best convey what I am trying to
remind you of by using some words of C. S. Lewis from another
context.

It is sobering and cathartic to remember, now and then, our collective smallness, our apparent isolation, the apparent indifference of nature, the slow biological, geological and astronomical processes which may, in the long run, make many of our hopes (possibly some of our fears) ridiculous. If *memento mori* is sauce for the individual, I do not know why the species should be spared the taste of it...Those who brood much on the remote past or future, or stare long at the night sky, are less likely than others to be ardent or orthodox partisans.

(C. S. Lewis, *Of Other Worlds* (1966), p. 67)

It is in the capacity to transcend the pettiness and egocentricity of most human concerns (including some of his own) that Tennyson seems to me among the supreme poets. He lives in a larger world than any other poet. Sometimes, it is true, the sheer immensity of the universe revealed by science is felt as a terrible alienation of man, as in *Maud* when the narrator speaks of modern scientific knowledge of the stars as:

> A sad astrology, the boundless plan
> That makes you tyrants in your iron skies,
> Innumerable, pitiless, passionless eyes,
> Cold fires, yet with power to burn and brand
> His nothingness into man.

But sometimes, as in Tennyson's translation of a famous passage of Homer, this very largeness is what gives consolation and perspective.

> As when in heaven the stars about the moon
> Look beautiful, when all the winds are laid,
> And every height comes out, and jutting peak
> And valley, and the immeasurable heavens
> Break open to their highest...

Nothing is more profoundly Tennysonian than the finale of *The Princess*, when the poet soars away from Victorian preoccupations to a timeless serenity.

> But we went back to the Abbey, and sat on,
> So much the gathering darkness charmed: we sat
> But spoke not, rapt in nameless reverie,
> Perchance upon the future man: the walls
> Blackened about us, bats wheeled, the owls whooped,
> And gradually the powers of the night,

> That range above the region of the wind,
> Deepening the courts of twilight broke them up
> Through all the silent spaces of the worlds,
> Beyond all thought into the Heaven of Heavens.

In Memoriam has many aspects, and I have left myself space only to mention this one, this largeness of vision.

> There where the long street roars, has been
> The stillness of the central sea.

Listening to the roar, and the stillness, I find myself reminded of a remark of A. J. P. Taylor's, that in politics and public affairs the nineteenth century thought of itself as very chaotic, but in fact was very stable. Perhaps something like this could be said about Tennyson in those parts of his work where he is truly classical.

And perhaps I may be allowed a final comment on that last word. Eliot in his essay on Kipling says Kipling and Dryden were both 'classical poets'. 'They arrive at poetry through eloquence. For both, wisdom has the primacy over inspiration...Both are more concerned with their own feelings in their likeness to those of other men than in their particularity.' (A romantic poet is presumably the opposite.) When I read these lines I wonder whether Tennyson was a classical or a romantic poet. Some of the poems and passages which may appeal most to modern readers reflect the struggles and frustrations of a divided nature and a sick soul. Here he seems a romantic poet. In other poems he strives hard to achieve the balance and serenity for which his soul yearned. But they strike a note which, while it may be sincere, is not authentic, if I can use Lionel Trilling's distinction. They say what he wanted to feel rather than what he really felt. It is my claim for *In Memoriam*, and the reason why I believe it to be the greatest of Tennyson's poems, that in it he unites the romantic and the classical. A personal voice, while never ceasing to be a personal voice, becomes at the great moments of the poem the voice of all humanity. That is, I believe, the present – and the permanent – value of Tennyson.

9
Robert Frost

I

An English critic (A. Alvarez in *The Shaping Spirit*, 1958) has this to say about Frost's present reputation in England:

Perhaps the only modern American poet who really is concerned with manners is Robert Frost...I think this is why Frost has been so readily accepted in England; he is peculiarly congenial; we are easy with the tradition of country poetry, simple language and simple wisdom. American cosmopolitanism, even Eliot's, has always seemed a suspicious virtue, whereas Frost seems assured, he does not have to strive; he has New England behind him...

Alvarez, perhaps unwittingly, gives the impression (which I do not share) that Frost's poetry is widely read in England. But otherwise this implicit placing of Frost ('country poetry, simple language and simple wisdom') in a familiar minor niche does, I think, convey a true account of Frost's actual standing here. His reputation is based, it would seem, on a handful of well-known anthology pieces. 'Everyone' knows 'Stopping by Woods on a Snowy Evening', just as 'everyone' knows Masefield's 'Cargoes', but that is not enough to put either poet in a context of active discussion. My own impression, for what it is worth, is that if Frost is mentioned at all, it is as a worthy but dull poet of about the rank of Masefield. And if this patronising attitude is accompanied by a more sympathetic note, that may derive from the memory of America's unofficial poet laureate as a white-haired old man pathetically inaudible at John F. Kennedy's presidential inauguration.

For those English readers who see more in Frost than Alvarez apparently does, this is a pity – especially since it was English readers in the first place who could very largely take the credit for discovering him. True, the first intelligent critique of his verse was written by an American, Ezra Pound. But the review of *North of Boston* in 1914 by the English poet Edward Thomas, though less well known, gives an equally incisive account of what must on any view be a large part of Frost's permanent claim to a place in the history of poetry. In its brevity and its clarity of description Thomas's review, modest as it is, is a model of good criticism, as this extract may suggest:

This is one of the most revolutionary books of modern times, but one of the quietest and least aggressive. It speaks, and it is poetry. It consists of fifteen poems, from fifty to three hundred lines long, depicting scenes of life, chiefly in the country, in New Hampshire. Two neighbour farmers go along opposite sides of their boundary wall, mending it and speaking of walls and of boundaries. A husband and wife discuss an old vagabond farm servant, who has come home to them, as it falls out, to die. Two travellers sit outside a deserted cottage, talking of those who once lived in it, talking until bees in the wall boards drive them away. A man who has lost his feet in a saw-mill talks to a friend, a child, and the lawyer comes from Boston about compensation. The poet himself described the dreams of his eyes after a long day on a ladder picking apples, and the impression left on him by a neglected wood-pile in the snow on an evening walk. All but these last two are in dialogue mainly: nearly all are in blank verse.

These poems are revolutionary because they lack the exaggeration of rhetoric, and even at first sight appear to lack the poetic intensity of which rhetoric is an imitation. Their language is free from the poetical words and forms that are the chief material of secondary poets. The metre avoids not only the old-fashioned pomp and sweetness, but the later fashion also of discord and fuss. In fact, the medium is common speech and common decasyllables, and Frost is at no pains to exclude blank verse lines resembling those employed, I think, by Andrew Lang in a leading article printed as prose. Yet almost all these poems are beautiful. They depend not at all on objects commonly admitted to be beautiful; neither have they merely a homely beauty, but are often grand, sometimes magical. Many, if not most, of the separate lines and separate sentences are plain and, in themselves, nothing. But they are bound together and made elements of beauty by a calm eagerness of emotion.

Thomas puts the stress where it could be put, in beginning his discussion of Frost: on Frost's technical innovation. Of course what Thomas himself, as a poet, owed to Frost was more than technical. That community of spirit between poets which makes it out of place to speak of 'imitation' of one by another is evident in passages like these I quote from Thomas; the similarity of accent to Frost's is obvious, but no informed admirer of Frost would suppose these passages to have been written by him:

> . . .Not till night had half its stars
> And never a cloud, was I aware of silence
> Stained with all that hour's songs, a silence
> Saying that Spring returns, perhaps to-morrow.
>   * * *
> And yet I still am half in love with pain,
> With what is imperfect, with both tears and mirth,
> With things that have an end, with life and earth,
> And this moon that leaves me dark within the door.
>   * * *

> > For I at most accept
> > Your love, regretting
> > That is all: I have kept
> > Only a fretting

> > That I could not return
> > All that you gave
> > And could not ever burn
> > With the love you have,

> > Till sometimes it did seem
> > Better it were
> > Never to see you more
> > Than linger here

> > With only gratitude
> > Instead of love –
> > A pine in solitude
> > Cradling a dove.

The last example reminds us of a note of longing, which sounds at the same time both stronger and sweeter than Thomas, in this poem by Frost:

> > Love at the lips was touch
> > As sweet as I could bear;
> > And once that seemed too much;
> > I lived on air

That crossed me from sweet things
The flow of – was it musk
From hidden grapevine springs
Down hill at dusk?

I had the swirl and ache
From sprays of honeysuckle
That when they're gathered shake
Dew on the knuckle.

I craved strong sweets, but those
Seemed strong when I was young;
The petal of the rose
It was that stung.

With that passage (from 'To Earthward') we have left the characteristic work in *North of Boston*, and the special qualities which Thomas in his review was concerned to bring to the attention of English readers. But displaying the likeness and difference between the sensibilities of the two friends in their most personal work may remove the suspicion that all Thomas learned from Frost was a trick of craftsmanship, a dodge for handling everyday material in those anecdotal/dialogue poems which are as characteristic of his work as of Frost's. What Thomas learned from Frost's work, whether in the lyrical or the 'dramatic' mode, was something that belonged to its essence.

But in his review Thomas *is* chiefly concerned with Frost's blank verse, and it is useful to note, in trying to decide what Frost's achievement meant to the English poet, just how Thomas counters the obvious objection to this blank verse, that it is no more than versified prose. He remarks that Frost 'would lose far less than most modern writers by being printed as prose'. But he continues: 'If his work were so printed, it would have little in common with the kind of prose that runs to blank verse: in fact, it would turn out to be closer knit and more intimate than the finest prose is except in its finest passages. *It is poetry because it is better than prose*' (my italics).

We have here a hint of the kind of influence Frost had on Thomas, the personal and technical impact that made him a poet – though his late flowering was tragically brief, covering only the years of the First World War (he was killed on the Western Front in 1917). What made possible his self-discovery as a poet was this: he had been shown the way out of the late Victorian literariness he had practiced in his previous writings. By being encouraged to admit the prosaic, he was enabled to deal at first hand with genuine experience and feeling; to resist the temptation to adapt them to a manner which seems to prescribe beforehand how one *should* deal with them: so that it is easy to go on to mistake (as conventional poets so often do) what one knows one is supposed to feel, for what one actually does feel – if anything. And this release from late Victorian poetic diction inevitably demanded – what was just as important – a release from conventional rhythm. One of the chief problems for poets at the end of the nineteenth century was how to emancipate themselves from the coarse measures, the emphatic movement, so prevalent in Victorian poetry. *Vers libre* was one seemingly unavoidable consequence of the reaction against the often over-emphatic metres of Tennyson or Swinburne or Meredith. But *vers libre*, in the hands of its inferior practitioners, became an excuse for carelessness, or exposed them as lacking the conviction that poetry is an art. Such an attitude was unthinkable in a poetic craftsman like Frost. His solution to the technical problem was to retain metre, but to incorporate into it the cadences of speech. It is the speech of New England speakers; its staple, the talk of an educated man at the point just before it crystallises into formal prose. We do not speak prose; Molière's M. Jourdain was wrong; we evolve it from the movement and syntax and cadence of educated speech. The artistic achievement of Frost was to evolve verse from these. Locutions like 'admittedly', 'to do that to', 'of course', he brought into impassioned poems. Yet he did so in a manner which does not disturb our sense that we are reading poetry, something with its origins in song. His versification can always go back to the *cantabile*, yet it includes little that does not belong to modern (if sometimes a little old-fashioned) educated speech. The contrast with an English poet like Edmund Blunden is significant. Blunden can write even in his best poems lines like 'The pole-tops steeple to the thrones / Of stars, sound gulfs of wonder', in which the rhythm imposed by the meaning seems not to fit the metrical pattern. This clumsiness, or constant slight artificiality, is what Frost banished from his poetry.

Frost's colloquialism is famous. It is also notorious, for in his anecdotal poems he can sometimes sink to an unparalleled flatness. But critics have sometimes misrepresented this quality of his work by over-statement, seeing in it the whole of his innovation. This does not do him justice. The most casual reader sees that Frost is colloquial; reading which is more than casual brings out how much of the 'archaic' and 'literary' language of traditional poetry he has retained. Thus no one familiar with Frost's work will find the following poem uncharacteristic; yet to call it 'colloquial' misdescribes it. So far from being the anecdotal jotting down of some incident of New England rural life, or a piece of gnarled rustic wisdom or country sentiment, it is a gracefully sustained literary fancy which (one might be inclined to say) could have come from an accomplished traditional poet:

> She is as in a field of silken tent
> At midday when a sunny summer breeze
> Has dried the dew and all its ropes relent,
> So that in guys it gently sways at ease,
> And its supporting central cedar pole,
> That is its pinnacle to heavenward
> And signifies the sureness of the soul,
> Seems to owe naught to any single cord,
> But strictly held by none, is loosely bound
> By countless silken ties of love and thought
> To everything on earth the compass round,
> And only by one's going slightly taut
> In the capriciousness of summer air
> Is of the slightest bondage made aware.

At first this seems to belong with 'literary' poetry; in its diction, syntactical organisation, and structure – the careful and explicit working out of the central idea – it is obviously a 'thing made', not a 'happening', like a jewel, not like a pebble or a snowflake, as so many of Frost's typical poems seem to be. But 'going slightly taut' – that is one's feeling about the poem: it is the reminder of the poet's formal control which here brings into unusual prominence Frost's usual firm grip on the sensory facts which provide the notation for his graceful compliment and comment; so that this delicate, consciously elaborated sonnet is, after all, of a piece with the most rugged of his poems. Frost's is a manner which can accommodate the literary and the artificial as well as other modes.

The critic I previously quoted, Alvarez, notes this retention by Frost of the literary and traditional, but sees it as a simple incongruity, inconsistent with his character as a realist in verse. 'Granted that Frost began to write a very long time ago', he says, 'so his archaisms are probably not all deliberate; and granted his singleness of colloquial tone must have needed great practice and hard work to perfect. Nevertheless the literariness is a surprising contrast both to his habitual air of plain wisdom and to the lucidity he reaches in his best work.' Alvarez seems to see Frost's 'singleness of colloquial tone' – his plain diction – as the distinguishing feature of his poetry. And literariness in a plain diction would be a blemish. But he has overlooked that for Frost tone and cadence of voice are not necessarily associated with conversational diction – or syntax. Edward Thomas once more shows his understanding of Frost's art when he writes to Gordon Bottomley to defend it against the criticisms of the traditionalist poet Sturge Moore:

All he [Frost] insists on is what he believes he finds in all poets – absolute fidelity to the postures which the voice assumes in the most expressive intimate speech. So long as these tones and postures are there he has not the least objection to any vocabulary whatever or any inversion or variation from the customary grammatical forms of talk. In fact I think he would agree that if the tones and postures survive in a complicated or learned vocabulary and structure the result is likely to be better than if they survive in the easiest form, that is, in the very words and structures of common speech.

What this perceptive statement brings out is that Frost, at any rate in intention, is a less *specialised* poet than some of his admirers, or detractors, have been prepared to recognise. Just as he was not merely offering, in *North of Boston* and the later work in resonance with it, pleasant material for the connoisseur of folkways or panegyrist of rural life, so his colloquialism was a development of something he thought an essential quality of *all* good poetry – an intrinsic naturalness which there is no reason to suppose he thought peculiar to the reported conversation of farmers. After all, there is no particular virtue in a conversational style as such; it is possible to be emotionally cheap, or tedious, or shallow, in a conversational style as in any other. In aiming to restore a vibration and human interest to poetry which late nineteenth-century poets seemed to have lost – and which had not been regained by Frost's immediate English predecessors, the poets among whom Yeats learned his trade, 'companions of the Cheshire Cheese' – Frost did not suppose that he could succeed by the simple expedient of writing as differently as possible from Dante Gabriel Rossetti. That may have been a necessary condition of what he did, but it was certainly not a sufficient one, nor do I see any reason for thinking that Frost himself believed it was.

Properly defined, then, Frost's technical innovation is a notable one, guaranteeing him a place in the history of poetry. A question that naturally arises is how far it was solely *his* innovation; and a related question, whether it should be regarded primarily as an American contribution to the poetry of the common language, or seen more in the terms of English poetic history. It would be ludicrous to deny that Frost's poetry is American poetry, not only in its manifest subject-matter, but in more impalpable qualities. But, as often, the definition of 'English' as opposed to 'American', in literary matters, is not simple. Notwithstanding the debt which American readers may perceive Frost to owe to Edwin Arlington Robinson, it seems clear that the development we note between the bulk of the poems in *A Boy's Will*, and the poems in *North of Boston*, has a vital connection with the work and study in which Frost joined with English poets in England. It was in the course of this association that Frost acquired a knowledge of other poetic experimenting, and a confidence in his own discovered 'voice' in poetry, which enabled him in the long run to exert an influence and attain a status denied to the isolated poet of Gardiner, Maine. What seems unquestionable is that Frost, in whatever other ways American critics may want to describe him, cannot be considered altogether apart from the Georgian phase of English literary history. To recognise that may not only be helpful in clarifying the study of his poetry; it may begin to do belated justice to the Georgian phase itself.

'Georgian' was once an honorific description; Wilfred Owen, a poet nowadays much in favour, was proud to be 'held peer by the Georgians'. But it has now become the reverse, being generally used to stigmatise all the weakness and spuriousness of the writers brought together in *Georgian Poetry* by Edward Marsh. Their work is associated with facile weekend-garden sentiment and a false affectation of simplicity. Schoolboys and undergraduates know that they were feeble escapists whom Modern Poetry consigned to the rubbish heap. What is sometimes forgotten, even by more mature students, is that Georgian poetry in its day was modern poetry. At least some of these poets thought of themselves as managing a revolt against established and popular traditionalists like Sir Henry Newbolt and Alfred Noyes. What they thought they were doing is doubtless irrelevant. And there is no need to have a very high opinion, or to weigh seriously the 'modernity' or otherwise of that terrain of Georgianism in which Rupert Brooke is the dominant figure and his *Grantchester* the representative poem. The more relevant consideration is that some gifted writers, as well as some less gifted, do seem in retrospect to have enough in common for some characterising adjective without a contemptuous overtone. The poets with whom Frost worked (Gibson, Abercrombie, Edward Thomas), Frost's own poetry, the short stories of A. E. Coppard, the early work of D. H. Lawrence – the period of English literature which contains these things reveals enough continuity between them and the work of weaker representative writers of the time, to need a historical description; and the word 'Georgian', notwithstanding its unfortunate associations, is the only one currently available.

What these writers have in common is a preoccupation, amounting in some cases to a positive obsession, with personal freedom. No reader of Frost will need to be reminded of his obsessive concern with it. This plays a large part, clearly, in that sanctification of whim and impulse for which Yvor Winters, his severest critic, has castigated him; many of the poems quoted for adverse comment by Winters show that this attitude of 'let me alone', a stubborn refusal to be pushed around by powers spiritual or temporal, is by no means confined to poems of playful whimsicality; a piece like 'The Objection to Being Stepped On' is itself trifling enough, but the protest it epitomises is the expression of something fundamental in Frost's work. No doubt in Frost it has to be related to the history of New England, and of the United States for that matter, as well as to his personal life and character. But it found a congenial environment, an echo of sympathy, in the Georgianism of 'old' England also.

This passion for privacy can be the foundation of a distinguished and strong personal art. But it can also come out in attitudes and mannerisms and tones of voice that have in them something tiresomely complacent and limited. In Frost we see the tiresome side of his cult of freedom in a certain cranky obscurantism in politics and a grumpiness in personal relations (see his letters). In the English Georgians we have something worse (at least from a literary point of view): the attempt to invest with spiritual distinction a self-congratulatory sensitiveness about country walks, garden suburbs, and afternoon tea. That poem by Brooke which begins 'Safe in the magic of my woods...' is a good example. The individual private responsiveness to nature on which the speaker in this poem congratulates himself, may be called the mysticism of the *rentier*; and mysticism in this context is apt to be the spiritual correlate of a vagueness about the sources of one's income. Certainly in Edward Thomas there is none of this Georgian complacency; the writing which he did for a living meant real hard work, and if it was hackwork it was perfectly decent. But when we read of Thomas's milieu in a book like Eleanor Farjeon's *Edward Thomas: The Last Four Years* we cannot but feel slightly depressed by that ethos of brown bread, knapsacks, 'rambles', and living on modest incomes in thatched cottages in the days when the pound was worth a pound. The characteristic note of Thomas's poetry, the note of yearning, recurrent and insistent, makes us feel all this as sad and restricted. It is remarkable how the entry into Eleanor Farjeon's pages of D. H. and Frieda Lawrence brightens things up.

Frost, like Lawrence, seems to have brought refreshment from outside into this somewhat stuffy atmosphere. That there was harshness and bleakness in what he brought was no disadvantage. But these are not the qualities to stress here. The distinction that Frost brought to Georgianism, the moral and emotional stimulus he gave to a poet like Edward Thomas (we think of poems of Thomas such as 'Bob's Lane') were due to a positive, attractive quality in his way of writing, a quality that distinguishes him not only from the Georgians but from almost any English poet since Chaucer. For this quality of feeling there is no satisfactory name. If, in default of better, we have to fall back on 'democracy', it must be in the full recognition that this word has little descriptive meaning, has become vapid; it belongs to political rhetoric, and – what in the present context is much worse – it suggests a backslapping *faux-bonhomme*, pretending friendliness which is utterly alien to the spirit of Frost's best work. And if we substitute 'fellow-feeling', it must again be without any suggestion of the easy gush of egalitarian emotion. There is, it is true, a trace of friendliness in some of Frost's invitations to his reader ('I shan't be gone long. – You come too'). But his manner of warm geniality frequently covers something much colder. No one can suppose that the fellow-feeling which is the subject of the poet or 'Snow' (in *Mountain Interval*) or 'The Axe-Helve' in *New Hampshire*) is a feeling which springs easily into the hearts of the hard, sometimes curmudgeonly, caste-conscious people Frost is writing about. No one can doubt that for Frost himself the impulse to 'let go' emotionally is not one that is easily yielded to, or that there is much of his own voice in the speaker of 'Wild Grapes':

> I had not learned to let go with the hands,
> As still I have not learned to with the heart,
> And have no wish to with the heart – nor need,
> That I can see. The mind is not the heart.
> I may yet live, as I know others live,
> To wish in vain to let go with the mind –
> Of cares, at night, to sleep; but nothing tells me
> That I need learn to let go with the heart.

Yet the capacity to express fellow-feeling with a deep and complete sincerity seems truly typical of Frost; and to describe it adequately is to give full weight to the importance for criticism of Frost's being an American.

There is, of course, a danger here of over-simplification. We must not sentimentalise away the realities of caste- or class-consciousness in American life, either in the present or the recent past. The recognition of them is obvious in Frost's poetry itself, and has clearly played an important part in his perception of his subject-matter. The situation in 'A Hundred Collars', when a professor has to share a room for the night with a travelling salesman, is just as uncomfortable as if they had been Englishmen. But it is uncomfortable in a different way; and to decide just what the difference is, is to bring out something essential in Frost's poetry. The difference is in the poet's attitude. We may imagine the situation treated by a liberal English writer of Frost's generation, like E. M. Forster. The vein might well be lightly ironical; the English writer, in the person of the professor, would have been ashamed of himself, would have known what he ought to feel, and would have done his best to feel it. Frost's attitude also includes an element of irony. But whereas the English writer would know what the professor felt, but would have to guess at what the salesman felt, Frost knows both. That is the difference. The conditions of American society and American life here give the American writer an advantage over his English counterpart.

Such an observation, however, could be made about a novelist or short-story-writer. In speaking of a poet we should be more closely concerned with technical considerations. What Frost brought home to some English poets in the early twentieth century was the truth in the famous description of a poet as a man speaking to men. The phrase is Wordsworth's; and the point in question may be brought home by suggesting the advantage Frost enjoys over Wordsworth in this capacity. Here are two passages from the earlier poet:

> 'Oh saints! what is become of him?
> Perhaps he's climbed into an oak,
> Where he will stay till he is dead;

> Or sadly he has been misled,
> And joined the wandering gipsy-folk.'
>
> ('The Idiot Boy')

>   . . .Once again I see
> These hedge-rows, hardly hedge-rows, little lines
> Of sportive wood run wild; these pastoral farms
> Green to the very door; and wreaths of smoke
> Sent up, in silence, from among the trees,
> With some uncertain notice, it might seem,
> Of vagrant dwellers in the houseless woods.
>
> ('Tintern Abbey')

Wordsworth, it is often said, has two voices, and lovers of his poetry will recognise them in these two passages, and recognise also an underlying harmony between them; but the immediate effect of the comparison is to show how 'unnatural' is the voice of the speaker in 'The Idiot Boy' passage, how little flavour or savour has been given to the speech of the old woman; in contrast, the 'literary' voice of the second passage is the 'natural' one. Frost's comparable 'two voices' have a much happier affinity:

> Mind you, I waited till Len said the word.
> I didn't want the blame if things went wrong.
> I was glad though, no end, when we moved out,
> And I looked to be happy, and I was,
> As I said, for a while – but I don't know!

> Somehow the change wore out like a prescription.
> And there's more to it than just window-views
> And living by a lake. I'm past such help –
> Unless Len took the notion, which he won't,
> And I won't ask him – it's not sure enough.
> I s'pose I've got to go the road I'm going:
> Other folks have to, and why shouldn't I?
>
> ('A Servant to Servants')

> There is a singer everyone has heard,
> Loud, a mid-summer and a mid-wood bird,
> Who makes the solid tree trunks sound again. . .

He says the highway dust is over all.
The bird would cease and be as other birds
But that he knows in singing not to sing.
The question that he frames in all but words
Is what to make of a diminished thing.

('The Oven Bird')

Here both voices, the poet's own, and that of someone very
different from himself in education and culture, seem equally
'natural'. The critical inference from this comparison of Frost
and Wordsworth might be generalised in a discussion of their
treatment of a common interest, 'humble and rustic life'. Wordsworth conveys the impression that he found 'speaking to men'
difficult – speaking to uneducated men belonging to a world and
a mode of life that he feels as external to him; and they find it
difficult to speak to him: as like as not they call him 'Sir'. In this
respect Wordsworth is typical of English poets belonging to the
central literary tradition, over several centuries; it is when they
have most sought to avoid the note of 'Yonder peasant, who is
he?' that they have most fallen into a stiff uneasiness which is
the forerunner of insincerity. The New England poet has no
such difficulty. But to suppose that this superiority just 'came
naturally' to him – the unearned advantage of an American
poet – is to forget the history of American poetry, and to forget
that Frost is above all an artist. It was the artist in Frost, not the
common man (whose notion of poetry may be a very banal and
'literary' one) which made him recognise that to *express* the
common man he must use words and rhythms very differently
from Longfellow or Whittier.

II

But when we have granted the value of Frost's technical innovation, have we said anything more than that he achieved a
style which (in Auden's words) is 'quiet and sensible'? Whether
one agrees with Winters's essay or not, it is surely its virtue to
insist that criticism – as distinct from 'appreciation' – *begins*
here. Frost may have developed an all-purpose style which he
could go on using for the rest of his life, and which other poets

could learn from – English as well as American poets: for if some present-day English poetry (as is often said) has gone back to Georgianism, it is a Georgianism which has learned the lesson of Frost, unpretentiousness, plainness, lightness; that 'pinch of salt', not taking everything seriously that is said solemnly, which William James is said to have brought back into philosophy, Frost brought back into poetry. But what is to be *done* with that style? And what did Frost himself do with it?

In considering the last question, an English critic's disadvantages are obvious. He has to consider Frost's New England, Frost's America, purely as a country of the mind. And he has to remember the warning conveyed by the answer a Frenchman gave when Matthew Arnold asked why the French thought Lamartine a great poet: 'He is a great poet *for us*.' But there may be one or two compensating advantages. The American critic appraising Frost is in danger of other disturbances of judgment, as examples have shown. He cannot but be concerned with politics in the widest sense of that word. It is his critical duty, for example, to consider whether or not Frost has been rated beyond his merits as a poet because of an idealisation of the older, rural America for which his work, and his supposed personal qualities, have been used as a sanction and a symbol. And it is his duty to consider how far Frost's work really does warrant this use. He must consider the issue, mentioned by Alvarez, of 'cosmopolitanism' against 'rootedness'; he must consider what conclusions for American criticism and American literature should be drawn from the fact – if it is a fact – that, as an American poet, Frost is the antithesis of Pound. Such questions can arouse heat and passion, as a distinguished New York critic found at the cost of much uproar. An English critic can pass them by.

The question he cannot avoid is whether Frost has ever written a really considerable poem. This is not very different from the question whether he is a great poet; but a critic might be discouraged from asking that question, partly no doubt because of the vagueness of the category, but in the main because of Eliot's authoritative insistence, over the years, on the relative unimportance of surmises about 'greatness' in comparison with considerations of 'goodness' or 'genuineness'. Yet it seems a reasonable condition even of the good and genuine poet that he shall have a poem to offer us. The search for it surely takes precedence over the historical inquiry (in itself of some interest) how the 'Georgian' poet of 1914 developed into the candidate for the status of American national poet – vacant since Whitman – which was urged for him when it began to be felt that Carl Sandburg somehow would not do. No amount of national appeal, country charm, regional flavour, or anecdotal personality can be a substitute for a poem; it is only in the world of the higher publicity and literary fashions that 'poems', 'poetry', a general poetical atmosphere, appear to compensate for the absence of a 'Sailing to Byzantium', a 'Cimetière Marin', a *Four Quartets*.

But it may be objected that Frost is not the kind of poet who invites description in terms of single masterpieces: that his claim to distinction is the impressive level maintained in a large body of work. In that case the question may be put in a different form, while remaining in essence much the same: what has he to say? What is the substance of his poetic achievement? And when we turn our attention to that question the frequent embarrassment of Frost's commentators is ominous. Something has gone wrong when we find an intelligent critic writing like this – his text being the poem 'Design', of which he is analysing the first line ('I found a dimpled spider, fat and white'):

At first we hear the cheerfully observant walker on back-country roads: 'I found a dimpled...' The iambic lilt adds a tone of pleasant surprise: 'I found a dimpled darling –' 'Little Miss Muffet sat on a tuffet!' But in 'spider' the voice betrays itself, and in 'fat' and 'white' the dimpled creature appears less charming. On a small scale the first line, like the whole poem, builds up a joke in tone, rhythm, and image that grows into a 'joke' of another sort.

Anyone holding an academic post must feel sympathy with this critic. But what is troubling, as we explore their commentaries, is the thinness which he and other writers on Frost seem to sense in their subject-matter, and their apparent need to import some density into it by paraphrasing Frost's thought and consider- ing Emerson, Thoreau, and a cultural tradition and habit of sensibility deriving from them. Of course this embarrassment of the commentators may reflect no more than the unsuitability of modern critical techniques, influenced by modern poetic fashions, to get hold of so traditional and unfashionable a poet. The kind of ironies, ambiguities, or 'polysemy' to which those techniques are adapted – and which indeed, in some poets of academic provenance, they may have actually inspired – are not there. Nor is Frost the kind of poet congenial to erudite exegetes; he has not constructed an esoteric world system, or a scheme of private allusions; there is no code to be broken. To be an adequate critic, it would seem, all you need is a heart and feelings and a capacity for independent thoughts about your life and your world; ingenuity and tenacious industry are not only not enough, they are irrelevant and distracting. Hence the plight of the commentator. But to take this line is to come dangerously near the position of those admirers who have institutionalised our poet, removed him from the talons of criticism, by insisting (in effect) that the scope of his achievement is no more open to rational discussion than the goodness of maple syrup. This kind of protectiveness really insults him. Frost's work may well require a different critical approach or procedure from that appropriate to discussion of Yeats's, Eliot's, or Valéry's; but the same final considerations of value, substance, and interest are as relevant in appraising it as to theirs.

If we do find a certain thinness in Frost's poetry, it is not because he has omitted to bolster it up with anything equivalent to Yeats's *A Vision* or Eliot's arcane allusiveness. Once again a comparison with the earlier poet, Wordsworth, seems in order; but this time the comparison is not to Frost's advantage. Frost has left us no poem of the quality of *Resolution and Independence*, a particular vision of man's life with its natural setting and tragic destiny. To avoid the charge of unfairness, we should at once turn to a poem of Frost which may come to mind as a counter-example, 'The Death of the Hired Man'. This is one of Frost's best-known and finest poems, and no better illustration could be given of the poignancy he can achieve in spare allusive dialogue. Yet something forbids us to call 'The Death of the Hired Man' great poetry, and what this is may come out when

we place it beside Wordsworth's 'Michael'. What strikes the
reader of Frost's poem in comparison with Wordsworth's is the
absence of something. There is nothing in it corresponding to the
poetic intensity with which Wordsworth invests the Dalesman's
feeling about his ownership of his bit of land, a man's elementary
desire to have something to hand on to his children. This inner
lack may be pointed out locally, when we consider those passages
of 'The Death of the Hired Man' in which we are most aware
that we are reading poetry:

> Part of a moon was falling down the west,
> Dragging the whole sky with it to the hills.
> Its light poured softly in her lap. She saw it
> And spread her apron to it. She put out her hand
> Among the harp-like morning-glory strings,
> Taut with the dew from garden bed to eaves,
> As if she played unheard some tenderness
> That wrought on him beside her in the night.
> 'Warren,' she said, 'he has come home to die:
> You needn't be afraid he'll leave you this time.'
> 'Home,' he mocked gently.
>   'Yes, what else but home?
> It all depends on what you mean by home.
> Of course he's nothing to us, any more
> Than was the hound that came a stranger to us
> Out of the woods, worn out upon the trail.'
> 'Home is the place where, when you have to go there,
> They have to take you in.'
>   'I should have called it
> Something you somehow haven't to deserve.'

This is the emotional centre of the poem, what the poem is 'about'.
But, moving and tender as it is, the effect of the 'background'
passage about the moonlight is curiously extraneous. Indeed, the
pathos of what is said in the poem about the life and death of
Silas depends largely on the *absence* from the dialogue of anything like this capacity to give a universal representation of
human sympathy; Frost's art, that is, is more akin to that of
the short-story-writer than the poet. The passages about the
moon seem something added to the story to make it poetry.

Wordsworth contemplates the mode of life of the Dalesman with the same poetic vision as he does the mountain landscape:

Among the rocks
He went, and still looked up to sun and cloud,
And listened to the wind; and, as before,
Performed all kinds of labour for his sheep,
And for the land, his small inheritance.

The significant difference between the poems – the difference in spiritual value – lies in the pastoral quality with which Wordsworth invests his simple story. He uses pastoral – normally a mode of irony for Frost – with complete seriousness; and the result is that generalising effect which we look for in poetry of the highest order. By including this pastoral element Wordsworth has got further away from his characters than Frost; but he has also given a greater universality to his theme.

Similar judgments might emerge from considering other poems in which Frost's art is that of the anecdote, sketch, or dramatic monologue. Pound has praised such work discerningly when he says: 'Frost has been honestly fond of the New England people, I dare say with spells of irritation. He has given their life honestly and seriously. He has never turned aside to make fun of it. He has taken their tragedy as tragedy, their stubbornness as stubbornness. I know more of farm life than I did before I had read his poems. That means I know more of "Life".' But in the same review (in *Poetry* for December 1914) he is clearly implying a limitation when he says: 'Mr. Frost's people are distinctly real. Their speech is real; he has known them. *I don't much want to meet them* [my italics], but I know that they exist, and what is more, that they exist as he has portrayed them.' The point of this observation is not that Frost's characters are sometimes simplified figures, done from the outside, for whom 'The Figure in the Doorway', glimpsed from a passing train might serve as an epitome; as Pound suggests, they are often done more inwardly. But even when they are done inwardly, they are not related to anything greater than themselves. Sympathy and understanding are surely not enough for a great poet; there must also be this suggestion of the larger perspective, the wider and finer mind. Frost's art is the antithesis of that practised by

Samuel Johnson in his poem on Levet, the man 'obscurely wise and coarsely kind'. Johnson, without losing sympathy, speaks with the voice of a highly literate culture on such a man; Frost, in refusing the responsibility of such a judgment, incurs corresponding disadvantages. We sometimes feel that he assumes his task to be complete when he has given a faithful record of particulars; an assumption which admirers of William Carlos Williams may approve, but which is one reason why English readers have found that poet's American reputation inexplicable.

The characteristic difficulty readers have with Frost is not 'What does he mean?' but 'What is the *point* of it?' Why has he chosen to crystallise *this* perception, rather than countless others? This kind of difficulty, it will be remembered, presented itself strongly – perhaps it still does – to Wordsworth's readers. But Wordsworth's little anecdotes, even if they do not always carry the charge of significance Wordsworth himself found in them, can be better understood in the context of Wordsworth's whole work – in the poems (by far the greater number) in which the poet speaks directly, not dramatically, sets out to communicate explicitly his thought or 'message'. Now Frost too speaks directly in the greater part of his poetry. And it will hardly be disputed that the quintessence of his work – his rarest and finest achievement – lies in the lyrical–reflective pieces in which he speaks with his own personal voice. But it is in that 'personal' work also that we are most conscious, not only of limitations, but of weakness.

His principal weakness – the one that makes for the most doubt about his claim to high poetic rank – is monotony. This may be attributed in part to the very nature of his gift. What is represented by *North of Boston*, the achievement praised so warmly by Thomas and Pound, is of a kind that could be represented in comparatively few poems. How much of Frost's whole corpus (we cannot help asking) do we really need? His work calls out for anthologizing, as Wordsworth's, I think, does not. No one will doubt that Wordsworth wrote a great many mediocre poems, or worse, but we have to have *The Prelude,* and much else, before we can form a fair estimate of him. Frost's distinction seems only notably present in a few poems. His average – to speak bluntly – is rather dull. Johnson observes of Dryden that 'he that writes much cannot escape a manner'; but 'Dryden is always *another and the same*'. This could hardly be said of Frost, at least of the later volumes.

For there are dangerous temptations in a colloquial style, and Frost has often succumbed to them. The chief danger is self-indulgence. So far from making an effort to 'escape a manner', he rather cultivates it. Old age can be the extenuation of much of the writing in *Steeple Bush*, where he seems at times to be maundering. But the same tendency can be observed in earlier work; Frost, like Hardy, seems to be a poet who, once he had formed his manner, stuck to it: there is no such technical (or personal) development as we find in a Rilke or an Eliot or a Yeats. This is both his strength and his weakness. He has achieved a continuous literary personality in a sense in which Pound, for example, seems not to have done: on the other hand, he does not appear to have experienced very strongly the need to check himself at the point when manner becomes mannerism (though, to be fair, it would seem that, considering his long life and not very large output, he did a good deal of tearing up).

In Frost's least satisfactory work, all that we tend to remember is the manner. 'Build Soil', the 'political pastoral', is a case in point. No poet deserves to be judged on the basis of his political ideas in a narrow sense. And 'Build Soil' itself shows that Frost is well aware of the warning conveyed in the words of Yeats: 'We have no gift to set a statesman right.' But as he adopts it in this poem the ironical plain-man manner comes to sound like a form of conceit. Frost has no 'public' voice; so that when, as is apparently the case, he is recommending unrestricted *laissez-faire* (in 1932, a singularly inopportune moment one would think) it sounds like an attempt to elevate personal selfishness into a lofty principle. Undoubtedly the basis of this attitude is that passion for personal freedom, that need to feel self-sufficient, which permeates Frost's best work. But the manner of this poem makes it seem unattractive and smug. Less injurious, perhaps, is the playful manner of Frost's excursions into 'astrometaphysics', though one understands the irritation of Malcolm Cowley at the 'cracker-barrel-in-the-clouds' effect of much of this writing.

Frost's 'metaphysics', it is true, are saved by the playfulness from sounding quite so hollow as those portentous reverberations, in cadences reminiscent of the later Eliot, which we hear in Wallace Stevens's philosophical poetry. His paraphraseable content is less empty; the poetry is less pretentious. But unless we find Frost's manner so congenial that we are critically disarmed, we must be tempted to ask why, if the poet himself (apparently) cannot take his ideas seriously, anyone else should be expected to do so.

A worse incongruity results when Frost brings the same manner into the field of tragic experience. In things like 'A Masque of Reason' he is plainly out of his depth. The manner of that 'masque', contriving as it does to be both smart and naive, would be an affront if we were to bring it seriously into comparison with the tragic poetry of the Book of Job. No doubt in its characteristic weakness, as in the weakness of some of Frost's political poetry, we may see that tendency to blur the edges of Job's terrible problem in an optimistic transcendentalism where 'evil tendencies cancel', and the waywardness, uncanniness, and utter incomprehensibility of the universe become somehow tokens of ultimate good. But optimism and reassurance are not qualities of Frost's deepest genius, which rests upon something hard and cold. Although a generalised geniality and a weak whimsicality are unfortunately common in Frost's work, they do not represent its strength. When he is a poet he is not genial: his true power, his peculiar sensitiveness, is closely bound up with those landscapes in which the season is always late autumn or winter, with flurries of snow, and a feeling of loneliness and danger impending; when a stranger is not a potential friend, but an object of suspicion. In his quasi-homiletic poetry Frost seems to be offering some vague theological equivalent of a friendliness and cosmic optimism which are antipathetic to his own creative powers.

III

But it is time now to draw to a conclusion about Frost's real strength, his personal poetry. This is not to be found in the most characteristic part of that poetry: the pithy observations, the wry gnarled apophthegms, engaging and quotable as many of them are; but in more elusive poems, where the personality, or *persona*, of the poet is not strongly felt at all; where what we are given is the *aperçu*, the glimpse, the perception crystallised, where the poet seems to be beside the reader, sharing his vision, not gesturing in front. In such poems Frost has affinities with Hardy, the Hardy of poems like 'The Wound':

> I climbed to the crest
> And, fog-festooned,
> The sun lay west
> Like a crimson wound:
>
> Like that wound of mine
> Of which none knew,
> For I'd given no sign
> That it pierced me through.

We may compare Frost's 'Dust of Snow':

> The way a crow
> Shook down on me
> The dust of snow
> From a hemlock tree
>
> Has given my heart
> A change of mood
> And saved some part
> Of a day I had rued.

In the nature of the case such poems are delicate achievements, and it must be a matter of critical controversy whether some of them succeed or fail. 'The Lockless Door', for example, seems to me to fail. These are the closing lines:

> Back over the sill
> I bade a 'Come-in'
> To whatever the knock
> At the door may have been.

So at a knock
I emptied my cage
To hide in the world
And alter with age.

The reader is asked to do too much; to keep pondering over a poem so slight and so imperfectly formulated until he has convinced himself of a significance which the poet may or may not have put there. On the other hand, 'Gathering Leaves' seems perfect. (Its method may be usefully contrasted with the beautiful earlier poem 'The Quest of the Purple-Fringed'.) That the tone of voice is utterly unpretentious, the rhythm light, even gay, far from detracting from the essential poignancy, actually increases it.

I make a great noise,
Of rustling all day,
Like rabbit and deer
Running away.

But the mountains I raise
Elude my embrace,
Flowing over my arms
And into my face.

The subject of the whole poem is the same as that of Tennyson's 'Tears, idle tears', but how much Frost gains from not *saying* anything like 'O Death in Life, the days that are no more.' Doing without sonority, doing without any play for a full-volumed response, Frost makes us live through (as we imaginatively participate in the simple actions he describes) the paradox of memory, real and unreal, intangible but substantial.

The obvious way of describing 'Gathering Leaves' is to say that it is symbolic. But this suggests another observation about Frost's poetic gift. Too many poets seem to imagine that they have made a thing symbolic by saying so – sometimes in so many words. They expect us to read profound meanings into what they have created, without having created anything. Here Frost's strength is apparent. He can make real to us, as freshly felt, objects, places, processes. His snow is truly cold, his hills barren, his woods impenetrably deep. This solidity, due to the poet's power to convince us that his image or fancy is based on a true and strong perception of a real world outside him, is felt even when, in a poem like 'Sand Dunes', the explicit topic is the human mind or spirit's independence of nature.

> Sea waves are green and wet,
> But up from where they die,
> Rise others vaster yet,
> And these are brown and dry.
>
> They are the sea made land,
> To come at the fisher town,
> And bury in solid sand
> The men she could not drown.

The reality of these dunes convinces us of their priority to the thought they suggest to the poet, and so seem to give an anticipatory guarantee of its firmness.

A preoccupation of these short poems is human transience, the poet's deep sense of flux and movement, and the brevity of 'the span of life'. For this immemorial subject of lyrical poetry Frost finds a note that is peculiarly his own. His strength here, as is customary with him, lies not in any very original formulation, or piece of consecutive thought or argument – the metaphysical passages in the title poem of *West-Running Brook* are not particularly convincing – but in the transmission of a sense of transience as a process which is at one and the same time experienced, lived through, and steadily contemplated. The emotional tone of this contemplation, as often in Frost, has to be described by remarking on an element that is missing. There is no wistfulness. Here Frost differs most strikingly from Edward Thomas:

> . . .When I turn away, on its fine stalk
> Twilight has fined to naught, the parsley flower
> Figures, suspended still and ghostly white,
> The past hovering as it revisits the light.

These lines of Thomas touch upon a recurrent preoccupation of Frost, but Frost's touch is different. Poems like 'The Sound of the

Trees' or 'The Road not Taken', beautiful as they are, are untypical; indeed, we are told that the latter poem is a deliberate exercise in Thomas's manner, and is as such a gentle rebuke to his friend's indecisiveness. Frost avoids the note of nostalgia about the past of an individual, as he does about the historic past; nothing strikes an English reader more in his poetry than his bedrock commonsense assumption that each generation starts from scratch, has to *make* its relationship with its environment. To say that Frost avoids nostalgia is not to say that his poetry lacks the note of longing. But it seems to have more affinity with what we find in Wallace Stevens's poetry. This poet of grey lives and grey landscapes suffers from 'the malady of the quotidian', is hungry for colour, radiance, everything that is unexpected, brilliant, spectacular.

> 'Oh, that's the Paradise-in-bloom,' I said:
> And truly it was fair enough for flowers
> Had we but in us to assume in March
> Such white luxuriance of May for ours.
>
> We stood a moment so in a strange world,
> Myself as one his own pretense deceives. . .
> ('A Boundless Moment')

The Frost of 'A Boundless Moment' is solicited by the same longing as the Stevens of 'Some Friends from Pascagoula', surely one of Stevens's finest poems:

> Tell me again of the point
> At which the flight began,
>
> Say how his heavy wings,
> Spread on the sun-bronzed air,
> Turned tip and tip away,
> Down to the sand, the glare
>
> Of the pine-trees edging the sand
> Dropping in sovereign rings
> Out of his fiery lair.
> Speak of the dazzling wings.

In 'The Middleness of the Road' Frost might seem to be replying to this sort of appeal; but his sober recall to the prose of life is qualified by his characteristic 'almost':

> But say what Fancy will,
>
> The mineral drops that explode
> To drive my ton of car
> Are limited to the road.
> They deal with the near and far,
>
> And have almost nothing to do
> With the absolute flight and rest
> The universal blue
> And local green suggest.

But most typical of Frost's finest work is 'Neither Out Far Nor In Deep'. This is the whole poem:

> The people along the sand
> All turn and look one way.
> They turn their back on the land.
> They look at the sea all day.
>
> As long as it takes to pass
> A ship keeps raising its hull;
> The wetter ground like glass
> Reflects a standing gull.
>
> The land may vary more;
> But wherever the truth may be –
> The water comes ashore,
> And the people look at the sea.
>
> They cannot look out far,
> They cannot look in deep.
> But when was that ever a bar
> To any watch they keep?

The poem represents in metaphorical form men's constant awareness that they must die; and it does this without appealing to pity or horror or any mode of evasion: we are invited to contemplate the fact within the metaphor quite steadily. Yet there is an emotional tone, however hard to describe; the 'they' of the poem are 'we' and 'I'; this fellow-feeling prevents the poem from sounding dry or abstract, or gnomic in the manner of Emerson. Poems like these are perhaps marginal in Frost's work; marginal perhaps in comparison with other poets' more ambitious statements. They offer no easy comfort, are never likely to be popular; they are as remote as they could be from the whimsical or crusty *persona* of the farmer–poet. Yet it seems to me that in their combination of apparent slightness with extraordinary depth Frost achieves something highly distinctive, and indeed unique.

10

Hopkins and Literary Criticism

There is a view, which goes back at least as far as Seneca, that poets are the best critics of poetry. And at one time T. S. Eliot seems to have held that poets are not only the best, but the *only* critics of poetry. It will be agreed that poets – creative artists generally – have things of the highest value to say, and things that only poets *can* say. We need not uncharitably recall the saying of Blake: 'The poison of the honey-bee / Is the artist's jealousy.' The insights of innovating poets into what they are trying to do – or not to do – have the highest value. But literature as a whole does not belong to any one writer, or group of writers, any more than to one critic or philosopher, or one school of thought. There is an ancient saying which James Joyce was fond of quoting: *securus iudicat orbis terrarum.* Literature belongs to all its lovers and appreciators, whoever and wherever they are.

Fortunately creative writers are not always narrow and partial critics of literature. Some of them have been men of great breadth of mind and sensitivity of reaction to the work of others: men like Dryden, Goethe, Baudelaire, Henry James, or Proust. It is into this company that I wish to introduce the name of Hopkins. But in some ways he cuts a strange figure beside them. Hopkins did not in the ordinary sense publish any literary criticism, or indeed any other kind of writing. His critical views have to be extracted from his letters, and this is a barbarous thing to do. They are real letters, meant only for one pair of eyes to read. And they are themselves a classic of English literature, rightly compared with the letters of Keats. The letters of Hopkins bring him into the room with us; humorous or poignant, affecting and natural, they draw us perhaps closer than the poems do to the 'wayfaring Christian' who wrote them. It is unpleasant to snip them up for so restricted a purpose. And there is another difficulty in grouping Hopkins with the poet–critics. His valuation of the art of poetry differed from theirs. 'When we met in London', he wrote to Robert Bridges on

19 January 1879, 'we never but once, and then only for a few minutes before parting, spoke on any important subject, but always on literature.' This remark shocks Professor Abbott, the editor of Hopkins's letters. He hopes it means 'we spoke superficially about the books of others rather than about ourselves'. Otherwise, he adds, 'the words are ominous'. Now it is important to remember the context of Hopkins's words. He was a priest talking about the salvation of a dear friend's soul. He tells Bridges: 'You understand of course that I desire to see you a Catholic or, if not that, a Christian or, if not that, at least a believer in the true God (for you told me something of your views about the deity, which were not as they should be).' All the same, Hopkins's way of referring to literature is representative of his general attitude. Here he is at the extreme opposite to Keats, who wanted to be nothing but a poet. Hopkins, as is well known, was in doubt whether he should be a poet at all. He had another calling, and (despite the protest of his friend Dixon) he came to think it not only higher than the calling of poet, but dubiously compatible with it.

Yet, apart from this question of rival vocations, it should not be too difficult to understand Hopkins's attitude. It may help us to go back a century before him, and consider the case of Samuel Johnson. Johnson, unlike Hopkins, may be said to have devoted his life to literature. But would he not have agreed with Hopkins that literature was not, in Hopkins's sense, an important subject? And there is another consideration to ponder. It may be that, as with Johnson, Hopkins's relegation of literature left him in a way freer to see it *as* literature than if he had followed the greatest critic of his time, Matthew Arnold, in seeing it as something that in due time would (and, as Arnold advocated, *should*) replace religion. Can it be that Hopkins's attitude to literature can actually help us more than Arnold's to achieve Arnold's declared aim of seeing 'the object as in itself it really is'? At any rate, my feeling that this may be so is my excuse for snipping up his letters.

Much of Hopkins's criticism is very narrow in scope, consisting of technical comments on the work of his poet friends (Bridges, Dixon, Patmore). How 'practical', in the more obvious sense, this criticism is appears in a letter to Bridges of 1 February 1882. Bridges had written for his Poems of 1880 a song containing these lines:

> Thou didst delight my eyes:
> Yet who am I? nor best
> Nor first nor last to test
> Thy charm, thy bloom to prize.

Hopkins saw that this would not do. 'Could you not get rid of *test* in "Thou didst delight"? Look here: rhyme on *first* and *durst* and you will get something very good. I dare not tell you my thought, for it wd. be to defeat my own purpose, but do it yourself, simple, suitable, and sweet.' And Bridges duly improved the lines to:

> Thou didst delight my eyes:
> Yet who am I? nor first
> Nor last nor best, that durst
> Once dream of thee for prize.

Then from time to time Hopkins comments on his own poems, as in this note on 'In the Valley of the Elwy': 'The frame of the sonnet is a rule of three sum *wrong*, thus: As the sweet smell to those kind people so the Welsh landscape is NOT to the Welsh; and then the author and principle of all four terms is asked to bring the sum right.' Bridges was able to use some of these explanations in his edition of Hopkins's poems. There is a recurrent controversy about poets writing notes to their own poetry. Wordsworth and Eliot were ridiculed for this – though I do not know of any complaints about William Empson or Marianne Moore. So it is interesting to discover from the letters that Hopkins thought it permissible, and perhaps desirable, for the author of lyric poems to include explanatory notes along with them – as it would not be for the author of dramas, or other forms of literature. The theoretical justification for this may lie in a generic difference between lyric poems and other literary forms. The composer of lyric poetry has more difficulty than a writer in other forms in establishing a context of utterance. Notes can help, not so much by 'explaining', as by putting the reader, so to speak, at the proper angle to the poem. At any rate, Hopkins's own notes are always helpful, and it is only to be regretted that he has not given us more of them.

This 'practical' criticism in Hopkins's letters also includes explanations of his theories of metre and diction, all the better because they are so informal and 'off the cuff'. It is to the letters that we shall turn in trying to understand what he means by 'sprung rhythm' – the use of counterpoint to the extreme of destroying the conventionally fixed metrical scheme; or his views on the survival of the Anglo-Saxon alliterative element in English verse; or the relationship between sound and meaning in poetry. With his aesthetic–technical cast of mind, there is no doubt that Hopkins could have been a very distinguished practitioner of 'practical criticism' in that broader sense of the term to which we have become accustomed since I. A. Richards used it as the title for his famous book. It has been much disputed whether Hopkins was a 'Victorian' or a 'modern' poet. However that may be, it seems clear that as a critic of poetry he is much nearer than any Victorian to the critics of the twentieth century.

But Hopkins's comments on poetry and poets often go beyond these technical observations. Amidst all his other pressing responsibilities, he kept a shrewd if intermittent eye on the contemporary literary scene. 'From notices in the *Athenaeum*', he says in passing, 'it would appear that Gosse, Dobson, and Co. are still fumbling with triolets, villanelles, and what not.' (To Bridges, 2 April 1878.) And his remarks on his greater Victorian contemporaries have an interest over and above the light they throw on his own poetic aims. What he says of Swinburne, for example, could be decanted into a whole critique of the Victorian poet who, with Browning, is almost his rival in strangeness. The piquant vivacity of his judgments on Swinburne suggests the involvement of his own subjectivity. The following comments occur in successive letters to Bridges.

...arrangements in vowel sounds, as Mallock says, very thinly costuming a strain of conventional passion, kept up by stimulants, and crying always in a high head voice about flesh and flowers and democracy and damnation.   (22 February 1879)

It is in the Swinburnian kind, is it not? I do not think that kind goes far: it expresses passion but not feeling, much less character... Swinburne's genius is astonishing, but it will, I think, only do one thing.   (22 April 1879)

Swinburn[e], perhaps you know, has also tried his hand – without success. Either in fact he does not see nature at all or else he overlays the landscape with such phantasmata, secondary images, and what not of a delirium-tremendous imagination that the result is a kind of bloody broth: you know what I mean. At any rate there is no picture.
                                                    (1 January 1885)

Swinburne has a new volume out, which is reviewed in its own style: 'The rush and the rampage, the pause and the pull-up of these lustrous and lumpophorus lines.' It is all now a 'self-drawing web'; a perpetual functioning of genius without truth, feeling, or any adequate matter to be at function on. There is some heavydom, in long waterlogged lines (he has no real understanding of rhythm, and though he sometimes hits brilliantly at other times he misses badly) about the *Armada*, that pitfall of the patriotic muse; and *rot* about babies, a blethery bathos into which Hugo and he from opposite coasts have long driven Channel-tunnels. I am afraid I am going too far with the poor fellow. Enough now, but his babies make a Herodian of me.   (29 April 1889)

Hopkins's good points casually thrown off, his impromptu felicities of description, are the kind of thing we expect in the correspondence of gifted poets. Everywhere we find memorable phrases, such as his remark about Wordsworth's sonnets: '...beautiful as those are they have an odious goodiness and neckcloth about them which half throttles their beauty'. But in the critical writings of some poets – Robert Graves may be an example – the good points seem incidental, they do not 'add up'. We feel that Hopkins's insights hang together, that he could have written a sustained critical essay, which Graves has never done. This sense of a coherent position in the background pervades his *obiter dicta*. Remarks like this on Milton: 'Milton is the great master of sequence of phrase. By sequence of feeling I mean a dramatic quality by which what goes before seems to necessitate and beget what comes after, at least after you have heard it it does' (to Dixon, 13 June 1878) or this on Burns: 'Between a fineness of nature which wd. put him in the first rank of writers and a poverty of language which puts him in the lowest rank of poets, he takes to my mind, when all is balanced and cast up, about a middle place' (to Bridges, 22 October 1879) – such remarks suggest rich possibilities of development.

But, interesting as an anthology of such things would be, I find even more impressive what Hopkins has to offer in the treatment of general critical questions. A topic to which – as we should expect – he often reverts is *originality*. 'People cannot, or they will not', he told Dixon, 'take in anything however plain that departs from what they have been taught and brought up to expect: I know it from experience.' He censures an Elegy of Bridges' as

unequal, because, as I told you and I now maintain my past judgment, there are two lines in it echoing Gray's. . .They are not at all the best lines and they can be easily changed and yet they echo lines which are held to be of faultless and canonical beauty. The subject and measure shd. of themselves have put you on your guard. Gray's poem may be outdone but, if you understand, it cannot be equalled.
(22 February 1879)

The sense of his own originality, and the demand which genuine originality makes on the critic, gives force to his memorable appeal to Bridges to open his mind to 'The Wreck of the Deutschland'.

Now they say that vessels sailing from the port of London will take (perhaps it should be/used once to take) Thames water for the voyage: it was foul and stunk at first as the ship worked but by degrees casting its filth was in a few days very pure and sweet and wholesomer and better than any water in the world. However that may be, it is true to my purpose. When a new thing, such as my ventures in the Deutschland are, is presented [to] us our first criticisms are not our truest, best, most homefelt, or most lasting but what come easiest on the instant. They are barbarous and like what the ignorant and the ruck say. This was so with you. The Deutschland on her first run worked very much and unsettled you, thickening and clouding your mind with vulgar mudbottom and common sewage (I see that I am going it with the image) and just then unhappily you *drew off* your criticisms all stinking (a necessity now of the image) and bilgy, whereas if you had let your thoughts cast themselves they would have been clearer in themselves and more to my taste too. I did not heed them therefore, perceiving they were a first drawing-off. Same of the Eurydice – which being short and easy please read more than once.   (21 May 1878)

The topic of originality must have a peculiar and poignant significance for students of the relationship between these two poets. This is a subject about which it is not easy to form a balanced opinion. For many of us, the first naked shock of Hopkins's originality has passed away; we have begun to learn his language, to take him on his own terms. Bridges, as is well known, found it hard to do this; to the end his sympathy was always imperfect. I will say only two things about this human and literary problem. The first is this. We think, understandably, of Bridges as standing for tradition and literary conservatism, whereas Hopkins is the champion of 'all things counter, original, spare, strange'. Yet in their critical disputes we often feel Bridges to be the opinionated, crotchety man and Hopkins in comparison to be humane and central. Over and over again, to use Hopkins's own words, he agrees against Bridges with the mob and the *communis criticorum*. The second point is that, to be just to Bridges, we must extend towards him the breadth of sympathy which many of Hopkins's admirers have held that he denied to Hopkins. For, to be fair to him, Bridges' attitude was not quite that of the expert who sighed exasperatedly over Hopkins's wayward ideas about music.

Indeed my dear Padre I *cannot* follow you through your maze of words in your letter of last week. I saw, ere we had conversed ten minutes on our first meeting, that you are one of those special pleaders who never believe yourself wrong in any respect. You always excuse yourself for anything I object to in your writing of music so I think it a pity to disturb you in your happy dreams of perfectability – nearly everything in your music was wrong – but you will not admit that to be the case – What does it matter? It will all be the same 100 Years hence.

(Sir Robert Stewart to Hopkins, 22 May 1886)

The best defence of Bridges would be on the lines Edward Thompson suggests.

I think it is now generally admitted that in his anxiety to conciliate readers brought up on established verse-forms Bridges was a little too cautious in praise and slightly overstressed what he explicitly admits were only minor features of Hopkins's work, its 'oddity', exaggerated Marianism, and other peculiarities.

But those faults are present, and the resentment of later critics has been unreasonable. All of us know completely conventional persons who are sure that if they had been on the Via Dolorosa on the original Good Friday *they* would at once have recognized what following ages were to learn through the witness of the army of martyrs and by infinitely slow stages. But why need intelligent readers assume that what to us, in the case of Gerard Hopkins, after a quarter of a century of constant discussion is now obvious ought to have been obvious when discussion was just beginning?. . .

The critics who are out of temper with Bridges are generally kind to Patmore, who saw merely confusion in Hopkins's verse, whereas Bridges saw freshness, originality, and imagination. His *Notes* are nothing like as ungenerous as they seem to our full and justified enthusiasm. . .his prefatory sonnet. . .proves that he made no mistake about the latter's quality as compared with 'the chaffinch flock' of poets who caught men's eyes. . .Even after [the] fuller publication [of 1918], the critics' reception was frigid and it took eight years to sell out a first edition of 700 copies. If it had not been for Bridges, no one would ever have heard Hopkins's name and his verse would have stayed unknown for ever.

(Edward Thompson, *Robert Bridges*, 1944, pp. 87ff)

To this I will merely add what Bridges himself says of his manner in criticism. In his study of Keats he says:

If my criticism should seem sometimes harsh, that is, I believe, due to its being given in plain terms, a manner which I prefer, because by obliging the writer to say definitely what he means, it makes his mistakes easy to point out, and in this way the true business of criticism may be advanced; nor do I know that, in work of this sort, criticism has any better function than to discriminate between the faults and merits of the best art.

All this could be said of Hopkins's own criticism: it may be free from acerbity, but it is always incisive.

Another critical matter which has a deep personal significance for Hopkins was the question of *literary fame*. Hopkins is always admirably firm about the public character of works of art. 'What are works of art for? to educate, to be standards. Education is meant for the many, standards are for public use. To produce is of little use unless what we produce is known, if known widely known, the wider known the better, for it is by being known it works, it does its duty, it does good. We must then try to be known, aim at it, take means to it.' He consoles his fellow-poet Dixon for the good Canon's neglect by the critics.

It is sad to think what disappointment must many times over have filled your heart for the darling children of your mind. Nevertheless fame whether won or lost is a thing which lies in the award of a random, reckless, incompetent, and unjust judge, the public, the multitude. The only just judge, the only just literary critic, is Christ, who prizes, is proud of, and admires, more than any man, more than the receiver himself can, the gifts of his own making. And the only real good which fame and another's praise does is to convey to us, by a channel not at all above suspicion but from circumstances in this case much less to be suspected than the channel of our own minds, some token of the judgment which a perfectly just, heedful, and wise mind, namely Christ's, passes upon our doings.   (13 June 1878)

He sees it as a serious issue when good work is neglected.

What I do regret is the loss of recognition belonging to the work itself. For as to every moral act, being right or wrong, there belongs, of the nature of things, reward or punishment, so to every form perceived by the mind belongs, of the nature of things, admiration or the reverse. And the world is full of things and events, phenomena of all sorts, that go without notice, go unwitnessed.   (*ibid.*)

Why then, given his views on the need for good work to be known, did Hopkins himself shrink from any serious effort to make himself known as a poet, and prohibit, with much agitation, Dixon's well-meant effort on his behalf? The nearest to an explanation is this from another letter to Dixon:

Moreover this kind of publication is very unlikely to do the good that you hope and very likely do the harm that I fear. For who ever heard of fame won by publication in a local paper, and of one piece? If everything of its intrinsic goodness gravitated to fame your poems wd. long since have been famous. Were Tennyson, putting aside marks of style by which he might be recognised, to send something to the *Nineteenth Century* or best circulated London magazine *without his name* it wd. be forgotten in a month: now no name and an unknown name is all one. But what is not near enough for public fame may be more than enough for private notoriety, which is what I dread. (31 October 1879)

But Hopkins's letters also discuss critical questions of a more impersonal kind. In an early dialogue on 'The Origin of Beauty' he had already shown himself aware, in the Oxford of Walter Pater, of the 'paradox of taste'. He has a speaker say:

In poetry purely common-sense criticism [is] not enough by itself... Criticism is not advocacy...Judicial, it should be...And judgments depend on laws, on established laws. Now taste has few rules, and those not scientific and easily disputed and, I might add, often disputed...If a man disputes your judgment in taste, how can you prove he is wrong? If a man thinks beautiful what you think bad, you must believe he is sincere when he tells you so; and if he is educated how are you to say that his judgment is worse than yours? In fact *de gustibus non est disputandum*. Criticism therefore in matters of taste cannot be judicial. And purely common-sense criticism is not enough, we agreed. So criticism in matter of taste has no weight at all. (*Journals*, ed. House and Storey, pp. 86–7)

This was not Hopkins's own position. But he was vividly aware of what there was to be said for it. His reaction, in his mature years, was to insist on the importance of *liberality* in the critic. On one occasion Bridges said (unjustly, I think) that the poetry of William Barnes lacked 'fire'. Hopkins agreed: 'I feel the defect or limitation...that offended you: he lacks fire.' But he adds: 'But who is perfect all round? If one defect is fatal what writer could we read?' 'The most inveterate fault of critics', he had just said, 'is the tendency to cramp and hedge in by rules the free movements of genius, so that I should say...The first requisite for a critic is liberality, and the second liberality, and the third, liberality.' In the like spirit Hopkins indicates the proper tone of the critic. 'I disapprove of damfooling people', he told Bridges. 'I think it wrong, narrows the mind, and like a "parvifying glass" makes us see things smaller than the natural size. And I do not like your calling Matthew Arnold Mr. Kidglove Cocksure. I have more reason than you for disagreeing with him and thinking him very wrong, but nevertheless I am sure he is a rare genius and a great critic.' (28 January 1883.) But although Hopkins is well aware of those pitfalls of judicial criticism, he is in no doubt that it is necessary. When he says he has reason for disagreeing with Arnold he may (*pace* Professor Abbott) be thinking of Arnold's views on religion, rather than literary matters. In any case, in matters of literary criticism Hopkins is Arnold's man: he always has at the back of his mind a concern for the best, the classical. Let us now look at some of the instruments he devised for the critic in search of it.

His youthful discernment of a kind of poetry which is *not* classical is well known, and has been influential. He gives a vivid account of his discovery in a letter to Alexander Baillie. 'Do you know, a horrible thing has happened to me. I have begun to *doubt* Tennyson...' And he introduces the term 'Parnassian'.

In Parnassian pieces you feel that if you were the poet you could have gone on as he has done, you see yourself doing it, only with the difference that if you actually try you find you cannot write his Parnassian...I believe that when a poet palls on us it is because of his Parnassian. We seem to have found out his secret...Well, it is notorious that Shakespear does not pall, and this is because he uses, I believe, so little Parnassian. He does use some, but little. Now judging from my own experience I should say no author palls so much as Wordsworth; this is because he writes such an 'intolerable deal of' Parnassian...I think one had got into the way of thinking, or had not got out of the way of thinking, that Tennyson was always new, *touching*, beyond other poets, not pressed with human ailments, never using Parnassian. So at least I used to think. Now one sees he is using Parnassian; he is, one must see it, what we used to call Tennysonian. But the discovery of this must not make too much difference... (10 September 1864)

Some of the other terms Hopkins introduces at the same time as 'Parnassian' have not had so much critical currency, but they are interesting. He speaks of 'a higher sort of poetry' which he calls 'Castalian'. 'Its peculiarity is that though you can hardly conceive yourself having written in it, if in the poet's place, yet it is too characteristic of the poet, too so-and-so-all-over-ish, to be quite inspiration.' Then there is 'Delphic', which is 'merely the language of verse as distinct from that of prose', 'used in common by poet and poetaster'. Finally, there is 'Olympian', which is 'the language of strange masculine genius which suddenly, as it were, forces its way into the domain of poetry, without naturally having a right there'. Although Hopkins gives examples of these different styles – from Wordsworth for the Castalian, from Rossetti and Milman for the Olympian – it may be that his definitions are too vague for the stylistician. But at least they bring home the paucity of the generally accepted stylistic vocabulary which those who discuss poetry today have to use.

In his rejection of *archaism* Hopkins has the moderns with him. Bridges had been praising some prose of Doughty, but Hopkins was sceptical.

You say it is free from the taint of Victorian English. H'm. Is it free from the taint of Elizabethan English? Does it not stink of that? for the sweetest flesh turns to corruption. Is not Elizabethan English a corpse these centuries? No one admires, regrets, despairs over the death of the style, the living masculine native rhetoric of that age, more than I do; but ''tis gone, 'tis gone, 'tis gone'. He writes in it, I understand, because it is manly. At any rate affectation is not manly, and to write in an obsolete style is affectation.   (7 September 1888)

In his poetic practice, as in his theory, Hopkins held that 'the poetical language of an age shd. be the current language heightened, to any degree and unlike itself, but not. . .an obsolete one'. His reason for maintaining this doctrine is that 'any artificial attempt. . .destroys earnest'. 'We do not speak that way; therefore if a man speaks that way he is not serious.' The moderns have agreed with Hopkins. But I wonder if there is not an element of the *a priori* in his position, which conflicts with his general liberality. I wonder also whether it was really archaic diction which was the main cause for the alienation of poetry from the ordinary reader. C. S. Lewis remarks:

Though the modern poet does not, like Pope, use *e'er* and *oft* nor call a young woman a *nymph*, his productions have really far less in common with any prose work than Pope's poetry had. The story of *The Rape of the Lock*, sylphs and all, could have been told, though not so effectively, in prose. The *Odyssey* and the *Comedy* have something to say that could have been said well, though not equally well, without verse. Most of the qualities Aristotle demands of a tragedy could occur in a prose play...But modern poetry, if it 'says' anything at all, if it aspires to 'mean' as well as to 'be', says what prose could not say in any fashion.

(C. S. Lewis, *An Experiment in Criticism*, 1961, pp. 96–7)

The rejection of archaism may have done less to bring poetry nearer to prose, and to men's business and bosoms, than its advocates, Hopkins among them, may have hoped. At any rate, the issue may be still more open than is always realised.

A critical idea which has had less influence is Hopkins's notion of what he calls *frigidity*. This is often associated by him with the poetry of Browning, for which Hopkins did not greatly care.

I remember a good case of the 'impotent collection of particulars' of which you speak in the description of the market place at Florence where he found the book of the trial: it is a pointless photograph of still life, such as I remember in Balzac, minute upholstery description; only that in Balzac, who besides is writing prose, all tells and is given with a reserve and simplicity of style which Browning has not got. Indeed I hold with the oldfashioned criticism that Browning is not really a poet, that he has all the gifts but the one needful and the pearls without the string; rather one should say raw nuggets and rough diamonds. I suppose him to resemble Ben Jonson, only that Ben Jonson has more real poetry.   (To Dixon, 12 October 1881)

In another letter to Dixon he illustrates the 'frigidity' of Browning by means of a technical comment.

I will give a glaring instance from Browning of false perspective in an image. In his *Instans Tyrannus* he makes the tyrant say that he found the just man his victim on a sudden shielded from him by the vault of the sky spreading itself like a great targe over him, 'with the sun's disk for visible boss'. This is monstrous. The vault of heaven is a vault, hollow, concave towards us, convex upwards; it therefore could only defend man on earth against enemies above it, an angry

Olympus for instance. And the tyrant himself is inside it, under it, just as much as his victim. The boss is seen from behind, like the small stud of a sleevelink. This comes of frigid fancy with no imagination. (16 September 1881)

And in the earlier letters he gives the topic a greater fullness of human reference.

Browning has, I think, many frigidities. Any untruth to nature, to human nature, is frigid. Now he has got a great deal of what came in with Kingsley and the Broad Church school, a way of talking (and making his people talk) with the air and spirit of a man bouncing up from table with his mouth full of bread and cheese and saying that he meant to stand no blasted nonsense. . .Now this is *one* mood or vein of human nature. . . .And Tennyson in his later works has been 'carried away with their dissimulation'. The effect of this style is a frigid bluster. A true humanity of spirit, neither mawkish on the one hand nor blustering on the other, is the most precious of all qualities of style, and this I prize in your poems, as I do in Bridges'. After all it is the breadth of his human nature that we admire in Shakespeare.

To call Browning 'frigid' seems a strange choice of words; one would think he was more conspicuous than most Victorian poets for his generous human warmth. But the very paradoxicality of the description is arresting: we have to think again.

More directly useful, perhaps, to the pedagogically minded reader is the special turn Hopkins gives to the term *rhetoric*. The context is a penetrating and sympathetic comment on Wordsworth.

What I suppose grows on people is that Wordsworth's particular grace, his *charisma* as the theologians say, has been granted in equal measure to so very few men. . .to Plato and who else? I mean his spiritual insight into nature; and this they perhaps think is above all the poet's gift? It is true, if we sort things, so that art is art and philosophy is philosophy, it seems rather the philosopher's than the poet's: at any rate he had it in a sovereign degree. He had a 'divine philosophy' and a lovely gift of verse; but in his work there is nevertheless *beaucoup à redire*; it is due to the universal fault of our literature, its weakness in rhetoric. The strictly poetical insight and inspiration of our poetry seems to me to be of the very finest, finer perhaps than the Greek; but its rhetoric is inadequate – seldom first-rate, mostly only just sufficient, sometimes even below par. By rhetoric I mean all the common and teachable element in literature, what grammar is to speech, what thoroughbass is to music, what theatrical experience gives to playwrights. If you leave out the embroidery (to be sure the principal thing) of for instance the *Excursion* and look only at the groundwork and stuff of the web is it not fairly true to say 'This will never do'? There does seem to be a great deal of dulness, superfluity, aimlessness, poverty of plan.

(To Dixon, 7 August 1886)

On a similar point I should like to cite what he says in his interesting and generalisable suggestion about Dryden's mastery of what Hopkins calls 'bare English'. He tells Bridges:

I can scarcely think of you not admiring Dryden without, I may say, exasperation. And my style tends always more towards Dryden. What is there in Dryden? Much, but above all this: he is the most masculine of our poets; his style and his rhythms lay the strongest stress of all our literature on the naked thew and sinew of the English language, the praise that with certain qualifications one would give in Greek to Demosthenes, the greatest master of bare Greek.

(6 November 1887)

As might be expected, all my examples of Hopkins's critical powers have been taken from his comments on poetry. But it is not always realised that he has interesting things to say about prose too. His own mastery of critical prose has, I hope, appeared in my quotations from him. And his discussion of Patmore's and Newman's prose styles incites much general thought, even in those who feel, as I do, that he is a little unjust to Newman.

When I read yr. prose [he tells Patmore], and when I read Newman's and some other modern writers' the same impression is borne in on me: no matter how beautiful the thought, nor, taken singly, with what happiness expressed, you do not know what *writing prose* is. At bottom what you do and what Cardinal Newman does is to think aloud, to think with pen to paper. In this process there are certain advantages; they may outweigh those of a perfect technic; but at any rate they exclude that; they exclude the belonging technic, the belonging rhetoric, the own proper eloquence of written prose. Each thought is told off singly and there follows a pause and this breaks the continuity, the *contentio*, the strain of address, which writing should usually have.

The beauty, the eloquence, of good prose cannot come wholly from the thought. With Burke it does and varies with the thought; when therefore the thought is sublime so does the style appear to be. But in fact Burke has no style properly so called: his style was colourlessly to transmit his thought. Still he was an orator in form and followed the common oratorical tradition, so that his writing has the strain of address I speak of above.

But Newman does not follow the common tradition – of writing. His tradition is that of cultured, the most highly educated, conversation; it is the flower of the best Oxford life. Perhaps this gives it a charm of unaffected and personal sincerity that nothing else could. Still he shirks the technic of written prose and shuns the tradition of written English. He seems to be thinking 'Gibbon is the last great master of traditional English prose; he is its perfection; I do not propose to emulate him; I begin all over again from the language of conversation, of common life.'

You too seem to me to be saying to yourself 'I am writing prose, not poetry; it is bad taste and a confusion of kinds to employ the style of poetry in prose: the style of prose is to shun the style of poetry and to express one's thoughts with point.' But the style of prose is a positive thing and not the absence of verse-forms and pointedly expressed thoughts are single hits and give no continuity of style. (20 October 1887)

And Hopkins has interesting and provocative judgments to make on the prose fiction of his own time.

In my judgment [he writes to Bridges], the amount of gift and genius which goes into novels in the English literature of this generation is perhaps not much inferior to what made the Elizabethan drama, and unhappily it is in great part wasted. How admirable are Blackmore and Hardy! Their merits are much eclipsed by the overdone reputation of the Evans–Eliot–Lewis–Cross woman (poor creature! one ought not to speak slightingly, I know) half real power, half imposition. Do you know the bonfire scenes in the *Return of the Native*, and still better the sword exercise scene in the *Madding Crowd*, breathing epic? or the wife sale in the *Mayor of Casterbridge* (read by chance)? But these writers only rise to their great strokes; they do not write continuously well: now Stevenson is master of a consummate style and each phrase is finished as in poetry. It will not do at all, your treatment of him. (28 October 1886)

Perhaps the most interesting of Hopkins's comments on prose fiction are his thoughts on a genre which, following Stevenson, he distinguishes as *romance*. 'Romance, which is fictitious history, consists of event, of incident...The type of pure Romance [is] the *Arabian Nights*: those stories have no moral, no character-drawing, they turn altogether on interesting incident' (to Dixon, 15 August 1883). His brief analysis of Stevenson's story 'The Treasure of Franchard' shows that Hopkins was a structuralist *ante litteram*.

His...stories are written on this principle; they are very good and he has all the gifts a writer of fiction should have, including those he holds unessential, as characterisation, and at first you notice no more than an ordinary well told story, but on looking back in the light of this doctrine you see that the persons illustrate the incident or strain of incidents, the plot, *the story*, not the story and incidents the persons...['The Treasure of Franchard'] is the story of an old treasure found, lost, and found again. The finding of the treasure acts of course and rather for the worse upon the finder, a retired French doctor, and his wife; the loss cures them; you wait to see the effect of the refinding: but not at all, the story abruptly ends – because its hero was, so to say, this triplet of incidents.

In another letter he applies this concept of romance to *A Midsummer Night's Dream*, suggesting lines of thought on Shakespeare's method of composition which might well be followed further, somewhat in the spirit of the neglected late-Victorian critic R. G. Moulton's studies of Shakespeare as a dramatic artist.

As a tail-piece to this presentation of Hopkins as a critic of prose, I will add this comment on Boswell's *Life of Johnson*.

I think Boswell is with the exception of St. Austin's Confessions, and some other spiritual works the most interesting book I ever read. Perhaps good novels are more so, but I don't know. Boswell himself was a dear good fellow. Some of his own repartees (and no one can doubt his truthfulness) are very good and his judgments in most things sound. It is not only that he cd. photograph Johnson; when he has occasion to draw another character it is lifelike: he hated Mrs. Thrale, yet her picture in the few scenes where she appears comes out as bright and witty as she could herself wish, because as an artist he was above doing an injustice.   (To Baillie, 19 November 1879)

This comment may serve to introduce my final topic: Hopkins's treatment of the relation between 'the writer' and 'the man', a subject of course bound up with the recurring problem of 'art and morality'. Hopkins is always well aware of the close relation between qualities that are specifically artistic and those that belong to humanity generally; his casual remarks show that, as when he tells Dixon that 'richness of imagery belongs especially to youth, broader effects to the maturer mind' (29 October 1881). But he sharply distinguishes aesthetic and moral judgments. In the same letter to Bridges (3 April 1877) in which he says that Milton's 'achievements are quite beyond any other English poet's, perhaps any modern poet's', he says bluntly,

Don't like what you say of Milton. I think he was a very bad man; those who contrary to our Lord's command both break themselves and, as St. Paul says, consent to those who break the sacred bond of marriage, like Luther and Milton, fall with eyes open into the terrible judgment of God. Crying up great names, as for instance the reviews do now Swinburne and Hugo, those plagues of mankind, is often wicked and in general is a great vanity and full of impious brag and a blackguard and unspiritual mind.

An early letter to Baillie (15 September 1867), apropos of the *Dame aux Camélias*, deals with the question of the 'morality' of a work, rather than of its author.

With regard to the morality it is true no doubt *haplōs* that any subject may be chosen for its art value alone and so will not, or rather need not, be any scandal in the writer or the reader. The question however is the practical effect, and is of course one of degree, where no line can be drawn. I mean for instance that it is impossible not personally to form an opinion against the morality of a writer like Swinburne, where the proportion of these subjects to the whole is great and secondly where the things themselves are the extreme cases in their own kind. Another thing is that what is innocent in a writer, if it must cause certain scandal to readers becomes wrong on that ground. This too is a question of degree for perhaps we are not bound to consider those who will take scandal from everything: it is required that the number only shd. be small. Then with the work itself the question is how far in point of detail one may safely go – another question of degree: one thinks e.g. *Othello* shd. be called innocent, Ovid immoral. To me then the question with your particular book wd. be just this practical balance, and without reading it I cannot say which way the balance wd. turn: that the subject by itself may be innocent or even commendable I have no wish to deny.

The American poet–critic Yvor Winters has objected of this position that it contains no idea that morality of any kind is involved in the *treatment* of a subject, confines it to the *choice* of subject.

The concept of art [he says in discussion of Hopkins's aesthetic views] is completely divorced from the concept of morality so far as any functional relationship goes. Swinburne is immoral because of the nature of his subjects, not because he falsifies them in the interests of excessive and sentimental decoration. In these terms, Baudelaire would be quite as immoral as Swinburne, because of his subjects, and Hopkins himself would be invariably a moral poet because of his subjects. Yet in my own terms, Baudelaire is at least very often a profoundly moral poet because of his understanding of his subjects, and Hopkins is very often an immoral poet for much the same reasons why Swinburne seems to me immoral.

(Yvor Winters, *The Function of Criticism*, 1962, p. 141)

Winter's essay is the most severe and radical criticism of Hopkins yet made by a critic of stature.

What are these mountains of the mind? One does not enquire because one holds them cheap, but because one has hung on so many oneself, so various in their respective terrors, that one is perplexed to assign a particular motive. One is inclined to ask: 'What do you know of these matters? Why are you so secretive? And above all, why are you so self-righteous in your secretiveness?'

So he interrogates the Hopkins of the later sonnets. And his critical attitude is summed up in this scathing sentence on 'The Windhover':

In no other literary period, I think, save our own, would a poet who was both a priest and a genuinely devout man have thought that he had dealt seriously with his love for Christ and his duty toward him by writing an excited description of a landscape.

Winters's essay has a special place in the history of Hopkins criticism. Hopkins's earliest important critics, such as I. A.

Richards, Herbert Read, and F. R. Leavis, applied themselves to vindicating him from the strictures of Bridges. There followed, first a trickle, and then a flood of elucidation and explication of Hopkins's strange language and unique poetic. The critical, or evaluative, question was ignored, or begged: it was taken for granted that Hopkins was a great poet: the only question at issue was the interpretation of what he wrote. It has been left to Yvor Winters to reopen the critical debate. There can be no pretence of dealing with Winters's position here. All I can say now is that I hope it has at least appeared from my presentation that, whatever the obscurity of meaning and motive Winters may find in Hopkins's poetry, in the thought of Hopkins the critic we see everywhere explicitness, candour, and plain terms. Those who love Hopkins the man and the poet may be permitted to hope that Winters will turn out to have been the devil's advocate. At any rate, coming from so harsh a critic, his final tribute is remarkable, and may serve as a final salute.

Hopkins in his later years passed through a period of psychological crisis in which his mental balance, if he really preserved it at times, was precarious. . .I suspect that his faith and vocation were his chief source of strength, and not, as some writers have supposed, a source of weakness. Whatever the nature of his difficulty, his struggle with it, so far as we may judge, was desperate, and, in spite of its lack of intellectual clarity, little short of heroic.

T. S. Eliot: a Poet's Notebook

In one respect T. S. Eliot is unusual among critics of eminence: he left on record (in 'To Criticize the Critic', 1961) an extensive and severe commentary on his own criticism. Opinions about this depend on one's view of Eliot. Those who dislike him will see it as a characteristically slippery action, a cunning bid to steal his opponents' thunder. Those who admire him will feel gratitude for his candour, and may reflect on how greatly we should have valued such an apologia – and *mea culpa* – on the part of Samuel Johnson or Matthew Arnold. Whatever view we take, Eliot's remarks on the scope, limitations, and shortcomings of what he wrote on other authors are so penetrating that there seems little for anyone else to add or subtract. Of course a man is not usually a good judge in his own cause; but in this case the task of judgment has been performed so well that one might think inquiry into Eliot's prose writings should now be left to those whose chief interest is in his accomplishment in the 'other harmony', or in material relevant to the study of his poems and plays. Or perhaps it should be left to those interested in appraising – nowadays often in a hostile spirit – his religious, social, or political point of view; or searching, with the F. R. Leavis of recent years, for evidence of impure motives and unworthy moral and emotional attitudes. The effect of Eliot's remarks on his own criticism has been to push into the background the question, how *true* – true for others, as well as true for him – is this or that judgment on this or that writer, and this or that injunction on points of literary principle. Eliot himself has become our main guide in helping us to see the extent to which his criticism can be 'placed' and 'dated'. As a writer of critical prose he had the great advantage, over some more recent pundits who invoke his name, of the ability to write interestingly. Yet it is he himself who tempts us to find in his criticism what Professor Raleigh found in *Paradise Lost*: a monument to dead ideas.

There is however one of Eliot's books, dealing with matters of literary criticism, which he does urge us to take account of for its intrinsic and not merely its documentary value. This is *The Use of Poetry and the Use of Criticism* (1933), based on the lectures he gave in 1932–3 on the Charles Eliot Norton Foundation at Harvard. Eliot changed his mind about these lectures. In the preface to the first edition he spoke of 'another unnecessary book', which he had been obliged to publish by the terms of the Foundation. But rereading them many years later he found to his surprise that he was 'still prepared to accept them as a statement of [his] critical position'. 'The lectures', he declared in the 1963 preface to the second edition (1964), 'seem to me still valid... I am ashamed neither of the style nor of the matter.' Although he '[did] not repudiate "Tradition and the Individual Talent"', he reprinted *The Use of Poetry* 'in the faint hope that one of these lectures may be taken instead of "Tradition and the Individual Talent" by some anthologist of the future'. So we have Eliot's own sanction for inquiring, in the spirit of the book itself, what is the *use* of what he offers us; how far he helps us to cope with the hard questions he raises about criticism and poetry.

But to play down the book's biographical interest is not to deny that this is considerable. Indeed, *The Use of Poetry* may be remembered now chiefly for that interest. It is to this book we turn to find what Eliot has to say about his intentions (or lack of them) in writing *Ash-Wednesday* (p. 30), the history of the development of his own taste in poetry (p. 33), Evelyn Waugh's father's attack on him and Ezra Pound as 'drunken helots' (p. 71), his partiality for the Scots (p. 72), his own experience in composing poetry (p. 144), his struggle, up to 1932, with the problems of writing poetic drama, and what he aimed at in the dramatic fragments he entitled *Sweeney Agonistes* (p. 153). Memorable, too, are the vivid glimpses we are given of the Eliot of the personal poetry. Writers on Eliot often quote the passage, doubtless autobiographical, about a child finding a sea-anemone for the first time (p. 78), placing it beside the lines on the 'old crab' in the early 'Rhapsody on a Windy Night'. Another passage is often related to 'Journey of the Magi'; it reveals also an affinity between Eliot's sensibility and Virginia Woolf's.

Why, for all of us, out of all that we have heard, seen, felt, in a lifetime, do certain images recur, charged with emotion, rather than others? The song of one bird, the leap of one fish, at a particular place and time, the scent of one flower, an old woman on a German mountain path, six ruffians seen through an open window playing cards at night at a small French railway junction where there was a water-mill: such memories may have symbolic value, but of what we cannot tell, for they come to represent the depths of feeling into which we cannot peer. We might just as well ask why, when we try to recall visually some period in the past, we find in our memory just the few, meagre, arbitrarily chosen set of snapshots that we do find there, the faded poor souvenirs of passionate moments.   (p. 148)

Here the lecturer's dais and the prose framework seem to vanish, and we are alone with the poet.

There is another way also in which the lectures sound personal – a rather disconcerting way. Towards the end, when Eliot cumbrously descends from the lecturing tone and endeavours to meet his fellow-men on equal terms, there are sudden lapses from that prim prose.

As things are, and as fundamentally they must always be, poetry is not a career, but *a mug's game*. No honest poet can ever feel quite sure of the permanent value of what he has written: he may have wasted his time and *messed up his life* for nothing. (p. 154: my italics)

Eliot's friend Frank Morley has plausibly suggested that in *The Use of Poetry* the figure of Coleridge is a *persona* or symbol of Eliot himself. This is the Coleridge whom he sees as a haunted and a ruined man, doomed to live with the knowledge that he could never again reach the level he had once reached in a few great poems. Here Eliot was in fact, as he came later to realise, unjust to Coleridge; he did not evidently know at that time how much the earlier poet managed to achieve in the long years after his *annus mirabilis*. But there is no doubt that Eliot himself, at the beginning of the 1930s, had grave doubts whether he would be able to write any more poetry. He thought of himself not as a 'poet' but as a man who occasionally wrote poems. It is natural that his thoughts should turn to this classic example of the poet from whom the Muse has withdrawn; however unaware he may have been of Coleridge's second career, not only as a compulsive talker, but as a writer on criticism, metaphysics, psychology,

political economy, and religious thought. And so he chose to end
the lectures with the sad ghost of Coleridge beckoning from the
shadows. (We may also remember, as Eliot himself perhaps did,
the tragedy of Coleridge's broken marriage.) All this is sympathetic. Yet the final reference to Coleridge seems tasteless.
Certainly Eliot had the right to suggest a parallel between himself and Coleridge. He was at least as great a poet and critic. But
he should have left it for others to do so.

Finally, the occasion of the lectures should be remembered.
Eliot had been brought back to the United States, after seventeen
years' absence, to deliver them. Before him was to stretch the
'low dishonest decade' of the 1930s. Time has not lessened the
force of those words which Eliot quotes from a letter of 1869 in
Charles Eliot Norton's *Life and Letters* (Norton is speaking of
the years after the American Civil War).

...I wonder...whether we are not to have another period of decline,
fall, and ruin and revival, like that of the first thirteen hundred
years of our era. It would not grieve me much to know that this were
to be the case. No man who knows what society at the present day
really is but must agree that it is not worth preserving on its present
basis.   (p. 15)

A minatory tone comes into the lectures whenever political and
social problems loom into view. For *The Use of Poetry* marks the
beginning of Eliot's major concern with public questions in the
age of Hitler, Franklin Roosevelt, and Stalin. Eliot's social and
political views are today unpopular. He is seen as the militant
issuer of reactionary 'calls to order'. It might be fairer to remember him as a detached – though far from dispassionate – observer
of the post-Christian world. As a Christian theorist he had, of
course, his confession, his 'commitment'. But he was enabled by
his philosophy, as some of today's ideologues may not be by
theirs, to allow for the contingent, contradictory, unpredictable
way things happen, and value is distributed, in art and literature
and life generally. Eliot's philosophical responsibility overlapped
with his duty as a poet: to maintain the contact between
language and reality which so many forces in the modern world
collaborate to destroy. It seems that he felt more in common

with people who manage to believe *anything* – such as sincere Communists – than with half-believers, lost in a mist of words. A remark about Wordsworth in *The Use of Poetry* may be applied to Eliot himself.

. . .when a man takes politics and social affairs seriously the difference between revolution and reaction may be by the breadth of a hair. . . Wordsworth may possibly have been no renegade but a man who thought, so far as he thought at all, for himself. (p. 73)

Some of that tone in Eliot's writing which readers today find disagreeable may be due to his feeling of frustration at having to contend, not with the opposition of the intellectual community, but with its indifference. It is this indifferentism that, with damaging consequences for his later reputation, he calls 'Liberalism'. Acerbity and increasing despair accompanied his efforts to explain to Liberals that Christianity is not a sentiment but a hypothesis about the world. On the other hand, Eliot did not feel happy among the zealots. For them too he speaks words to ponder, in the appendix to *The Idea of a Christian Society* (1939).

So far as a man sees the need for converting *himself* as well as the World, he is approximating to the religious point of view. But for most people, to be able to simplify issues so as to see only the definite external enemy, is extremely exhilarating, and brings about the bright eye and the springy step that go so well with the political uniform. This is an exhilaration that the Christian must deny himself. (pp. 95–6)

W. B. Yeats, writing to Lady Gerald Wellesley (6 July 1935), struck a similar note; but his alternative to zealotry was different.

When there is despair, public or private, when settled order seems lost, people look for strength within and without. Auden and Spender, all that seem the new movement, look for strength in Marxian socialism, or in Major Douglas; they want marching feet. The lasting expression of our time is not in this obvious choice but in a sense of something steel-like and cold within the will, something passionate and cold.

Eliot's humility may be more attractive.

This sombre contemporary background is always present in *The Use of Poetry*. But for the most part the book is concerned only with literary criticism. As such, it has sometimes been judged inferior to Eliot's earlier essays. This judgment may be right: but some of the things that have been said to support it seem unfair. Thus more than one writer thinks Eliot mistaken in adopting a chronological approach, which did not suit him. But Eliot had good reason to seek for a place in that line of poet–critics who adorn English literature: Sidney, Ben Jonson, Dryden, Addison, Johnson, Wordsworth, Coleridge, Shelley, Keats (of the letters), and Arnold. All these poets are discussed in *The Use of Poetry*, and to discuss them in their historical succession seems right and natural. Furthermore, over and above his personal authority as a distinguished poet, Eliot was qualified as an expert in at least some of the literary periods that his undertaking required him to traverse. His connoisseurship of the drama of Shakespeare's time is well known from *Elizabethan Essays*, and it is put to good use in the second lecture. His examination of Dryden's critical terminology shows keen historical awareness, and does something to atone for his irritable cavilling, in the sixth lecture, at some of Arnold's phrases. Similarly he may be forgiven for his inadequate and petulant remarks on Addison because of his admirable comments afterwards on Johnson. (It is interesting to see how in his later lectures on 'Johnson as Critic and Poet' (1944) some of the ideas he tried out in *The Use of Poetry* are developed in a more mature style.) Here and there, it is true, the scholarship of *The Use of Poetry* is faulty, and Eliot did nothing to correct it in the second edition. We still read there, for example, that Coleridge did not 'acclaim' Donne (p. 72), though by 1963 Eliot knew that Coleridge did indeed acclaim Donne, and repeatedly. The hasty composition of the lectures is no doubt responsible for such blemishes. (In the preface to the second edition Eliot says that they were written during the course.) They do not invalidate *The Use of Poetry* as a contribution to literary history at least as valuable as anything by the academic writers Eliot mentions with respect, such as Ker and Saintsbury.

But the main concern of the book is not with literary history but with matters of critical principle, and it is into these that we should now look. Early on, in the first lecture, Eliot makes an often quoted pronouncement.

The rudiment of criticism is the ability to select a good poem and reject a bad poem; and its most severe test is of its ability to select a good *new* poem, to respond properly to a new situation.   (p. 18)

This pronouncement, like other dicta of Eliot's, can be paralleled in Sainte-Beuve, who remarks, in his book on Chateaubriand and his literary group, that the sagacity of the judge and the perspicacity of the critic are tested by works not yet tried by the public. 'To judge at first sight – that is the critical gift; how few possess it!' *Combien peu le possèdent,* says Sainte-Beuve, and our first reaction is to wonder whether Sainte-Beuve possessed it himself. Proust thought that Sainte-Beuve failed to appreciate *all* the great writers of his time, and contrasts him with Anatole France, who laid no claim to the *magisterium* of the judge, and offered solely his personal impressions; and yet in spite (or because) of this, was far more generous and perceptive about his rivals than Sainte-Beuve ever was. Could one make a similar *ad hominem* retort to Eliot? Into the field of contemporary literature Eliot rarely ventured; and when he did, he seems not to have come out with any valuable recommendations. At any rate, I have never met anyone who concurred in his grave praise for the poems of Harry Crosby. It would seem that few of those who have been recognised by posterity as important critics – and no academic critics whatsoever – have been good talent-spotters. We might conclude, on practical grounds, that the test Eliot proposes is too severe. A more reasonable demand of critics *de carrière* would be that they write informatively about works that other readers have discovered for them. (Even in this, some fail.)

A more theoretical kind of objection might be made to Eliot's seeming assumption that the goodness of a poem is an essence or quality, which it either has or has not. This way of looking at poetry is only plausible if we confine our attention to poems which are universally recognised as good, and to poems which are by-words for failure. But these two categories exclude the bulk of poems that have been written. Tastes notoriously vary, and most of us would agree that there is a vast range of poetry in which variations of judgment are perfectly legitimate. In any case, is goodness (or badness) an essence or quality at all? One might take the view that to call a poem good or bad is to do no more than give or refuse endorsement to the judgment that it possesses or lacks certain properties which happen to be held in esteem by the individual critic, or by readers in a particular literary period. And the course of literary history makes it clear that such properties vary greatly from time to time, and from reader to reader. The test of a critic's ability might then be whether he can recognise the properties that a given poem possesses; not whether he arrives at a judgment of merit or demerit which many of his contemporaries assume to be automatically supervenient or consequential upon them. The test of his quality is his descriptions, not his evaluations. The trouble with this, as with all other efforts to find objective literary criteria, is that the properties of poems, as of other works of art, seem actually to undergo change. They appear to possess certain properties at one time and not at another. Some improve with the years, some deteriorate, some vanish. The poetry of Edward Young, and perhaps the poetry of Boileau, glowed brilliantly for about a hundred years; then the light went out. Perhaps the painful search by academic critics for stable and enduring material – 'literary artefacts' – on which to base their judgments is as delusory as the similar belief, common among philosophers, in the supra-historical persistence of 'concepts'.

All the same, Eliot's dictum – that new poems are the test – retains some value. But it should be regarded as a counsel of perfection, or word of caution, to those who attempt criticism, a reminder of the long history of their failure to anticipate the verdict of posterity. The next critical principle he proceeds to lay down is a revival, in modified form, of the old doctrine of the dramatic unities. Clearly there is something in this doctrine. An audience grows restless, without necessarily knowing why, when the parts of a play do not pull together. A modern discussion would have to take into account the expectations of theatrical audiences in particular historical circumstances ('conventions'). The possible influence of films would also have to be considered.

In its Renaissance form the doctrine of the unities is perhaps not very interesting. It is historically important as regards the French stage; but on its invalidity as an account of the practice of ancient Greek drama A. W. Verrall long ago pronounced incisively. It is, he says, 'a mere piece of confusion, arising from a false attempt to justify practices which, *so far as they existed* had a totally different origin' (*Lectures on Dryden*, 1914). One's first reaction, in reading of the wrangles of the sixteenth and seventeenth centuries on this topic, might well be one of wonder. How could intelligent men have for so long been spellbound by so arbitrary a prescription? (After that, it is sobering to speculate on what future literary historians will see as a comparable dogmatism of our own time.) But the exposure of the fallacies involved can be interesting. We can read with pleasure a classic piece of common sense on this subject, the remarks of Johnson in his *Preface to Shakespeare* (1765). And for a more subtle discussion we may go to Johnson's contemporary Lessing, who in his *Laokoon* (1766) draws the distinction between 'delusion' and 'illusion' that is indispensable for a proper treatment of the problem. Then, as a paradoxical defence of the doctrine of the unities, we might consider the peculiar pleasure we feel when they are violated to good purpose. This may be part of the pleasure we take in the treatment of place in Barrie's *The Admirable Crichton*, or of time in Bennett and Knoblock's *Milestones*. Is it part of the pleasure we take in *The Winter's Tale*? When I last saw that play the dramatising of the change of generations, between the beginning and the end, had a most moving effect. F. R. Leavis has a fine suggestion in an essay in *The Common Pursuit* (1958), when he puts forward as a possible superiority of *The Winter's Tale* over *The Tempest* – a play that has often been praised on account of Shakespeare's ingenious elimination of the time gap – the 'depth and richness of significance. . .given, in *The Winter's Tale*, by the concrete presence of time in its rhythmic processes, and by the association of human growth, decay and rebirth with the vital rhythms of nature at large'.

No critic was better qualified than Eliot to add something of real value to this durable debate. His own increasing struggle with the problems of play writing should have been enough to ensure that. But what he says is brief and disappointing. He endorses Sir Philip Sidney's strictures on the drama of his day, without arousing our interest in the conventional pedantry which is all Sidney has to offer on the topic of the unities. Nor is the attitude Eliot strikes as a defender of neo-classicism, invoking the name of Aristotle, strengthened by his appearing to realise only belatedly (p. 47, fn) that 'the Unities' can claim no support from the *Poetics*. Aristotle says nothing about the unity of place, and his reference to the unity of time is casual; he merely remarks that the usual practice of tragedy was to confine itself, as far as possible, to the action of twenty-four hours. There is nothing prescriptive about it. Nor is Eliot's case improved by his citing, as a case of triumphant faithfulness to the unities, of Joyce's *Ulysses*. (No doubt he did so with a twinkle, since Joyce was not yet a respectable author in the Harvard of 1932.) It is true that the action of *Ulysses* – and of *Mrs Dalloway* – like that of *Oedipus Rex*, takes place in one day. But the reason is different in each of these works. In any case, no one has ever thought the unities had to do with anything but plays.

The conclusion Eliot soon comes to is that the unities of time and place are merely special cases of what he calls unity of action. And this in its turn proves to be a special case of unity of senti-ment, ignored to their detriment, Eliot thinks, by some Eliza-bethan plays, for example *The Changeling*. (Eliot was writing before the appearance of William Empson's ingenious defence of the double plot of that play in *Some Versions of Pastoral*, 1935.) The unity of sentiment is, then, to use Eliot's own terms, a law, not a rule. And it is this law that the defenders of the traditional unities were really – and legitimately – upholding. This may be so. But the trouble with the updated doctrine Eliot offers us is that it has no teeth. The traditional unities may be arbitrary, but at least we are in a position to decide whether a particular play observes them or not. Mr Curdle in *Nicholas Nickleby* could have found plenty of plays which answer to his demand for 'a kind of universal dovetailedness with regard to place and time'. Perhaps the same could be said of the unity of action, though when Eliot mentions Shakespeare's *Henry IV* plays as an example it is not clear what he is thinking of: if *Henry IV*,

Part II exhibits unity of action it is hard to imagine any play that could be fairly said to lack it. But the final over-riding prescription of unity of sentiment is very vague. Does *The Dynasts* show it? does *Cavalcade*? Does it amount to more than asking that a play should have unity of *some* kind? to requiring, with Mr Curdle, 'a sort of general oneness, if I may be allowed to use so strong an expression'? It has always been the trouble with neo-classicism that the more reasonable its propositions, the more they slide towards analyticity.

But Eliot's stance as the stern neo-classicist seems to disappear in the course of the argument. Was it anything more than a pose? Perhaps he felt that his appearance in this role was something he owed to his old teacher Irving Babbitt, or to the twentieth-century French neo-classicists he so admired. If so, he compares unfavourably, when he adopts it, with some of the French critics. He does not show the willingness of Julien Benda, for example, to see merits in his opponents' position. The neo-classicism for which Eliot became famous in the 1920s seems to bring out the least alluring quality of his writing: that frosty, self-important tone which mars *The Use of Poetry*. 'The majority of critics can be expected only to parrot the opinions of the last master of criticism...' (p. 109). 'What I *call* the "auditory imagination"...' (p. 118: italics mine). This tone is insufferable. Eliot says of Matthew Arnold that 'he is most at ease in a master's gown', but this does not seem to be true of Eliot himself. At *ease* is what he never sounds. These lectures lack the quality that charms us in Addison (to whom he is so harsh). I am thinking of things like Addison's discussion of true and false wit in the *Spectator* for 7 May 1711:

I intend to lay aside a whole week for this undertaking, that the scheme of my thoughts may not be broken and interrupted; and I dare promise myself, if readers will give me a week's attention, that this great city will be very much changed for the better by next Saturday night.

In *The Use of Poetry* it seems that Eliot cannot smile.

But the important objection to Eliot's neo-classicism is not that it is chilly, but that it is half-hearted. It is interesting to learn from Quentin Bell's *Virginia Woolf* (1972) that in September 1933 Eliot told Mrs Woolf he was no longer sure there could be a 'science of criticism'. This is ironic, coming from T. S. Eliot, the last of the great literary pundits, the idol of the academies, more responsible than any other single individual for this very influential conception of criticism. His loss of faith in it may account for a bored, perfunctory element we sense in *The Use of Poetry*. It may also be the reason why those *enquêtes* into Shaw, Wells, Kipling, and other modern 'heretics', now and then promised in the *Criterion*, never appeared. Perhaps Eliot had come to recognise that his own interest as a critic was in what he *liked* in another writer's work. He was also coming to have forebodings about his own influence on criticism. These are suggested here by his deprecatory reference to a 'criticism which seems to demand of poetry, not that it shall be well written, but that it shall be "representative of its time"'. While agreeing with this, we might agree also with Yvor Winters, a more full-blooded literary conservative than Eliot, when he tartly retorts that it was Eliot and Pound and their disciples who had always been demanding that poetry should be 'representative of its time'. Nowhere is the relation in Eliot between the innovating poet and the literary traditionalist more uneasy than in *The Use of Poetry*.

But as the lectures proceed the self-conscious neo-classicism becomes merely a notional basis for the development of ideas which belong to Eliot's mature thinking. This remark about 'communication', for instance, is a better phrasing of his thought on this topic than any he had found before.

If poetry is a form of 'communication', yet that which is to be communicated is the poem itself, and only incidentally the experience and the thought which have gone into it. (p. 30)

We think here of his later remark in 'The Frontiers of Criticism' (1956), when he is deprecating the claims of Herbert Read and F. W. Bateson to have illuminated some of Wordsworth's poems by reference to his biography and purported psychology. 'When the poem has been made, something new has happened, something that cannot be wholly explained by *anything that went before.*' And to strengthen the force of this warning to the practitioners of *Quellenforschung* (of all kinds) we can sub-join a remark by a later author writing from a very different point of view – Sartre in *What is Literature?* (1947): 'The appearance of the work is a new event which cannot be *explained* by anterior data.' Eliot's discussion of this subject shows a maturity of thought and clarity of expression lacking in passages more often quoted, such as the famous pronouncement on the 'objective correlative' in the essay on *Hamlet*, or the lofty sentence on the 'auditory imagination' in *The Use of Poetry* itself. Such passages offer portable phrases for our notebooks; but they bring an arrest to thought rather than an advancement, and they are not free from the suspicion of attitudinising.

The question of poetic greatness or, as he calls it, of differences of degree among poets, is one to which Eliot recurs in the lectures. He observes in the appendix to the first lecture, where he is considering the place of the study of literature in the educational process, that it is not a matter which is easy to clarify for school-children or undergraduates. It seems to have puzzled Eliot himself, and for good reasons. He was anxious to retain judgments of scale in the criticism of poetry. Yet he wanted to reject the ethical criteria proposed for them by Matthew Arnold. His solution here, in so far as he finds one, is to emphasise the *historical* constituent in judgments of greatness. In the course of some sensible comments on Herbert Read's too-eccentric post-Eliot map of the history of English poetry he remarks that

the great poet is, among other things, one who not merely restores a tradition which has been in abeyance, but one who in his poetry re-twines as many straying strands of tradition as possible.   (p. 85)

And, while praising Landor, for whom Pound had a cult, Eliot draws a useful distinction between him and Wordsworth, who was 'an essential part of history', while Landor was 'only a magnificent by-product'. Here Eliot generalises: 'in estimating for ourselves the greatness of a poet we have to take into account also the *history* of his greatness'. This generalisation could be used as a caveat against Winters's cult of Greville, as well as Pound's cult of Landor. The development of English poetry might well have been much the same if they had not lived; they were not influences. But though Eliot's suggestion seems acceptable so long as we are thinking of a Landor or a Greville, it seems less persuasive when we think of Blake. Blake is in such critical favour today – and, I believe, on the whole justly – that there is some discomfort in denying him greatness. Yet it cannot be denied that he had little or no influence on later poets. This is a case in which we see the value of distinguishing, as Eliot does, between a poet's place in literature and his place in its history. It is the *relation* between these two placings which is mysterious. Matters would be simpler if we could regard 'greatness' as purely – or primarily – a historical term. But it is difficult to use the word like that, and Eliot himself does not so use it, for he speaks of 'estimating for *ourselves* [my italics] the greatness of a poet'. And I imagine that those who consider a Blake or a Greville or a Landor great would reply that he is a great poet for them, whatever his influence or lack of it. Eliot's discussion has the merit of crisply restating the problem rather than suggesting a plausible solution.

This may also be said of a more controversial part of the lectures, which deals with a subject much canvassed in the 1930s, the so-called 'problem of beliefs'. Eliot's discussion of it, though tentative, is of value. But the issue is clouded by his decision to make it the occasion for disparaging the poetry and personality of Shelley. In some ways Eliot's frankness is commendable. I wish all literary eminences had been equally frank about their predecessors. And he makes it plain that he is reporting his personal reaction to Shelley: he lays no claim to judicial impartiality. But to make these remarks in a context of such solemnity gave them, for many of his followers, the force of a papal edict. And we cannot banish the suspicion – in view of his repeated sniping at Shelley in previous essays – that Eliot uses the occasion for one of those carefully planned and executed literary assassinations which Conrad Aitken recalls from the early days of the *Criterion*. However that may be, Eliot's remarks were very influential. (They were to be reinforced a few years later by Leavis's chapter on Shelley in *Revaluation*.) As a result, Shelley has become the least known of the major English poets. Younger school and university teachers took their cue from Eliot and Leavis, and their pupils did not properly get to know a poet who might have become one of their greatest friends. The oracle had spoken: Shelley the man was 'almost a blackguard', and Shelley the poet 'almost unreadable'. To this day Shelley has not recovered the fame he enjoyed in the nineteenth century. A writer in *Essays in Criticism* (October 1975) notes that 'in Britain at least he is still out of favour'.

But the problem Eliot raises can be discussed without considering the justice or otherwise of his remarks on Shelley (or his references to Goethe, which are much more outrageous). This is the problem of how far, if at all, it is possible not only to enjoy, and rate highly, but even fully to *understand*, a poet who propagates or assumes a point of view from which the reader seriously dissents. There is no agreed solution to this problem among literary critics, theoretical or practical, at the present day, and the revival in the West of Marxist criticism has made it again a live issue. Eliot's contribution is to divide poets' 'beliefs' into three categories. First, there are beliefs which the reader finds 'acceptable', which he may actually share with the poet. Second, there are beliefs which Eliot describes as 'tenable'. These are beliefs which the reader does not share, but can imagine himself sharing, which can be respected as worthy of credence by a sane and intelligent person. Finally, there are beliefs which the reader can neither share nor imagine himself sharing; and it is these which, Eliot thinks, animate Shelley's major poems and prevent Eliot's enjoyment and real comprehension of them.

An objection might be made to Eliot's position, that he draws the distinction between poetry and philosophy too sharply. He approves of Lucretius and Dante because they did not philosophise on their own, but got on with the poet's job. But even if we grant (as some would not) the thoroughgoing Epicureanism of Lucretius and the thoroughgoing Thomism of Dante, we do not have to admit that they are in this respect typical of great poets. It might rather be thought that their alleged subordination to an external system of beliefs makes them untypical. There have been poets who thought for themselves, and some of them have even influenced philosophers, as in the case of Goethe. But at the time of *The Use of Poetry* Eliot despised Goethe, and one of his major aims in this book is to discredit the notion of poets as independent thinkers.

What seems to be the really crucial issue Eliot evades. This is the difference between ideas which can safely be relegated to the *musée imaginaire*, which may require intellectual understanding but are no longer a serious challenge and, on the other hand, ideas which are still alive and kicking. It is surely these which constitute the 'problem of beliefs', for those for whom there is one. For this reason we might judge that Eliot only skirmishes with it here. But his distinction between acceptable, tenable, and untenable points of view seems good common sense. It should, however, be supplemented by the practical conclusion, which Eliot himself was to come to later (though not in the 1930s), that when a critic finds a writer's point of view utterly unsympathetic he should refrain from writing about him at all. It is true that sometimes a sincere attempt to understand a difficult author may result in unexpected insights. As Eliot remarks, with a Yeats-like flourish:

. . .a critic may choose an author to criticise, a role to assume, as far as possible the antithesis to himself, a personality which has actualised all that has been suppressed in himself; we can sometimes arrive at a very satisfactory intimacy with our antimasks.   (p. 112)

(He says something like this about his state of mind in writing his critique of Kipling, published in 1941.) But the sense of a moral obligation to be fair is not usually enough to sustain the imaginative effort of entering a point of view one finds odious. One should leave such authors alone.

Eliot's entanglement in the difficulty about 'beliefs' is noticeable throughout the later part of *The Use of Poetry*, which is concerned chiefly with Matthew Arnold and his modern successors. The treatment of Arnold has been the object of some adverse comment, and rightly. In some ways it shows Eliot at his worst. He seems to write in a mood of peevish irritation. He is unjust to Arnold's lasting achievement in propagating a humane conception of culture, and sometimes descends to mere gibes, as in his reference to Arnold's school-inspecting (p. 110). And his tone in general is unpleasantly reminiscent of the animosity shown towards Arnold by Walter Raleigh and Lytton Strachey in their essays. The irritation may be due in part to his dislike of Arnold's habit of presenting a Low Church point of view in a High Church manner. But his deeper objection is evidently not to Arnold's style, but to something else, something that Eliot seems to have felt as a challenge to his own existence as a poet, an attempt to block the sources from which his poetry came. This comes out in his often quoted demur to Arnold's saying, apropos of Burns, that 'no one can deny that it is of advantage to a poet to deal with a beautiful world'.

...the essential advantage for a poet is not to have a beautiful world with which to deal: it is to be able to see beneath both beauty and ugliness; to see the boredom, and the horror, and the glory.   (p. 106)

Similarly, taking his turn in the long series of castigators of Arnold's famous dictum: 'Poetry is at bottom a criticism of life', Eliot comments:

At bottom: that is a great way down; the bottom is the bottom. At the bottom of the abyss is what few ever see, and what those cannot bear to look at for long; and it is not a 'criticism of life'. If we mean life as a whole – not that Arnold ever saw life as a whole – from top to bottom, can anything that we say ultimately, of that awful mystery, be called criticism? We bring back very little from our rare descents, and that is not criticism.   (p. 111)

These retorts have often been quoted. But they have been admired for what they tell us about Eliot himself, not about Arnold. To me they show a trace of attitudinising – Eliot's worst fault as a critic. And to concentrate on them is to ignore the merits of Eliot's discussion, his ability to take further the questions that Arnold had raised. Many of the points he makes are fair comment, and show a deep knowledge of his subject. His brief critique of Arnold's poetry may be too severe, and it contains one or two judgments which sound odd, as when he calls 'The Forsaken Merman' a charade – has one really to suppose, in reading that poem, that the speaker has a tail? But a judicious admirer is likely to find that Eliot, while dwelling on Arnold's

faults as a poet, does also mention the things that make us like
Arnold's poetry, and describes them as well as any critic has
done. And his closing reference to Arnold's essay 'The Study of
Poetry' is the best summary ever made of Arnold's distinction as
a literary critic.

...to be able to quote as Arnold could is the best evidence of taste.
The essay is a classic in English criticism: so much is said in so little
space, with such economy and with such authority.   (p. 118)

This is something that could be said of Eliot himself when he is
at his best; and I would add that when he is at his best he is an
even better quoter than Arnold.

When he comes to Arnold's modern successors the heated
tone disappears from Eliot's writing. He sounds more troubled
and more tentative, an inquirer rather than an inquisitor. The
position of I. A. Richards, then the most influential modern
critic (apart from Eliot himself), Eliot regards as essentially the
same as Arnold's; but his objections to it are made with a courtesy
and a sympathy he denies to Richards's Victorian predecessor.
He puts forward reasonable, if somewhat laborious, strictures on
Richards's 'ritual for heightening sincerity' – the recommendation that we should meditate on the immensity of the universe,
and other portentous subjects, as a preparation for reading
poems. (Curiously enough, Eliot does not make the point –
perhaps he thought it too obvious – that there are many poems
to which so solemn an approach is plainly unsuited: The Rape of
the Lock, for example.) Eliot's real target here is modern secular-
ist religiosity – Russell's 'bad prose' in the Conrad-like 'Free
Man's Worship', the sentimental verbiage issuing from the
twentieth-century equivalents of Arnold's attempts to 'mediate
between Newman and Huxley'. Later attempts in this vein only
serve to strengthen the conviction that Eliot was right. 'Culture'
in the honorific sense has become an irritatingly vague word,
conducive to complacency and woolly thinking.

It seems even possible to defend Eliot's reference, taken from
Jacques Maritain, to the influence of the devil on modern literature (p. 137). This was much ridiculed at the time, and Eliot
may have been unwise in his wording, which made him sound

like Peacock's Mr Toobad ('He said, fifty times over, the devil was come among us'). Belief in the devil is optional for Christians: he is not mentioned in the Creeds. In the second edition Eliot dropped the footnote promising further treatment of this subject – which looks forward to *After Strange Gods* – and he came to regret the later book and, in effect, to expunge it from his canon. Yet since Eliot wrote these words a growing proportion of the serious literature of the Western world has been perverse and abnormal. Only a reader totally at one with the sceptical-permissive climate of our time would deny that; and if many do, the continuity of humanity would appear to be in peril. Fear of the 'stock response' seems to have led some writers and readers into a state of mind in which any recognisably human reaction is stigmatised as sentimentality. How far this disturbing trend actually affects the lives of most people is not certain. But we may reflect that in the cinema the pornography of the sixties yielded to the sadism of the seventies, while the proponents of the new enlightenment are distinguished by their insistence – shades of Peter Quint and Miss Jessel! – on their right to deprave children. So Eliot does not seem to have been tilting at windmills. That the evil trend he discerns has something to do with the decline of Christianity there is no doubt; and the questions he asks in the closing pages of *The Use of Poetry* remain very pertinent – even, or especially, for agnostics.

But in the end the book may be remembered, not for its treatment of this or any other problem, but for its *obiter dicta*. It is a poet's notebook, especially memorable when concerned with a subject on which Eliot is always interesting: the responsibility of the poet. This, of course, is a theme which has occasioned much frenzied insincerity, and one of the attractive aspects of Eliot is that he is quite free from that frantic insistence, so common in bad artists and critics, so rare in good ones, that we are all madly concerned with art and poetry at every moment of our lives. Equally sympathetic, and as salutary now as when he wrote, is his effort to divert attention from the poet to the poetry. He disagrees with Bremond over the relation between poetry and divine inspiration; and surely Eliot is right here, and Cowley also right when he addresses the departed Crashaw:

> Poet and Saint! to thee alone are given
> The two most sacred names of Earth and Heaven
> The hard and rarest union which can be
> Next that of Godhead with Humanity.

And Eliot already foresaw the exaltation of personality which in our times has produced such phenomena as Norman Mailer, or the intense curiosity about the sex lives of minor Bloomsbury figures. His own personal restraint and sobriety makes the seriousness of his claims for poetry the more impressive.

The people which ceases to care for its literary inheritance becomes barbaric; the people which ceases to produce literature ceases to move in thought and sensibility. The poetry of a people takes its life from a people's speech and in turn gives life to it; and represents its highest point of consciousness, its greatest power and its most delicate sensibility.   (p. 15)

And in another of these dicta we have an example of something familiar to readers of Eliot's poems, a point at which a characteristic self-observation turns into a statement of general truth.

[Poetry] may make us from time to time a little more aware of the deeper, unnamed feelings which form the substratum of our being, to which we rarely penetrate; for our lives are mostly a constant evasion of ourselves, and an evasion of the visible and sensible world.
                                                        (p. 155)

For the rest, when the neo-classical trappings are laid aside, what Eliot really appeals for is a catholic taste in poetry. His virtue is that he is always reminding us how hard it is to acquire this: most critics' statements about 'poetry' only apply to a limited range of it, the poetry they themselves can appreciate. The moral he draws can be found in what he said in writing of Dryden some years before.

Our valuation of poetry, in short, depends upon several considerations, upon the permanent and upon the mutable and transitory. When we try to isolate the essentially poetic, we bring our pursuit in the end to something insignificant; our standards vary with every poet whom we consider. All we can hope to do, in the attempt to introduce some order into our preferences, is to clarify our reasons for finding pleasure in the poetry that we like.

                                           (*Selected Essays*, 1932, p. 309)

At a time when in the literary world 'fashionable madmen raise / Their pedantic boring cry', we should be grateful for what Eliot gives us in the best parts of *The Use of Poetry*: that memorably expressed good sense which we honour with the name of wisdom. He does not offer new things, but enables us to see familiar things anew. 'But to say this is only to say what you know already, if you have felt poetry and thought about your feelings' (p. 155).

12

I. A. Richards

Christopher Isherwood has given in *Lions and Shadows* (1938) a lively description of the first impact of I. A. Richards in Cambridge:

Here, at last, was the prophet we had been waiting for...he was infinitely more than a brilliant new literary critic: he was our guide, our evangelist, who revealed to us, in a succession of astounding lightning-flashes, the entire expanse of the Modern World...Poets, ordered Mr. Richards, were to reflect aspects of the World Picture. Poetry wasn't a holy flame, a fire-bird from the moon; it was a group of interrelated stimuli acting upon the ocular nerves, the semi-circular canals, the brain, the solar plexus, the digestive and sexual organs. It did you medically demonstrable good, like a dose of strychnine or salts. We became behaviourists, materialists, atheists. In our conversation we substituted the word 'emotive' for the word 'beautiful'; we learnt to condemn inferior work as a 'failure in communication', or more crushing still, as 'a private poem'. We talked excitedly about 'the phantom aesthetic state'.

This well suggests the dual attraction of Richards's early writings. On the one hand, he sounded austere, clinical, disinfectant, the man in a white coat. In this respect, his criticism was a counterpart to T. S. Eliot's early verse. Eliot had administered a cold douche after the over-poetical poetry of the Georgians: Richards's dry astringent style counteracted the rhapsodical excesses of critics in a late nineteenth-century tradition, such as A. C. Bradley with his 'Poetry is a spirit.' On the other hand, with all its dry scientific air, the early work of Richards made (as Mr Isherwood testifies) a strongly 'emotive' impact. There is in it an atmosphere of buoyant optimism, a sense that age-old mysteries are being at last unravelled, the 'chaos of aesthetic theories' brought to order. It is possible that contemplating the remarkable diagram in *Principles of Literary Criticism* which is supposed to depict schematically what happens in the nervous system when the eye reads a line of Browning, some readers may have received a fleeting suggestion of the Grand Academy of

Lagado. But more must have been impressed by the Aristotelian sweep and breadth of Richards's concerns, and the promise of new and powerful intellectual disciplines.

All that was in the 1920s, before Richards made his home in the United States. Today his vogue-reputation is over. On this side of the Atlantic he was superseded, as an influential literary critic, by his one-time admirer F. R. Leavis; on the other side, perhaps by the ebullient Canadian 'anatomist' of criticism, Northrop Frye. And his book of essays, *So Much Nearer*, though in its studies of 'communication' it plunges enthusiastically into the world of computers and advanced technology, is unlikely to range him, in the world of cultural fashions, beside a Marshall McLuhan or a Noam Chomsky as a 'maker of the modern mind'. He came to be widely regarded as a mere survivor from the *avant-garde* of the day before yesterday. Once it appeared to be Richards's strength that he could bridge the communication gap between general readers and the technically qualified – the psychologists, the philosophers, the linguists. Today he may have lost the interest of both publics. He fell, as he once rose, between two stools. Many readers today will accept as their own the account of him which Jerome P. Schiller, in his excellent analytic study *I. A. Richards' Theory of Literature* (1970) ascribes to 'the average critic':

Richards may be important as one of the founders of the New Criticism. This can be due only to his conviction that poetry is important and to his technique for studying it. His theory of poetry is absurd: he claims that the only way to study poetry is through psychology; he maintains that poetry does not say anything, so it has nothing to do with our beliefs. No wonder he lost interest in poetry years ago and started worrying about Basic English and general education.

But if we go and read Richards, and if we also read this book by Mr Schiller, and the longer book on Richards by W. H. N. Hotopf (*Language, Thought and Comprehension*, 1965) we shall soon find reasons to revise that account. One way in which it is unfair is in its ignoring of the unity of Richards's work – notwithstanding occasional shifts of nomenclature and emphasis.

His concern throughout his career has been the same: a concern with understanding, and with misunderstanding. It should be remembered that his first major work was *The Meaning of Meaning* (1923), written in collaboration with C. K. Ogden, that idiosyncratic genius who translated Wittgenstein's *Tractatus* and invented Basic English.

The Meaning of Meaning deals with the influence of language on philosophical theories: it has something in common with the attempts of contemporary philosophers, under the influence of Russellian logic, to create an ideal unambiguous language. In the background are books like Bertrand Russell's *Philosophy of Logical Atomism* (1918) and Wittgenstein's *Tractatus Logico-Philosophicus* (1921). Perhaps the most memorable part of *The Meaning of Meaning* is the authors' exposure of the role of 'word-magic' in traditional modes of thought: here they enlisted the help of modern anthropology (Malinowski contributed a long appendix). Its copiousness and gusto, its exuberant if eccentric erudition, and its cheerful iconoclasm, make the book highly enjoyable, and help us to overlook its philosophical crudities and the improbability of its general thesis – for surely it is very doubtful whether the long history of metaphysics can be explained merely as the result of 'word-magic', or of grammatical confusions. But *The Meaning of Meaning* was less a sober treatise than a manifesto. Human thought, it proclaimed, had become diseased through the misuse of language. The cure was the cultivation of the right kind of linguistic awareness. The authors were not slow to offer their therapeutic programme. Something of the book's essential aim – and something too of its youthful confidence and over-optimism – have survived in Richards's work in all its phases.

In the books that followed, down to *The Philosophy of Rhetoric* (1936), Richards made that long excursion through literary criticism during which his most popular writings were published. *Principles of Literary Criticism* (1924) made his reputation current. It is his best book, because it is more of a *book*, and less of a paste-up, than any of the others. In *Principles* Richards denied that poetry (there his main concern) belonged to a separate aesthetic realm. He defined a poem as 'a class of experiences which do not differ in any character more than a certain amount, varying for each character, from a standard experience'. And this 'standard experience' he defined as 'the relevant experience of the poet when contemplating the completed composition'. Richards does not specify in what way, or how much, experiences may permissibly differ from the standard experience. Nor does he explain the usefulness, as a standard, of an experience which presumably is inaccessible to us. But his phrasing does serve to suggest the psychological bent of his work, his determination to disentangle criticism from mystifications and metaphysics.

Richards believed that aesthetics was in principle amenable to science. Yet, contrary to the average critic's belief, he did not offer to make *criticism* a science. Nor did he think aesthetics at present susceptible to laboratory methods. What he did do was to sketch a *possible* psychological analysis of the effects and value of poetry. Literary readers tended to be mystified or repelled by this analysis, with its talk of 'impulses' and 'the nervous system'. They did not recognise its purely speculative character. Nor did they give Richards due credit for the ingenuity with which he connected the technical psychology of his day (expounded in text-books like George F. Stout's) with his quasi-utilitarian theory of value, and both in turn with his aesthetic theory.

It may indeed be as a 'scientific' *jeu d'esprit* that *Principles* is most vulnerable. But its lasting interest is to be found in its aesthetic theory – or rather, in its articulation of a modern taste which the new poetry of Eliot was doing much to form: a taste which rated complex poetry above simple, encouraged intellectuality and irony, and promoted an attitude Eliot had already detected in Marvell's poetry, 'a recognition, implicit in the expression of an experience, of other experiences which are possible'. (Irony, Richards maintained, is a quality of the greatest poetry.) But besides this 'period' interest, *Principles* also demonstrates clearly the most engaging aspect of Richards's work: his lifelong enmity both to pedantry and to preciousness. The one emerges, with lasting effect, in those parts of the book which demolish the pretensions of formalists, prosodists, and *a priori* literary theorists of all kinds; the other is seen in those passages which insist on the continuity between the 'values' of poetry and the 'values' of general living.

One of the most controversial elements in *Principles* is the idea Richards was soon to popularise in *Science and Poetry*: that the 'Magical View' of the world, on which poetry and art had hitherto depended, cannot now be sincerely held. Richards always stressed the vital importance of sincerity, even proposing a 'ritual' for inducing it in *Practical Criticism*. 'I would meet you upon this honestly' is a note he constantly strikes. His acclaim for the Eliot of *The Waste Land* was founded on his conviction that Eliot had succeeded where Yeats or D. H. Lawrence had failed: Eliot had achieved sincerity by accepting 'the neutralization of nature' and freeing his poetry from dependence on any beliefs. This last suggestion was to bewilder many readers, including, it soon appeared, Eliot himself. The average critic takes it to mean that poetry is meaningless. But Richards did not think that. The beliefs he had in mind seem to have been religious beliefs; and Richards's concern was, rather in the spirit of the later Matthew Arnold, to retain the beneficent effect of 'literature' while dropping untenable 'dogma'.

In this spirit, employing the distinction adumbrated in *The Meaning of Meaning* between 'emotive' and 'referential' uses of language, Richards allocated poetry to the emotive use. Here again he was often misunderstood. He was thought to have pronounced – with manifest unsoundness – that certain *words* were emotive (rather than certain uses of words). And he was much criticised for his use in *Science and Poetry* of the term 'pseudo-statement' to distinguish 'emotive' utterances like 'God's in His heaven' from 'referential' ones like 'There is life on Mars.' Richards was accused of dismissing poetry as beautiful nonsense in abject deference to a shallow scientism. And the term he used is certainly unfortunate, since the prefix 'pseudo' sounds derogatory, though it is not meant to be. In fact, his concept of 'pseudo-statements' can easily be interpreted so as to satisfy the most exalted traditional claims for the poet. For when Richards says that 'a statement in poetry arouses attitudes much more wide and general in direction than the references of the statement', he could be taken as saying not that the statements of poetry, in contrast to those of science, are meaningless, but that they are more general, or even universal, in their application.

The Meaning of Meaning had been concerned with therapy of the intellect: *Principles*, and *Practical Criticism* (1929), were more concerned with therapy of the sensibility. Richards agreed with those who stress the importance of literature and its capacity to fulfil social needs (though his emphasis, as Mr Hotopf complains, is 'individualist', and he dwells almost wholly on personal self-culture). In *Principles* he describes art as both the product and (if properly received) the source of a greater and more various and, above all, a more *ordered* set of experiences than can be got elsewhere. The 'release', the 'repose in the midst of stress', the 'balance and composure' we should find in art were for him given most of all by great tragedy; for it is tragedy which supremely provides a 'balance and reconciliation of opposite and discordant qualities'. Richards's interest in Coleridge, which was to become a cult, is apparent here. But his usual way of speaking about art, in his early work, is like Pater's, as when he speaks of 'those hours', experienced by the artist and conveyed to the recipient, when 'habitual narrowness of interests or confused bewilderment are replaced by an intricately wrought composure'. He criticises Pater, however, for stressing the intense 'moments' that art can give us, rather than the lasting dispositions and emotional habits which it encourages us to form.

Art, then – above all, poetry – is, according to Richards, not a luxury but a necessity, for that 'self-completion' and 'increased order' without which our mental life is shapeless and confused. To appreciate it is to defeat the fixations of habit and convention, to overcome our 'stock responses' in favour of ever finer and more discriminating ones. But when Richards carried out the well-known experiment he describes in *Practical Criticism* – of setting poems without authors' names before Cambridge students, and recording their sometimes hilarious misapprehensions – he became convinced that much more educational work was necessary before poetry could perform its function. The analytic part of this book has had a great influence, not only on the incipient 'new criticism', as John Crowe Ransom was to call it, but on pedagogic practice in schools and colleges. That 'practical criticism' has now often become at the same time irresponsible, and a sterile routine, is acknowledged, regretfully, in *So Much Nearer* (1970).

Richards himself went on from *Practical Criticism* to explore the theoretical implications of his growing conviction that poetry is best seen, not as 'the emotive use of language', but as language requiring multiple interpretation. In *The Philosophy of Rhetoric* he wrote some of the few valuable pages there are on metaphor – pages which should enlighten those who think of it too simply in terms of likeness between 'vehicle' and 'tenor' (to use the helpful terminology Richards introduced). In *Interpretation in Teaching* (1938) he applied the methods of *Practical Criticism* to the study of prose, criticising elementary books on logic, rhetoric, and grammar, and finding them full of mistaken doctrines. Once again Richards showed himself the enemy of pedantry. He came forward as the advocate of 'ordinary fluid language with full settings', against those logicians and grammarians who are 'stuck fast in an injudiciously technicalized set of words'. And in *So Much Nearer* he has some spirited and amusing criticisms to make of the new pedantries and abstractionist illusions (such as 'the fluent speaker') in the linguistics of Chomsky and his school.

How much has Richards achieved? If the answer is uncertain, this is because (as he good-humouredly complained) he has been found hard to interpret. And this is not entirely on account of the intrinsic difficulty of his subject-matter, or the obtuseness of his readers. Richards's procedures are frequently confusing. The most obvious obstacle is stylistic. Sentence by sentence he can write trenchantly and wittily. But all too often the reader is distracted by sudden coynesses, ambiguous obscurities, the unexplained presence of out-of-the-way quotations or enigmatic Chinese fables. Cryptic hints are dropped, tips thrown out, bright ideas gleam and vanish in opaque contexts. We feel that Richards often digresses waywardly, goes off at tangents. He seems too capricious to submit himself to any particular discipline of thought. Sometimes his exposition is roundabout to the point of perversity. Thus in *Interpretation in Teaching* he is concerned to discuss the common belief that grammar summarises usage. But we have to pick our way through his intricate commentary on the ill-formulated opinions of immature protocolists on what an old-fashioned grammarian said in attacking the views of another author, before we can divine what Richards's own views are – if then.

It is noteworthy that Mr Schiller, a philosopher, and Mr Hotopf, a psychologist, constantly remark on Richards's obscurities, inconsequences, and vagueness. Richards recognises that 'talk about poems may have all sorts of purposes behind it: social, suasive, literary, comparative, analytic, scientific'. The trouble is that he himself is apt to switch without warning from one purpose to another; whether the aesthetician's or the critic's, the psychologist's or the logician's, the linguist's or the lexicographer's. This greatly adds to the ambiguity which – with ironic appropriateness in an opponent of the One Proper Meaning superstition – is the main defect of his work. Above all, ambiguity overhangs the nature of the *claim* Richards makes for what he does. Sometimes he seems only to make a modest claim, for the value of clarity in thinking and writing. But at other times his tone suggests that his proposals are truly momentous: he promises 'a general theoretical study of language capable of opening to us new powers over our minds comparable to those which systematic physical inquiries are giving us over our environment'. Yet the use he makes in *Coleridge on Imagination* (1935) – from which this quotation comes – of Coleridge's distinction between fancy and imagination cannot be thought to advance that 'theoretical study'. His claims for it are unconvincing.

As a theorist, then, Richards seems to promise more than he performs. His place in the history of criticism is secure: but as a critic in his own right he is insubstantial. Apart from interesting pioneer essays on writers like Gerard Manley Hopkins or E. M. Forster, his contribution here is small. In the end the best of his writings may survive in a generous selection from those asides, those pregnant suggestions, those insights into 'words and their ways', which abound in his work. It may be that he could have achieved more if he had not insisted on always being a 'loner' and confined himself to a discipline not invented by himself. His work as a whole leaves us with a sense of squandered talents. But, as George Orwell said of H. G. Wells, what a thing it is, after all, to have any talents to squander.

13

Yvor Winters: Counter-romantic

Forms of Discovery begins with a short introductory chapter, in which Yvor Winters summarises his theory of poetry.

A poem is a statement in words about a human experience; since language is conceptual in nature, this statement will be more or less rational or at least apprehensible in rational terms, or else the medium will be violated and the poem weakened. But the language has connotation as well as denotation. . .for man is more than a merely rational animal. In so far as the rational statement is understandable and acceptable, and in so far as the feeling is properly motivated by the rational statement, the poem will be good.

(He goes on to explain the functions of metre, rhythm, syntax, and grammar in poetry.) It should be noted that Winters's account of poetry omits all reference to invention, imagination, or feigning. The core of it is his insistence that a poem is a 'rational statement' about 'reality'. And as 'reality' is defined as 'the realm which we perceive with our unaided senses', it is not easy to see how invention, imagination, or feigning come in. We may also wonder how the critic is to decide whether a poem's 'rational statement' is 'understandable and acceptable', and whether the 'feeling' it motivates is 'proper'. To take an example. The poet wishes to say 'I think longingly of my beloved's beauty.' He then (if he is Yeats) invests the statement with feeling and writes 'I dream of a Ledaean body.' How is the critic to decide whether the initial statement is 'acceptable', and that the feeling it motivates, when turned into poetry, is proper? The only answer seems to be that he must have a look at the poet's beloved, or pictures of her, if she is not available. And this Winters duly does – with negative results: '. . .the portraits of Maude [*sic*] Gonne which I have seen are not very convincing' (p. 218).

Usually, however, Winters does not apply his test for rationality and proper feeling so literally. His general position is, rather, what might be called Platonic realism – though he prefers to call it 'absolutism'. It comes out in such typical remarks as:

'The romantic lover of nature dislikes universals and can neither see nor describe nature.' In other words – to quote from an old anecdote about Turner's paintings – if a lover of nature wants to describe a sunset properly, what he must try to describe is not his idea of it, or your idea, or my idea, but God Almighty's idea. Similarly with human subject-matter, and its literary expression. 'To write about human experience with distinction, one must know the relevant universals; to manage poetic form with distinction or to perceive it clearly when managed by others, one must know the relevant universals.'

The obvious difficulty in this theory is how we are to *know* that we know the relevant universals; that we have attained, or at least approximated to, the point of view of God. Winters never deals directly with this difficulty. But we may infer from his practice that he believes we at least know when we are 'getting warm', from the feeling of moral conviction which a great poem induces in us. For Winters describes his theory of literature as 'moralistic'. This he distinguishes, in the foreword to *In Defence of Reason*, from the 'didactic' theory, which holds that 'literature offers us useful precepts and moral instruction'. Winters rejects this theory. But it should be noted that he says he rejects it because it accounts only for the 'paraphraseable content' of literature. Literature, then, on Winters's view, *has* a paraphraseable content; and this content is important. And he does not deny that it does, or ought to, consist of useful precepts and moral instruction. It would seem, moreover (to judge from the way in which he deals with many poems), that the moral wisdom he requires from poetry is not merely 'implied' or 'embodied' in the poem – to use the present-day critical patter which Winters would reject. It is something actually stated and explicit. But the difference between Winters's theory, and the didactic theory as described by him, still stands: because his poet, as distinct from the mere didact, not only states moral truths but, by means of his art, makes us feel them.

Winters's conception of art, then, is that it is the same as technique. ('The term *art*, as I use it, signifies *method*.') Like the ancient Greeks, he does not draw the customary modern distinction between pure and applied art, or between art and craft. He proposes an analogy between poetry and athletics. ('The great poet resembles the great boxer in the ring.') It may have escaped Winters that this analogy is in at least one respect defective. While there is a convincing public test for the greatness of a boxer (namely whether he knocked out strong opponents) where is the equivalent test for the great poet? None, at any rate, that I can imagine Winters accepting. I am sure he would not accept widespread academic approbation as conclusive; still less, a poet's notoriety or worldly success. At any rate, the analogy with athletics suggests that Winters thinks of a good poem as a successful performance according to antecedent specifications. This view also seems to emerge from his account of the expert critic, whom Winters, drawing on his own experience, compares to a dog-breeder. Where the untrained eye would only see a lot of Airedales (or perhaps just a lot of dogs) the trained eye of the breeder can see all sorts of interesting individual differences. And out of his long familiarity with these he gradually forms a conception of the ideal or standard which the prizewinning Airedale must comply with (the Form of the Airedale, so to speak). Applying the analogy to criticism, then, the critic's situation, as Winters sees it, should be something like this. Where the ordinary observer would merely see fourteen lines of verse (or perhaps only fourteen rows of black marks, if he is dyslexic) the trained critic sees a Petrarchan sonnet. And out of his long experience of Petrarchan sonnets he gradually forms a conception of the ideal Petrarchan sonnet, with which he compares, to its advantage or otherwise, the particular Petrarchan sonnet before him.

This may be a tenable, if today very unfashionable, account of the procedure of literary critics. But what is baffling about Winters's own procedure is that, although he appears to invite us to judge a poem as a performance according to antecedent specifications, he never makes it clear what these are. For one of the many perplexing things about this strange book is that we never learn just what 'a short poem' is supposed to be. The title refers to its 'forms', yet we are offered no discussion of traditional kinds such as the ode, elegy, epistle, etc. This failure to be specific is all the more surprising, because elsewhere, in *The Function of*

Criticism, Winters affirms his conviction that the short poem is the supreme literary genre, ranking above the epic, the drama, or the novel. But as he never makes it plain what its scope is supposed to be, he cannot give a clear account of their limitations. All that we can reasonably infer about what he has in mind is that it is (in the seventeenth-century phrase) 'a paper of verses'; that is, a non-dramatic and non-narrative composition not much longer than about 200 lines ('Lycidas', which he discusses, has 193).

So much for Winters's critical theory. We must now examine his practise, as exemplified by the rest of the book. The first, and longest, chapter is a revision and expansion of his well-known essay on 'The Sixteenth Century Lyric in England', first published in 1939. Its main thesis is that the best sixteenth-century poetry is that written in what he calls the 'plain' style, rather than the 'Petrarchan' or 'courtly' style. He prefers, that is, what C. S. Lewis called the 'Drab' poets to Lewis's 'Golden' poets. 'The wisdom of poetry of this kind lies not in the acceptance of a truism, for anyone can accept a truism, at least formally, but in the realization of the truth of the truism: the realization resides in the feeling, the style.' One of the poets discussed with especial enthusiasm is Thomas Lord Vaux (1510–56). A poem called 'When all is done and said' is cited as evidence that 'even a simple and commonplace medium can be managed with extraordinary polish'. Vaux's poem of four verses is 'one of the most urbane fusions of wit and wisdom to be found in the miscellanies'. Here are the first and last verses of this urbane fusion:

> When all is done and said, in the end thus you shall find
> He most of all doth bathe in bliss that hath a quiet mind;
> And, clear from worldly cares, to deem can be content
> The sweetest time in all his life in thinking to be spent.
> . . .
> Our wealth leaves us at death, our kinsmen in the grave;
> But virtues of the mind unto the heavens with us we have.
> Wherefore, for virtue's sake, I can be well content
> The sweetest time of all my life in thinking to be spent.

But for Winters the chief figure of the early Renaissance poets, 'one of the greatest masters of the short poem in this century', is

George Gascoigne (1542–77). One of the passages quoted from Gascoigne, of which Winters says that its 'seriousness, passion and power should be obvious', is this:

> If fortune favoured him, then may that man rejoice,
> And think himself a happy man by hap of happy choice.
> Who loves and is beloved of one as good, as true,
> As kind as Cleopatra was, and yet more bright of hue,
> Her eyes as grey as glass, her teeth as white as milk,
> A ruddy lip, a dimpled chin, a skin as smooth as silk,
> A wight what could you more, that may content man's mind,
> And hath supplies for every want that any man can find,
> And may himself assure, when hence his life shall pass,
> She will be stung to death with snakes, as Cleopatra was.

Other sixteenth-century poets discussed include Wyatt, Alexander Scott, Surrey, Barnabe Googe, Raleigh, Nashe, and John Heywood. We now come to the Petrarchan or courtly movement. Winters has a low opinion of Spenser, but grants certain merits to Sidney, though he does not think him a great poet. Nor does he think Shakespeare one, at any rate in the sonnets. Of these Winters regards LXXVII as the most impressive, though its impressiveness may be accidental. His real enthusiasm is reserved for two other poets of this period, Ben Jonson and Fulke Greville. Donne, on the other hand, he judges to be fashionably over-rated. He thinks Donne obsessed with sex, a bad metrist, and often irritatingly perverse and artificial. He censures 'A Valediction, Forbidding Mourning', and 'The Canonization', and decides that the greatest of the love-poems is 'A Valediction of my Name, in the Window'. (Donne's 'divine' poems are not discussed.) Other poets dealt with hereabouts are Daniel, Drayton, Greene, Peele, Lodge, Lyly, the anonymous poems of the songbooks, and the work of composer–poets such as Morley, Campion, and Dowland.

We are now in the seventeenth century. Winters praises Lord Herbert's 'Elegy over a Tomb' and George Herbert's 'Church Monuments', the metre and rhythm of which he analyses at great length (he is a keen prosodist). But his general opinion of George Herbert is not high: Herbert's poems mostly 'exhibit a cloying and almost infantile pietism'. He has words of praise for

Henry King's 'Exequy', though finding it unequal. Crashaw he sees as an unsatisfactory poet, full of erotic religiosity, but he has some praise for the 'Shepherds' Hymn'. Henry Vaughan is judged a great poet on the strength of 'The Lamp' and 'To his Books'. We come now to Marvell, who receives some praise for his brilliance, but is not judged a great poet. Winters takes the opportunity, while praising Traherne's 'On News', to disparage Wordsworth's 'Immortality Ode'. 'Traherne seems to give us the life, the movements of the soul. Wordsworth gives us bad oratory about his own clumsy emotions and a landscape that he has never really perceived.' Philip Pain, Edward Taylor, and some of the seventeenth-century continuators of the Elizabethan song tradition are then discussed. Herrick receives some praise, but is judged trivial in comparison with Ben Jonson. Winters does not think Milton a great poet, at any rate in his shorter poems. (And there are suggestions that Winters does not admire *Paradise Lost* either.) For him the later sonnets are the best of Milton. 'Lycidas' is examined and disparaged later, as a forerunner of the 'sentimental–romantic decadence' of the eighteenth and nineteenth centuries.

'The greatest English poem of the 18th century, and one of the greatest in our language', is Charles Churchill's 'The Dedication (to Warburton)'. Dryden and Pope are dealt with only in passing, and judged inferior to Churchill. He gets a whole chapter, a compliment not paid in this book to any other poet. Nor does Winters supply for any other poem the long historical and biographical commentary he offers on the 'Dedication'. We have now reached the sentimental–romantic decadence, which has gone on till the present time. It derives mainly from the third Earl of Shaftesbury, and the work of Emerson. Among its pernicious doctrines are the following: '...whatever is, is right; our impulses are good and can only lead us to virtue; human reason is the principal source of error and evil; study and the effort to improve ourselves are unnecessary and in fact dangerous; and whoever sees any contradiction among these ideas or between these ideas and experience is unworthy of refutation'. In close alliance with these doctrines is the theory of the 'association of ideas', which maintains that 'all ideas arise from sensory perceptions and then from associations among these; by the end of the 18th century it was often held that all ideas could be expressed in terms of sensory impressions, and this notion is still with us; Pound tells us that the natural object is always the *adequate* symbol'.

After discussion of the Countess of Winchelsea, Swift (dismissed as a poet), and Gay, Winters comes to the poetry of Samuel Johnson. He admires Johnson for opposing romanticism, but cares for him as a critic and master of English prose rather than as a poet. 'Poetry appears to have been an acquired language in which he was never entirely at home...The force of the great character comes through some of the poems, especially through a few remarkable lines, but with labor.' 'His two most famous poems, the two imitations of Juvenal, are, in my opinion, very dull reading.' With Dyer's 'Grongar Hill', Collins's 'Ode to Evening', and Gray's 'Elegy written in a Country Churchyard', we reach the full flowering of the sentimental–associationist tradition. Winters is caustic about all these poems, especially the first two. He finds some words of praise for Smart's 'Song to David', notwithstanding its 'enthusiasm'; for some passages here and there in Crabbe; and for a poem called 'The Hasty Pudding', by an American, Joel Barlow. Of Burns he praises 'Holy Willie's Prayer' and 'To a Louse'. Blake he clearly finds a critical problem. 'I find it impossible either to accept Blake as a serious poet, or to discard him outright.' In the end Blake is disparaged by the application of two of Winters's favourite touchstones, 'Down in the depth of mine iniquity', by Greville, and 'Low Barometer', by Bridges.

The period commonly called 'romantic' Winters dismisses altogether. Wordsworth was 'a very bad poet who nevertheless wrote a few good lines'. Coleridge is likewise dismissed; in 'Dejection', and in everything else but the 'Mariner', he is 'merely one of the indistinguishable bad poets of an unfortunate period'. And the 'Mariner' is only 'a story for children with the Sunday-school moral attached'. Byron is 'amusing but shallow', 'popular journalism'. In Shelley 'one can find no single poem that is not weak or worse in conception and predominantly bad in execution'. Landor is given moderate praise for 'Rose Aylmer' and one or two other things, but he is compared to his disadvantage with Winters's friend and fellow-American poet J. V. Cunningham. As for Keats, 'the "Ode to a Nightingale" is a mediocre poem with a few good lines and some of the worst lines of the century'. The Victorians fare no better. 'Tennyson has nothing to say, and his style is insipid.' Browning is unique among these poets in that he succeeded in escaping from the 'pseudo-political clichés' which make most of these poets so 'abominable', but he did not achieve 'precise concentration'. His language is 'fresh, brisk, shallow, and journalistic'. Arnold is 'sentimental to the point of being lachrymose...he offers the worst pseudo-poetic diction imaginable; he is capable, though not invariably guilty, of very crude rhythm'. Apart from one or two poems Christina Rossetti is 'for the most part mild, diffuse and sentimental'. Swinburne 'wrote no poems that will endure serious reading'.

In short, according to Winters, 'the 18th and 19th centuries were low periods in the history of English poetry; the text-books will convey this message to my reader's grandchildren'. But his story has a happy ending. 'The period from Jones Very to the present, an American period except for the inclusion of Bridges, Hardy, and T. Sturge Moore, is one of the two greatest periods of poetry in English and, I think, the greater of the two.' (The other period is from Wyatt to 1700.) Hardy, like Emily Dickinson, was 'essentially a naif, a primitive, but one of remarkable genius'. He had the 'best eye for natural detail in all British poetry'. Bridges was 'a poet whose native talent and whose immediate background appear to have been at odds'. He wrote too much, and rarely freed himself from the sentimental language and pseudo-spirituality of Wordsworth and Shelley. But he reached great heights in 'Low Barometer' and 'Eros', and in his poetic drama on Nero. Yeats, on the other hand, is subjected to prolonged castigation. 'A good deal of scholarly work has been done on Yeats in recent years; unfortunately, the better one understands him, the harder it is to take him seriously.' Of 'A Coat' Winters remarks: 'Yeats never learned to walk naked, although he managed to shed a few of the more obvious ribbons of the 1890s.' The main reason why Yeats is so highly admired

today is 'his power of self-assertion'. His 'bardic tone' is for most
readers synonymous with greatness. We learn that Yeats's contemporary T. Sturge Moore was a far greater poet. Moore's great
achievements are the poetic drama *Daimonassa*, the first sonnet
entitled 'Silence', and 'From Titian'.

Finally, the Americans arrive. 'The Cricket', by F. G. Tuckerman (1821–73) is a very great poem. Poe and Whitman are
dismissed elsewhere as worthless, like Robinson Jeffers. But
Winters has high, though judicious, praise for Emily Dickinson;
and E. A. Robinson, on whom he wrote a whole book, is one of
his great poets. Frost he deals with elsewhere, dismissing him
here as minor and Wordsworthian. Of Wallace Stevens we are
asked to admire 'Sunday Morning' and 'The Course of a
Particular', and a few other poems, but otherwise Stevens's
work is said to be mannered, fanciful, and essentially trivial.
Poems by Louise Bogan, Edgar Bowers, and N. Scott Momaday
are singled out as great. Ezra Pound receives severe criticism,
both for his theory and practice, but also some praise; the case of
Hart Crane is similar. 'Early Pound is not great poetry; it is
superior Swinburne. As Crane makes us more acutely aware of
the defects of Whitman, so Pound makes us more acutely aware
of the defects of his predecessors. In both poets there is something
admirable, which sharpens our sense of the defects.' Winters
speaks at some length of William Carlos Williams, Pound's
associate in the free-verse movement, which once claimed
Winters's own allegiance, before his shift to 'classicism'. Williams
is praised and blamed, the blame predominating ('he was a
thorough bore in print except on a few occasions'). Marianne
Moore was a 'birdwit', but Mina Loy a 'talented eccentric'.
T. S. Eliot is 'inferior to Pound'. None of Eliot's poems is
examined in detail, though the opening of 'Burnt Norton' is
characterised as 'simple-minded profundities' followed by 'sad
little clichés'. Eliot is dismissed as thoroughly mediocre. 'He has
inspired generations of imitators because he is easy to imitate.'
Allen Tate is praised for 'The Cross', but otherwise regarded as
'eccentric', along with Yeats, Hopkins (adversely analysed in
The Function of Criticism), and most of Stevens. The book ends
with a short account of Winters's own work, that of his wife

Janet Lewis, and other poets associated with him at Stanford University. He has had 'neither the time nor the inclination' to deal with John Masefield, Alfred Noyes, Edgar Lee Masters, Carl Sandburg, Vachel Lindsay, Amy Lowell, Elinor Wylie, Edna St Vincent Millay, E. E. Cummings, Archibald Macleish, Dylan Thomas, W. H. Auden, Robert Lowell, Richard Wilbur. ('I name them lest the reader think that I do not know about them.') He ends with a parting admonition: 'Let us beware of saying that the best poets of our time deal with the subjects which are most important to our time. . .Five hundred years from now the subjects which will appear to have been the most important will be the subjects treated by the surviving poets who have written the most intelligently.'

We must wait, then, for A.D. 2473 to settle these questions. In the meantime, I will summarise the mature conclusions of this eminent critic and poet, after a lifetime of devotion to the study, teaching, and composition of English poetry. His definition of a great poet is a poet who has written at least one great poem. When he applies this definition, his list of great poets in English after 1500 excludes, among others, Shakespeare, Donne, Marvell, Milton, Dryden, Pope, Gray, Johnson, Blake, Wordsworth, Coleridge, Byron, Shelley, Keats, Tennyson, Browning, Arnold, Hopkins, Yeats, Pound, and Eliot. The great poets are Gascoigne, Greville, Ben Jonson, the Herberts, Vaughan, Churchill, Hardy, Bridges, Tuckerman, Emily Dickinson, Robinson, Stevens (in 'Sunday Morning'), Louise Bogan, Edgar Bowers, J. V. Cunningham, and N. Scott Momaday. We note that of the seventeen great poets writing in English since 1500, eight were American.

Thus *Forms of Discovery* offers a drastically revisionary account of the history of poetry in English. It has provoked widely different reactions. Mr John Fraser, discussing it in the *Southern Review* (Winter 1969), considers that 'Winters is very largely right. . .I do mean right, not just courageous, forceful, challenging and so on – right in his general view of the history of poetry in English, and right in a great many of his particular judgments.' On the other hand, other reviewers have dismissed the book as mainly revealing the obsessions of a crass and blundering pedant, a belated Donatus or Rymer. The British reviewers who took that view have also judged the author a painful case of American provincialism, confirming Eliot's remark about the drawbacks of being born into an unsettled society.

I must now make my own attitude explicit. I cannot admire this book. It does not seem to me, as a whole, either sound literary history or sound criticism. Clearly Winters is not a writer like W. P. Ker, who tries to give as thorough and impartial an account of his subject as he can, given the inevitable limitations of his knowledge, taste, and capacity. He writes as an advocate, in causes in which he feels justice has not yet been done. And this is a perfectly legitimate way to write: T. S. Eliot's essay on Dante is a distinguished example. But the critical advocate does best when he takes us, his readers, by the hand, and shows us the evidence on which we can form our own opinion. He always remembers that critical argument can at most be persuasive, never demonstrative. In these respects Winters seems to me often to fail.

Then there is much in Winters's critical theory which I find unsatisfactory, and which I think has led him into wrong or blinkered judgments. I cannot see that the issue of 'absolutism' versus 'relativism' is worth all the fuss Winters makes about it. Presumably the absolutist does not claim to be actually in possession of absolute truths – at any rate, Winters does not. But in that case all he can do is what any other critic does: give reasons for his views, make plain what his judgments apply to, and allow them (in Plato's phrase) to run the gauntlet of argument; always bearing in mind that the criteria he employs, and his mode of arguing, are themselves open to further discussion. And if he succeeds in convincing a number of people who are interested in the subject, open-minded, and as unlike himself as possible, he may reasonably conclude that there is something in his views. The only way in which Winters seems to me to satisfy these requirements is his praiseworthy habit of specifying the poems on which his judgments are based. He says that he was rebuked for this by Austin Warren; but I agree with Winters against Warren that a critic should always do it. As for the critical approach Winters recommends, I think it wrong to judge a literary work according to whether it meets antecedent specifications (even if he had stated them). And the proposal that a critic should compare the work in front of him with some ideal, non-existent work I think quite misguided. Nor do I think Winters actually does this when he is at his best as a critic: like most critics, he compares and analyses existent poems. As to his general standards of judgment, they seem to be very narrow, and to attach far too much importance to a poet's explicit moral valuations. While the conventional wisdom may also be un-satisfactory, with its cant about 'dramatisation' or 'tension' or 'the distancing of an attitude' etc., at least it recognises, as Winters does not, the presence in most poems of a dramatic or fictional element. At the same time I think he has performed a service to literature in calling attention to poems of grave, reflective generalisation, which the conventional wisdom of our day tends to overlook. There may be geese among his swans, but he has found fine poems, both old and new, which had not been noticed. He was himself a distinguished poet, if of limited gifts; his best poems I find beautiful in a rather aloof way (I am struck by the recurrence in them of the word 'cold'). And I can believe that he was a gifted teacher of poetry. I think he also performed a service in questioning the conventional valuation of Shake-speare's sonnets, Donne, Hopkins, and Yeats, though I disagree with much that he says in those discussions. His dismissal of Wordsworth and Eliot, however, seems to me quite inadequately based; he hardly bothers to conceal a hostility too strong for argument. It might be urged on Winters's behalf that these poets have been so extravagantly extolled by other critics that a little iconoclasm will do no harm. But that is not a becoming attitude in one who purports to write 'in defence of reason'.

Winters's conception of a great poet, as one who has written a great poem, seems to me also inadequate. (It goes with his habit of awarding ticks or crosses to individual lines and passages – sometimes in a way which seems inexplicably arbitrary.) Surely the definition of a great poet should include some reference to an *œuvre*, or to the need for range and variety? The definition Winters favours seems in part tactically motivated: he wishes to play down 'the cult of personality', to emphasise the poem rather than the poet. This seems to me in itself laudable. And with Winters's general anti-romanticism I have some sympathy. I share his dislike for modern irrationalism and emotionalism (probably increased, in Winters's case, by his friendship with Hart Crane, in whose life he seems to have played something like the role of Rowland Mallet to Crane's Roderick Hudson). But I am unconvinced by Winters's account of its origins. I cannot believe that Shaftesbury, or even Emerson, are so important (they are much less important, surely, than German idealism). And I also feel misgivings about the tone of voice in which Winters proclaims his conviction that his 'absolutism' is the only alternative to the madness of the romantics. A rationalism more confessedly fallibilist would surely be more appropriate, just as a more effective tone might be that of a balanced, classical critic.

Even when Winters expresses his conservatism so temperately, it seems to allow too little for men's capacity to adapt themselves to change. He constantly appeals to 'human experience'. But human experience changes, and one of the things which change it is experimental art – something that Winters, after his early free-verse phase, unvaryingly condemns. Yet history shows that much experiment is eventually accepted as normal, and indeed becomes part of the conventionality which the next experimental artist has to challenge. I agree with Winters that in a time like ours, so full of confusion about what is or is not good, a critic should strive for a comprehensive philosophy of life, of which his literary opinions are the partial expression. What I regret is, not that he has a philosophy, but that his philosophy seems so rigid – and so censorious. In this respect I prefer the implied philosophy of the 'new' critics, though I agree with Winters in rejecting their formalism, and in wanting to connect literature directly with life and society.

The most attractive aspect of Winters's criticism is its style. He can write on subjects like the function of the university, as a symbol for the disinterested search for truth, with a moving dignity which rebukes the shallowness and corruption of our times. And he is surely a master of incisiveness and wit. Just as I suspect that he was a better prose-writer than poet, so I sometimes wonder if he may not be eventually judged a better critic of prose than of verse. At any rate, he seems to me to have written especially well on some American prose-writers – on Henry James, for example, in *Maule's Curse*. But he himself seems to have wished to stand or fall as a critic of poetry. To judge his achievement, we can only do what he asks us to do: read the poems on which he based his standards, decide if he was right to do so, and then see if he has applied them relevantly and consistently to other poems. I must admit that so far I myself am unconvinced. But I would be willing to accept the application to Winters of what C. B. Tinker says of Samuel Johnson: his opinions 'pique our pride, make us review the evidence, restate the case, and criticize the critic. They certainly do not terminate the discussion, but initiate a critical inquiry in us, the readers.'

Winters's *Uncollected Essays and Reviews* have been edited with a very able introduction by Mr Francis Murphy. I found them disappointing. Winters's *forte* seems to have been the full-dress discussion of an author (such as his treatment of Henry James in *Maule's Curse*). He did not have T. S. Eliot's gift for making a memorable essay out of an occasional review. The good formulations in this book are all to be found, better stated, elsewhere in his writings. Nor did he have Eliot's extraordinary power of quotation. But above all his particular judgments are again and again quite unconvincing. It is true that most of the book deals with American poetry, and perhaps an Englishman is not qualified to disagree. But Winters himself showed no hesitation, as we have seen, in dismissing virtually the whole of English poetry since 1700, and in this volume he pronounces, with characteristic confidence, that 'the daughter of Robert Bridges, Mrs. Elizabeth Daryush, is one of the few first-rate poets to appear in the British Isles since the generation which produced her father and Thomas Hardy; aside from Yeats, T. Sturge Moore, and Viola Meynell, I can think of no poet now [1937] writing in England or Ireland sufficiently interesting to bear comparison with her' (p. 271). Distinguished critics have, of course, sometimes made very odd judgments. Johnson praised Blackmore; Leavis saw 'no room for doubt' about Ronald Bottrall; Graves and Riding took E. E. Cummings very seriously; Edmund Wilson was impressed by Gertrude Stein. But aberrations simply abound in Winters's pages.

Only a few examples need be given. On p. 30 Winters quotes this passage from Mina Loy:

> Lepers of the moon. . .
> unknowing
> How perturbing lights
> our spirit
> on the passion of Man
> until you turn on us our smooth fool's face
> like buttocks bared in aboriginal mockeries
> . . .
>   in the raw caverns of the Increate
> we forge the dusk of Chaos
> to that imperious jewelry of the Universe
> ——the Beautiful. . .

and praises it at some length, calling it 'a proof of genius – and of a genius that rises from a level of emotion and attitude which is as nearly common human territory as one can ever expect to find in a poet'. On the other hand (p. 52) 'the poetry of Mr. Eliot is a catastrophe'; and on p. 136 Eliot's 'Marina' is called 'a loosely written affair with several charming lines'. On p. 139, T. Sturge Moore is said to be a greater poet than Yeats; one of the passages quoted in support (p. 147) concludes with the lines:

> Like, ah! like on midnight hush
> Tears that under eyelids gush.

Winters stood by Sturge Moore to the end, but some of his other enthusiasms waned, conspicuously William Carlos Williams. In 1928 Williams is 'the most magnificent master of English and of human emotions since Thomas Hardy'. In 1939 Winters thought that he 'will prove as nearly indestructible as Herrick. . .the end of the present century will see him established, along with Stevens, as one of the two best poets of his generation'. But by 1965 Winters had come to the conclusion that 'to say that Williams was anti-intellectual would be almost an exaggeration: he did not know what the intellect was. He was a foolish and ignorant man, but at moments a fine stylist.' (What has become of Winters's theory of style?)

There is no need to raise the question of 'right' and 'wrong' here: the first test is persuasiveness, or otherwise. And the effect on me of so many odd judgments is that I begin to lose interest and feel no impulse to investigate when I hear, for example, that one Grant H. Code 'is one of the most distinguished poets living' [in 1932]. And when Winters pronounces (p. 168) that 'Randall Jarrell is wholly without the gift of language', I reflect, with a shrug, that this may be so, but Jarrell's novel *Pictures from an Institution* and his critical book *Poetry and the Age* still seem to me more worth reading than most of the poets Winters 'discovers' in this volume.

Not all of it is dull and unconvincing. Winters is amusing about Conrad Aiken, whose 'heroes commit murder to appropriate music, fall from skyscrapers, or wander in the lamplight in the rain (to steal a cadence from him) in exactly the same frame of mind and in the same colorless vocabulary' (p. 89). And there are passages which only a distinguished critic could have written; for example, this objection to Edmund Wilson's assumption, in some of his poems, of the Yeatsian mantle:

It is not a sufficient discipline for the wearing of that particular costume to admire the grand manner in general and the Yeatsian grand manner in particular. A traditional grand manner, ready for anyone to assume, occurs only when there is a traditional discipline and morality by which everyone is prepared. No such discipline now exists; Mr. Yeats's manner has grown out of his...strenuous and lifelong, if somewhat idiosyncratic discipline; it is an intensely personal thing. It might conceivably be taken over in a measure by another poet, but only by a poet who had in a sense earned the right, who had performed a comparable amount or kind of moral labor. Mr. Wilson sometimes seems to rattle a trifle loosely in the armor.

(p. 84)

Another interesting paragraph compares the poetry of Wilfred Owen with minor Elizabethan drama, adding this suggestive comment: 'This kind of rhetoric requires a drama back of it to sustain it and justify it; just as we tend to imagine the play that Dekker should have written when we come to a great passage, we are forced here to reconstruct the drama in which these lines were spoken, which Owen took for granted as a part of his environment, but which for us has fallen away, the War' (p. 118). But I doubt whether enough of the book is on this level to justify high claims for Winters's criticism.

To establish his real interest and value – at any rate for a non-American reader – we have to stand a little further back than these essays mostly permit us to do. We have to separate off Winters the minor poet and the propagandist for a special brand of minor poetry, from Winters the challenging critic of the conventional wisdom about poetry in the English-speaking world. The main objection to this conventional wisdom is that it has for many years evaded, or equivocated over, the problem of the truth-value of poetry. Thus I. A. Richards said in *Science and Poetry* that 'the greatest poets, as poets, refrain from assertion'. Apparent counter-examples were to be classified as 'pseudo-statements'. 'How true!', on Richards's view, is never an appropriate reaction to great poetry. Cleanth Brooks said that 'poems never contain abstract statements'. According to T. S. Eliot, poetry does not advocate certain beliefs, but tells us what it feels like to hold certain beliefs. A poem is variously defined as a 'gesture', or a 'verbal icon'. It is often said to be composed of a system of conflicting tensions or impulses. Ambiguities and paradoxes are typical of poetic language. (A recent version of this position is W. K. Wimsatt's 'tensional' theory of poetry, explained in his *Hateful Contraries*, 1965.) We must not inquire into the truth, or even the rationality, of what a poem says. Indeed, it is misleading to talk of a poem as 'saying' anything. 'For Hopkins', said F. R. Leavis, 'his use of words is not a matter of *saying* things with them; he is preoccupied with what seems to him the poetic use of them, and that is a matter of making them do and be.' But if poetry *says* nothing, why should anyone read it? The answer seems to be that poetry (of the right kind) conveys, and creates in the reader, a complicated mental state, which is worth having for its own sake – something like Pater's 'not the fruit of experience, but experience itself' (though the 'new' critics do not endorse Pater's hedonism). The conventional wisdom sees the 'dramatising' or 'realising' of 'experience' as the paradigm of poetry. 'In poetry', said Allen Tate, 'the disparate elements are not combined in logic, which can join things together only under certain categories and under the law of contradiction; they are combined in poetry rather as experience, and experience has decided to ignore logic. Experience means conflict, our natures being what they are, and conflict means drama. Dramatic experience is not logical.' 'Words in poetry', said Leavis, 'invite us, not to "think about" and judge, but to "feel into" and "become" – to realize a complex experience that is given in the words.'

This is not the place to go into the sources and validity of these doctrines. I suspect that they represent a desperate, if tacit, concession – all the more impressive because made by critics who are for the most part anti-positivist – to the positivist claim for science as the only domain of (non-tautological) truth. However that may be, I wonder if the effect of these doctrines is not to reduce still further the already small number of voluntary readers of poetry. After all, people may well make great efforts to follow the thoughts of a writer who is struggling, if with only partial success, to convey what he believes to be the truth. But if the only upshot of the reader's efforts is that he is enabled to contemplate 'the dancing of an attitude', or 'a play of conflicting tensions', or whatever formula the conventional wisdom may nowadays have hit upon, it is understandable that he doesn't bother. It is understandable, too, that a reaction is provoked, which disparages reason and intelligence altogether. 'The new American poetry as typified by the SF Renaissance', according to Jack Kerouac, '(which means Ginsberg, me, Rexroth, Ferlinghetti, McClure, Corso, Gary Snyder, Phil Lamantis, Philip Whalen, I guess), is a kind of new–old Zen lunacy poetry, writing whatever comes into your head as it comes, poetry returned to its origin, in the bardic child, truly ORAL, as Ferlong said, instead of gray faced Academic quibbling.' (*Chicago Review*, vol. 12, no. 1.)

Winters was a poet and critic who made it his business to find a third possibility, more consonant with the traditional high claims for poetry. The main thrust of his polemic is directed against the romantic theory, which he sees as still the dominant one in our time. This theory holds that literature is mainly or even purely an emotional experience. Behind it lies the conviction that man is naturally good; if he will rely upon his impulses, he will achieve the good life. When Pantheism is added, as it often is, he will achieve a kind of mystical union with the Divinity. Literature thus becomes self-expression, which is good in itself. Many romantics are also determinists. 'Determinism is Romanticism in a disillusioned mood; Henry Adams is little more than the obverse side of Emerson, the dark side of the moon.' Hedonists too are often determinists, because determinism is hostile to the intellect.

Winters, unfortunately, calls his own position 'absolutist' – unfortunately, because some have been led to suppose that he believes himself to be in possession of absolute truths. But he did not believe that he personally had free access to these absolutes and that his own judgments were final. What he *did* believe was that such absolutes exist and that it is the duty of every man and of every society to endeavour as far as may be to approximate to them.

Our universities, in which relativistic doctrines are widely taught, can justify their existence only in terms of a doctrine of absolute truth. The professor of English Literature, who believes that taste is relative yet who endeavours to convince his students that *Hamlet* is more worthy of their attention than some currently popular novel, is in a serious predicament, a predicament which is moral, intellectual, and in the narrowest sense professional, though he commonly has not the wit to recognize the fact' (*In Defense of Reason*, 1947, p. 10)

Similarly, speaking of Henry Adams, he says:

Throughout *Mont Saint-Michel and Chartres* he insists that the judgment of art is wholly relative; at the same time that insistence causes him deep regret. He prefers the older tower of Chartres cathedral to the later…but he cannot defend the preference. He apologizes, and says that after all the later tower was better for the people who made it and it may be better for his reader: a position which is defensible, needless to say, only if one is willing to push it to its unmistakable conclusion, and assert that the latest roadside horror is better for its builders than either tower and may be better for the reader. *There is no defensible compromise in this matter between a thorough relativism and a thorough absolutism.* (my italics)

Compare the introduction (p. xx) to *Forms of Discovery*:

Many critics…will disagree with my judgments of certain poems; they will believe that I am wrong and that they are right, and a good many will write bitterly on the subject. Some of these will be gentlemen who regard themselves as relativists, but a relativist doctrine provides no justification for argument in these matters. Argument implies a belief that there is a basis for argument, a true judgment which both arguers are trying to reach.

Winters was well aware of the difficulties in the 'absolutist' position. He confronted them more squarely than any other modern 'evaluative' critic I know, apart from those who, like Eliot, were content to assign final authority to the Church. This Winters was unable to do, though at one point, it is true, he was driven to commit himself to what must be the most reluctant version on record of the sequel to 'I fled Him, down the labyrinthine ways', when he writes in *In Defense of Reason* (p. 14):

If experience appears to indicate that absolute truths exist, that we are able to work towards an approximate apprehension of them, but that they are antecedent to our apprehension and that our apprehension is seldom and perhaps never perfect, then there is only one place in which these truths can be located, and I see no way to escape this conclusion. I merely wish to point out that my critical and moral notions are derived from the observation of literature and of life, and that my theism is derived from my critical and moral notions. I did not proceed from the opposite direction.

But Winters's occasional excursions outside literary criticism are best seen as reminders that the value of an idea cannot be judged in a vacuum. 'The hedonistic view of literature', he says, 'or the relativistic view of literature or morals, might appear sound in isolation, but either idea implies a fairly complete description of a large range of human experience, and if the description does not agree with the facts as we are forced to recognize them, then something is wrong.' The ideas Winters is fighting are not mere epiphenomena of literary fashion; they can be (as the suicide of his friend Hart Crane reminds us) literally matters of life and death.

To give literary application to this 'classical' position Winters worked out a theory of poetry, which he set forth in formulations that recur frequently in his criticism, with only slight variants. A poem is a statement in words about a human experience. The poet makes his statement in such a way as to employ concept and connotation as efficiently as possible. (By 'concept' Winters means something like the literal sense of a word or phrase; and by 'connotation' its suggestive overtones.) The poem is good in so far as it makes a defensible rational statement about a given human experience (the experience need not be real but must be in some sense possible) and at the same time communicates the emotion which ought to be motivated by the rational understanding of that experience (see *In Defense of Reason*, pp. 11ff). Poetry has also rhythmic and formal aspects (Winters does not approve of the common use of the term 'poetry' to refer to some kinds of writing which are not in verse). Rhythm communicates emotion, and as part of the poem it qualifies the emotion. The form of a poem can be seen both as its rational structure, the orderly arrangement and progression of its thought, and as a broader, less easily measurable rhythm than the rhythm of the line; in this sense, form might be called the rhythmical progression of the poem.

Winters's fundamental theses are clearly vulnerable as they stand, and they have attracted much adverse comment (the most cogent I know is John Holloway's in the *Critical Quarterly*, Spring 1965). But they should, I think, be treated with a charitableness which Winters himself does not always extend to other critics, when he castigates their looseness of expression. They should not be pressed too hard as *definitions* of poetry (to define a poem as 'a statement in words' is obviously unsatisfactory). What he achieves is not a definition but a reorientation of the reader's point of view, away from the romantic and post-romantic notions of our day towards something like the position of Matthew Arnold in the 1853 Preface, or of Sidney in the *Apology*, where Sidney speaks of 'peyzing each sillable of each worde by just proportion according to the dignitee of the subject'. But Winters has the advantage over earlier writers, in reinstating 'the dignity of the subject', of his familiarity with French symbolist and post-symbolist developments, in which 'the subject' becomes a very subtle matter. He was no archaiser, but a man very much alive to the literary problems of his own time.

Winters's particular judgments on poems and poets may seem narrow, cranky, and ill-founded. I confess that many of them seem so to me. And they must be taken into account when we are assessing the value of his theory. But his critical reputation should not stand or fall by his extravagant praise of dull English poets of the sixteenth century, or dull American poets of the twentieth. The proper claim for him should rest first of all on his passionate seriousness, sincerity, and dignity; and then on the courage and incisiveness with which he confronted the impasse of all modern criticism which purports to be judicial. Few readers of Winters are going to be satisfied in the future with facile talk about 'imitative form', or 'the stylistic advances of Eliot and Pound', or the thoughtless assumption that 'colloquial language' is a guarantee of poetic value. But the claim for him can best be defended by appeal to the best parts of his full-length books.

To dwell too much on the Winters of these *Uncollected Essays and Reviews* would be to fix him in memory as a fire-breathing dragon whose hoard, whatever it is, is not gold.